Advancing the World of Literacy: Moving into the 21st Century

The Twenty-First Yearbook
A Peer Reviewed Publication of
The College Reading Association
1999

Co-Editors

JoAnn R. Dugan
Clarion University of Pennsylvania

Wayne M. Linek
Texas A&M University-Commerce

Patricia E. Linder
Texas A&M University-Commerce

Elizabeth G. Sturtevant
George Mason University

Editorial Assistants

Devika Gollapudi
Texas A&M University-Commerce

Vicky G. Spencer
George Mason University

ISBN 1-883604-05-2

Printed at Texas A&M University-Commerce

COLLEGE READING ASSOCIATION BOARD MEMBERS 1999-2000

Executive Officers

President, Nancy Padak, Kent State University
President-Elect, Jack Cassidy, Texas A&M University, Corpus Christi
Past President, Timothy Rasinski, Kent State University
Executive Secretary, Linda L. Thistlethwaite, Western Illinois University
Treasurer/Business Manager, Gary L. Shaffer, State University of West Georgia

Directors

Donna Alvermann, University of Georgia
Elizabeth Sturtevant, George Mason University
Wayne M. Linek, Texas A&M University-Commerce
Barbara Walker, Oklahoma State University
Robert Rickelman, University of North Carolina-Charlotte
Gwendolyn Turner, University of Missouri-St.Louis
Alan Frager, Miami University, Ohio
Judy Richardson, Virginia Commonwealth University

Divison Chairs

Teacher Education, Joan Elliot,Indiana University of Pennsylvania
College Reading, Phyllis Kremen, Middlesex Community College
Clinical, Madlyn L. Hanes, Penn State University-Great Valley
Adult Learning, Sarah Nixon-Ponder, Southwest Missouri State University

Editors

Reading Research and Instruction, Robert Rickelman, University of North Carolina-Charlotte; Ernest Dishner, Penn State University-Harrisburg; William Henk, Penn State University-Harrisburg; Samuel Miller, University of North Carolina-Greensboro
The Reading News, Ellen Jampole, State University of New York-Cortland
CRA Monograph, Barbara Martin Palmer, Mount St. Mary's College
CRA Yearbook, JoAnn R. Dugan, Clarion University of Pennsylvania; Elizabeth Sturtevant, George Mason University; Wayne M. Linek, Texas A&M University-Commerce; Patricia E. Linder, Texas A&M University-Commerce

Committee and Commission Chairs

Conferenece Coordinator, Maria Valeri-Gold, Georgia State University
Program, Jack Cassidy, Texas A&M University-Corpus Christi
Membership, Peggy Daisey, Eastern Michigan University; Cindy Gillespie, Bowling Green State University
Professional Affairs, Michael Martin, University of Southern Mississippi
Public Information, Jane Matanzo, Florida Atlantic University
Awards, Timothy Rasinski, Kent State University
Media, Nancy Bertrand, Middle Tennessee State University; John Bertrand, Tennessee State University
Historian, J. Estill Alexander, University of Tennessee
Photographer, Frederick Fedorko, East Stroudsburg University
Research, Evangeline Newton, University of Akron; Jacqueline Peck, University of Ohio
Elections, Marino Alvarez, Tennessee State University
Resolutions and Rules, William Dee Nichols, University of North Carolina-Charlotte; John Helfeldt, University of Arkansas
Publications, Michael McKenna, Georgia State University
Legislation and Social Issues, Betty Goerss, Indiana University-East Richmond

TABLE OF CONTENTS

ADVANCING THE WORLD OF LITERACY:
MOVING INTO THE 21ST CENTURY
INTRODUCTION

Advancing the World of Literacy: Moving into the 21st Century reflects the ongoing efforts of a group of scholars and educators who have dedicated their professional lives to the advancement of literacy through inquiry that is linked with actual teaching and learning. Their involvement in the formation of school/university partnerships has done much to move the preparation of prospective teachers into the schools where teachers, school administrators, and university professors can collaborate to provide upcoming teachers with more extended teaching experiences that involve children in a variety of instructional settings. These efforts have created opportunities for long term mentoring of new teachers and serves to smooth the way for their transition into the classroom. These mentor relationships also encourage reflection about teaching that is conducive to self-improvement and have created many opportunities for professional development for classroom teachers through teacher research and collaborative programs. As classroom teachers and university faculty work together, they have many more opportunities to talk about instruction, engage in problem solving and inquiry, and share in decision-making. This dialogue is both intellectually challenging and refreshing as it brings positive and sometimes controversial issues to the surface. Everyone stands to benefit from such experiences because they learn and grow together as a community.

To advance the world of literacy, some of the areas explored in this volume include field teaching experiences, instructional practices, sociocultural contexts, literary reading and writing, and the integration of literacy, instructional technology and the arts. We realize that we must prepare teachers to meet the diversity and technological challenges of the 21st Century. As educators we wish to inspire our students think critically and to construct their own understandings of the world. Yet we must not lose sight of the underlying driving force that motivates us. That is an overwhelming passion for reading, writing, and learning. We really do enjoy our work. If we let our students see our passion, and share with them our enthusiasm for reading and writing, we can make it possible for them to experience the same joy and satisfaction that we do. With that passion in mind, we dedicate this volume of the CRA Yearbook to prospective teachers who will inherit the enormous responsibility of educating children and perpetuating the world of literacy in the new millennium. May the force be with them.

It goes without saying that this volume would not be possible without the authors who devoted much energy and thought toward writing the articles presented here. Also, we are especially grateful for the expertise of the Editorial Review Board members who make possible the review and the selection of manuscripts. The selection of reviewers and administrative details are facilitated by the CRA Publications Committee, which is chaired by Michael McKenna of Georgia Southern University. Because the CRA Yearbook is a peer reviewed publication, we encourage all presenters at the CRA annual conference to submit articles for consideration. We are also thankful for the unwavering commitment of the CRA Board of Directors who have supported the editorial team and the publication of the CRA Yearbook year after year. We are indebted to them all.

The editors feel privileged to have had out standing editorial assistants who were most attentive to the finest details and tracking of the articles. We commend graduate assistant Devika Gollapudi at Texas A&M-Commerce, and doctoral candidate Vicky Spencer at George Mason University, for their hard work and long hours spent reading and rereading manuscripts and communicating with authors. We also appreciate the clerical support provided by our secretarial staff, Frances Norman and Jan Hazelip, at Texas A&M-Commerce.

Editors are grateful for the extensive support provided by our universities. At Clarion University of Pennsylvania, we thank President Diane Reinhard and Dean Gail Grejda, College of Education and Human Services, for supporting the Yearbook during the final stages of publication.

At Texas A&M University-Commerce, we thank President Keith McFarland, Provost and Academic Vice President Donald Coker, and Dean Jerry Hutton for the ongoing financial assistance. We also extend a warm thanks to faculty in the Department of Elementary Education for supporting the publication. Finally, we thank Vivian Freeman and Lyndal Burnett for facilitating the printing and production of the Yearbook.

We appreciate the financial assistance and encouragement of Dean Gary Galluzzo and Associate Dean Martin Ford in the Graduate School of Education at George Mason University. Also, we thank President Alan Merten, administration, and faculty of the Graduate School of Education for creating a collaborative academic community.

Lastly, we extend a heartfelt thanks to our families, colleagues, friends, and readers who have supported our professional efforts with encouragement, acknowledgement, and genuine interest. THANKS!

JRD, PEL, WML, EGS
September, 1999

PRESIDENTIAL ADDRESS

Outside of a Dog, a Book Is Man's Best Friend. Inside of a Dog, It's Too Dark to Read. (With Apologies to Groucho Marx)

1998 CRA Presidential Address

Timothy V. Rasinski

Kent State University

Timothy Rasinski is a Professor of Curriculum and Instruction in the College and Graduate School of Education at Kent State University. After several years of classroom and Title I teaching in Elkhorn, Nebraska, Tim earned his Ph.D. from Ohio State. Prior to coming to Kent, Tim was a faculty member in the Department of Reading Education at the University of Georgia. Tim's professional interests include working with struggling readers, early literacy development, reading fluency, and parent involvement in reading. During the past decade he has served as co-editor of both The Reading Teacher *and the* CRA Yearbook. *Tim has also authored, co-authored, or edited several books on reading education. He and his wife Kathy have four children, Michael, Emily, Mary, and Jenny, and one dog—a beagle named Ginger.*

Have you heard the one about the man who walks into a bar with his dog and bets the bartender 20 bucks that his dog can talk. The bartender takes on the bet. So the dog's owner asks the dog a series of questions. First he asks, "Where will a bad golf shot end up?" And the dog answers, "RUFF." Then the owner queries, "What's on the top of a house?" And the dog answers, "ROOF." Finally, the guy says to the dog, "Who's the best baseball player of all time?" Immediately, "RUTH" comes out of the dog's mouth. "Alright," says the bartender, "I've had enough of this baloney," and he throws the man out of the bar with the dog right behind. The dog trots over to his master, looks up with pleading eyes and asks, "Was it Dimaggio?"

Dogs and books, dogs and reading, dogs and language—What's the connection? Actually, there are plenty of connections. There are dog lovers and there are book lovers. (And judging from my chats with CRA members, those two categories have a lot of overlap.) Just as reading has become an integral part of contemporary life, dogs seem to have made themselves right at home in our world too. Just consider some of the everyday expressions we use that make reference to dogs:

Who here has ever been in the doghouse?

How many of you have ever felt like you've been treated like a dog?

How many people feel that the world is going to the dogs?

Have you ever been hounded by your boss?

And after a hard day's work, it's not unusual to feel dog tired.

Who can remember their first puppy love?

Oh, and lets not forget that some of us believe that it's the evaluation tail that wags the reading instruction dog.

And then there is the way that literary quotes always seem more vivid and memorable when they involve dogs. Take for example:

Some days you're the dog, some days you're the hydrant. (Unknown)

Dogs feel very strongly that they should always go with you in the car, just in case the need should arise for them to bark violently at nothing right in your ear. (Dave Barry)

In dog years, I'm dead. (Unknown)

A dog teaches a child fidelity, perseverance, and to turn around three times before lying down. (Peter Benchley)

I wonder if other dogs think poodles are members of a weird religious cult? (Rita Rudner)

Cat's motto: No matter what you've done wrong, always try to make it look like the dog did it. (Unknown)

No one appreciates the very special genius of your conversation as the dog does. (Christopher Morley)

No dog should ever jump on the dining room furniture unless absolutely certain that he can hold his own in the conversation. (Fran Lebowitz)

There is no psychiatrist in the world like a puppy licking your face. (Ben Williams)

Since CRA is an association dedicated to excellence in reading, just think of all the dogs that have graced the pages of books for children, adolescents, and adults. There's that stage struck pooch Gloria in *Gloria and Officer Buckle* by Peggy Rathbone, and then there's Bandit and Slider from Beverly Cleary's *Dear Mr. Henshaw* and its sequel. *Shiloh* is now into his third book. There's *Old Yeller* and *Sounder,* and we shouldn't forget Old Dan and Little Ann from Wilson Rawls' classic *Where the Red Fern Grows.* And Jack London's *White Fang?* What about Beverly Cleary's *Henry and Ribsy* and Cynthia Rylant's *Henry and Mudge?* You also can't leave out *Clifford the Big Red Dog*, and oh yeah, *Harry the Dirty Dog.* Oh, and let's be sure to mention good old *Wishbone*, and of course, we couldn't leave out *Spot.* I'm sure I could add many more pooches to the list; but you get the idea.

But beyond quotations and expressions and books, there is more. The ways that dogs garner our attention and affection should be a model of the way we get our students, young and old alike, to become excited about reading.

Last year, after 22 years of marriage and 4 kids, my 2 youngest children convinced my wife to buy a dog for the family. The dog we got is a little beagle; we named her Ginger. We didn't know much about how to feed or discipline dogs. We still don't have much of a handle on training her. In fact, I think she has trained us better than we have trained her. But this little pup has woven herself into our family and in many ways enriched our lives—not only in our interactions with the dog, but in our interactions with one another.

This is an important point that seems to me to have direct and often neglected implications for reading and writing. How did Ginger enrich our lives? Mainly through the sheer vigor and playfulness and sense of wonderment she brings with her. That same sense of wonderment and passion and playfulness needs to be part of our literacy teaching. We need to have fun with reading, and we need to let our students see us have fun with reading. Indeed, we need to include them in that passion we have for the written word. How are students ever going to enjoy reading if they never see the joy we get out of it?

And yet the evidence suggests that many students do not see our own passions and playfulness for reading. In a survey study of students' reading perceptions, reported recently on the National Reading Conference Listserve, elementary students were asked toward the end of the school year if their teacher liked to read. A third said that their teacher "did not like to read," 47% responded they "didn't know," and only 20% said their teacher "liked to read." If students can't tell if their teacher has that playfulness about reading and language, how can we expect students to develop the passion and love for literacy that needs to develop concomitantly with any skills learned? Before we bring tests, skills, worksheets, and assignments to the reading classroom, we need first and foremost to bring a dog—well maybe not a *real* dog, but the playfulness we see in dogs has to be the same sort of playfulness we have about reading. William Steig put it nicely in his book *Caleb and Kate*, "Being a dog among dogs could be joyous sport." When we engage in that joyous sport of reading, we will inexorably draw our students into this web of meaning and wonderment and satisfaction. Reading will win its way into our students' hearts just as Ginger has won her way into my family's life. And even if she never masters any of those doggy tricks or skills or never passes any of the puppy obedience tests, or is not perfectly responsive to us in her own poochy ways, well that's okay, because we're sold on her no matter what happens. And if we can sell reading to our students in the same way, well let's just say if we win the heart over first, the rest of the reader will soon follow and they'll be in pooch paradise as they wolf down books one after another.

There's a lot we can learn from dogs. These include:

When you're happy, dance around and wag your entire body.

If what you want lies buried, dig until you find it.

Delight in the simple joy of a long walk.

Avoid biting when a simple growl will do.

Take lots of naps and always stretch before rising.

When loved ones come home, always run to greet them.

On hot days, drink lots of water, lie under a shady tree, and let yourself dream.

And now one more:

Run, romp, play, and read every day.

Children's Literature Cited

The Adventures of Wishbone. (1999). Milwaukee, WI: Gareth Stevens Inc.

Armstrong, W. H. (1987). *Sounder.* Saint Petersburg, FL: Pages Inc.

Bridwell, N. (1985). *Clifford, the big red dog.* New York, NY: Scholastic, Inc.

Cleary, B. (1984). *Dear Mr. Henshaw.* New York: NY: Dell Publishing.

Cleary, B. (1954). *Henry and Ribsy.* Madison, WI: Demco Media.

Gipson. F. B. (1956). *Old Yeller.* New York, NY: Scholastic, Inc.

Hill, E. (1999). *Spot helps out.* New York, NY: Putnam Publishing Group.

London, J. (1935). *White Fang.* Old Tappan, NJ: MacMillan Publishing Co.

Naylor, P. R. (1991). *Shiloh.* New York, NY: Dell Publishing.

Rathmann, P. (1995). *Gloria and Officer Buckle.* New York, NY: Putnam Publishing Group.

Rawls, W. (1961). *Where the red fern grows: The story of two dogs and a boy.* New York, NY: Doubleday.

Rylant, C. (1996). *Henry and Mudge under the yellow moon.* New York, NY: Simon & Schuster Trade.

Steig, W. (1977). *Caleb and Kate.* New York, NY: Farrar, Straus & Giroux, Inc.

Zion, G. (1956). *Harry the dirty dog.* New York, NY: Harper Collins Children's Books.

KEYNOTE ADDRESS

ARE WE TREND SPOTTERS OR TALE SPINNERS? A REPORT FROM THE FIELD

CRA Keynote Address

Donna E. Alvermann

University of Georgia

Donna E. Alvermann is a University of Georgia Research Professor in Reading Education. Her most recent research explores the potential of feminist pedagogy and poststructural theory for interpreting gendered literacy practices in middle school, high school, and college level classrooms. Having minored in history throughout her undergraduate and graduate programs, she is particularly interested in tracing personal experiences and theoretical underpinnings that guide her present research.

This paper was a keynote address for the 1998 CRA meeting in Myrtle Beach, South Carolina. Its purpose was to report and interpret the results of an informal survey sent to members of CRA earlier that year. The survey, which consisted of only five questions, was a means through which the members could express their views on the probable future of CRA. Looking toward the year 2020, the membership's responses to the five questions were grouped into ten themes. These themes were explored through the lens of what current research and theory imply. The question of whether we are an organization of trend spotters or tale spinners is addressed in the final section of the paper.

When Nancy Padak invited me to speak on a topic of my choice at the 1998 annual meeting of the College Reading Association, my first inclination was to focus on some aspect of literacy that would involve all of us in thinking about reading, literacy, and CRA in the new millennium. Then I recalled Bill Sheldon's advice (Bill was on my doctoral committee at Syracuse University). He advised staying as far away from crystal ball gazing as possible. So, I compromised and made only one of the five questions that I posed on a mail survey distributed during the summer of 1998 pertain to crystal ball gazing. Briefly, these were the five questions I asked:

1. If you could begin your career anew in reading and literacy education, what would you likely choose as your dissertation topic, and why would this be your choice of topics?

2. What do you want the students whom you teach and advise to say about you after they have completed their programs?

3. If you had to give assistant professors in the field a few words of advice, what would they be?

4. As you look into your "crystal ball" toward the year 2020, what do you see in store for CRA?

5. What additional questions/issues do you think I should address in my talk this Fall?

Participants

With Gary Shaffer's assistance, I obtained a complete mailing list of all CRA members as of May 1998. This list was used in distributing the survey. Eight surveys were returned because of no forwarding address, and several graduate students who received the survey indicated that they felt the questions did not pertain to them and hence chose not to respond. A return rate of approximately 25%, which, while not statistically valid[1] for representing the membership, was considered acceptable for the purpose of this paper— to determine if we, in CRA, are *trend spotters* or *tale tellers*.

Demographically speaking, those who completed the survey represented a broad cross-section of CRA's membership. The northeastern and southeastern sections of the United States accounted for 70% of the returned surveys, with each of these sections representing 35%. The midwestern states (with 14%) and the southwestern states (with 11%) accounted for the next largest group of returned surveys. The northwest (with 3%) and Canada (with slightly less than 2%) accounted for the smallest group of returned surveys. This distribution is fairly representative of the membership of the College Reading Association at large.

Analysis and Results of the Survey

In analyzing the results of the survey, I used a constant comparative method that involved rereading the responses to each of the five questions and then coding them according to key words used by the respondents. This method of analysis allowed me to retain the actual language of those who responded and to find themes within the overall data set. For example, the term *balance* was implied or appeared verbatim in responses to questions about what people would change about their dissertation topics, what they wanted their students to say about them, what advice they would offer new assistant professors, and what they believed is in store for CRA by 2020. Three other themes, *intellectual pursuits, practical matters,* and *teacher education,* were also implied in the responses to the first four questions. The term *technology* appeared in response to the question about what respondents would choose as a topic if they were to re-do their dissertations today, as well as to the question about what they saw in store for in for CRA by the year 2020.

In all, ten themes were identified across the first four questions on the survey. These themes included: a balancing act, intellectual pursuits, matters of reading, mentoring and modeling, motivating factors, political issues, practical matters, professional organizations, teacher education, and technology.

The responses to question 5 (What additional questions/issues do you think I should address in my talk this Fall?) were so variable that they defied easy classification. For example, some respondents indicated that they had "no other ideas" (with one person adding, "I'm sure you will have more than you can address!"), while others wanted me to provide an "overview of where we have been as well as where we are going" in the literacy field. One person wanted me "to take a stand on phonics and its role in meaningful reading instruction" while another requested that I "provide leadership in determining the focus of the profession." As you can well imagine, I had difficulty deciding how to code the diversity of responses I received to question 5. Many respondents simply omitted answering the question, while a number suggested that I answer the same questions I asked everyone else. This latter suggestion seemed one way of addressing question 5 while at the same time providing a way out of the problem I had in classifying people's varying responses to the question. I will share my responses to the first four questions after providing a brief summary and interpretation of the data survey data.[2]

Interpretation of Data from Survey

A Balancing Act

The notion of seeking balance in one's professional life was a major theme. This showed up in respondents' choices in alternative dissertation topics. For example, one person said she would choose to do a dissertation this time around on the "use of informational text in K-2 because the focus is presently on narratives." Another person would study adolescent literacy "because [it] is being overlooked in the current focus on early literacy."

The importance of balance was reflected, as well, in how professors said they wanted to be remembered by their students. They would prefer to be remembered for loving both their students and their subject area, for focusing on both reading and writing, for being well informed about both theory and practice, and for being tough but fair .

CRA members also had words of advice for new assistant professors that echoed the need for balance in one's professional life. For example, they recommended helping undergraduates and graduate students understand theory while concentrating on the practical, balancing university commitments with civic responsibilities, researching and writing both collaboratively and independently, and striving for diversity since "specialization is for insects." Managing stress on the job was a big factor in the balancing act. One respondent advised CRA members to remember that in interacting with new assistant professors, "a little kindness, support, and humor can go a long way in easing stress," while another believed that the key to stress management was learning how to handle the wearing of many hats with many different demands.

In terms of balance and the future of CRA as an organization, one person saw growth in the organization as "both a curse and a blessing," while another sought a more geographically balanced membership, brought about perhaps by holding the annual conference "in different locations, like the Midwest." Still another remarked that CRA "needs to become less of an Eastern U.S. organization."

Intellectual Pursuits

This theme was marked by comments having to do with the inquiry process. For instance, one respondent, if given the opportunity to change dissertation topics, would choose to do a study that explores students' inquiry processes. Most professors wanted to be remembered for challenging students to think critically. They also wanted students to examine their own beliefs about literacy, teaching, and learning. Two respondents specifically noted that they wanted to be remembered as active learners who are always learning new things. Others wanted to be remembered for helping students stretch their thinking in new and complex ways.

As for how new assistant professors might invest in worthwhile intellectual pursuits, the respondents focused on inquiry processes that involve reseaching, writing, and publishing. For example, several people advised that new assistant professors develop a program of research and establish a reasonable agenda for publishing. Others were more specific about how younger faculty might engage in intellectual pursuits. One respondent, for example, advised new assistant professors to read John Dewey, while others advised them to "spend time in the library" and "join a writing group."

Intellectual pursuits involving inquiry also figured into people's crystal ball gazing about CRA's future. One person wanted to see more collaboration among CRA members, particularly in the area of inquiry. Another person predicted that by the year 2020, "CRA will be encouraging of creativity, inquiry, invention, and the reconstruction of knowledge in schools."

Matters of Reading

When it comes to matters of reading, a number of respondents would not change a thing about their dissertation. Citing reasons such as, "I'd focus on early intervention because first grade reading instruction continues to interest me," or "I'd choose the same topic-narrative text analysis—because I still find it fascinating," these respondents were adamant that their first choice would not change. Others were not so sure, however. For instance, one person noted that phonological awareness would be a good topic to explore "because the phonological deficit hypohesis is all the rage in the LD area." Another person would choose a topic related to "the role of women in the field of reading instruction." Some would choose topics that they deem worthy of making a difference, such as studying emergent literacy and "turning kids 'at-risk' on to reading because it is this population that often drops out."

CRA members want their students to say the following things as a result of having taken classes with them: that they enjoy reading and that they metacognitively know what to do as readers. In terms of the role CRA is likely to play in matters of reading in the year 2020, respondents said they saw "a renewed interest and appreciation for reading specialists" and "a need to incorporate worldwide literacy issues into our definition and vision of literacy."

Mentoring and Modeling

Although no one mentioned mentoring and modeling as a topic they would choose to study if they were to do another dissertation, they did mention this topic when they responded to the question about what they would like their students to recall about them. Generally, CRA members want to be remembered as caring, having the time to listen, being supportive, and practicing what they preach. Their advice to new assistant professors includes choosing with care the faculty members who will be their mentors, and working closely with their mentors "to learn the what and how about all university requirements."

Overall, CRA is perceived as continuing its mentoring role well into the year 2020. Respondents predicted that the organization will "keep its congenial, family atmosphere," will continue to be "a nurturing environment," and will remain "a friendly, collegial organization that welcomes new members . . . [especially] a lot of newer, younger faces."

Motivating Factors

After reading as a topic, the largest number of changes in dissertation topics came from respondents who said that if they were to begin their careers anew, they would choose to do a study that involved some type of motivating factor. For example, several mentioned doing studies on the affective dimensions of life-long reading. Specifically, there was interest in studying the attitudes of under-prepared community college readers, the decline of interest in reading at the middle and high school levels, and the building of self-esteem in multiethnic settings.

Motivation plays a major role in terms of what CRA members would like their students to say about them as a result of taking their classes. Expressions of enjoyment, encouragement, and confidence building were among the major motivating factors mentioned by respondents. For instance, one person wanted to be remembered by her students for turning them on to literacy; another, for motivating them to do well by pointing them in the right direction; and still another for helping them think about new options.

As for motivational advice to new assistant professors, the word from CRA members was to "reject the medical model; you're not here to heal or fix problems, but to help readers discover their own success." Another member advised, "If you don't enjoy what you're doing, find something else to do, or go somewhere else; life's too short to be miserable."

Political Issues

Two respondents were explicit in their desire to incorporate the political in any new dissertation that they might write. As one of them noted,

> Back in the '60s when I, as so many others, was a political activist, I never saw politics as affecting literacy and school practices. Thus, I put my interest and enthusiasm for politics aside in the '70s and concentrated on teaching methods and materials. Only in the '90s did I realize the synergistic relationship between politics and education, specifically literacy education. Hindsight is always 20/20, but I wish I had stayed politically active in combination with "literacy active."

Advice to new assistant professors was also explicitly political. For example, respondents urged people new to the field to "try to reclaim in our various states the generation of reading specialists we seem to have lost," "stay away from the negative people; learn how to find 'the high road' of professional conduct by associating with professionals already on that road," and "keep a low profile if your senior faculty are at war over philosophical differences."

Hope was expressed that CRA would become more politically active by the year 2020 by speaking up "for what we know to be best practices" and by focusing on "new ways to voice our position on educational issues." One respondent worried, however, that CRA, while continuing to be supportive, would not be strong enough to affect federal policy.

Practical Matters

How to organize and manage language arts instruction and how to teach learning disabled youngsters in the college-prep classroom were practical questions that respondents posed as alternative dissertation topics. One person stated that for practical purposes "[she] would still probably pick a topic that would make an 'easy-to-complete' dissertation." She believed that the process of writing a dissertation was more valuable than the actual content, and that "the important thing is to finish it."

CRA members would like to be remembered for being "realistic, connected to the real classroom," for teaching practical material that can be applied in the classroom, and for providing "real-life experiences that enable [their students] to become better teachers and diagnosticians." This same emphasis on the practical is echoed in the respondents' advice to new assistant professors. For example, academics new to the literacy field are advised to "spend time in schools and keep current," to "coordinate classes so that projects and experiences relate to each other," and to "select service and teaching opportunities closely related to [their] research interests." Other words of advice include being organized, staying calm, doing "a solid job of teaching," saying no to a multitude of committee assignments, and being disciplined enough to spend time at the word processor writing for publication.

The practical also entered into respondents' predictions about what is in store for CRA twenty years hence. For instance, one person wrote, "I see the literacy field as we know it becoming increasingly classroom and teacher focused. . . . We will become even more applied in our research than we are now."

Professional Organizations

With the exception of one person who predicted that by the year 2020, CRA will be "bigger and better, always involved in growth," respondents focused almost exclusively on what they perceived to be a *decline* in CRA's membership. Comments such as "CRA will have fewer members as travel funds continue to dwindle," "I'd like to see CRA grow; it qualifies now as a best kept secret," and "I hope it has found new life (it seems to be fading a bit now)" are representative of the respondents' concerns. Suggestions for how CRA might revitalize itself included the following: reshape the organization's mission to appeal to practitioners, change its name to be more representative of its membership, do a better job of publicizing itself, increase its emphasis on diversity, and participate in activities with other professional organizations that have literacy as a focus.

As for CRA members' advice to new assistant professors in terms of joining professional organizations, the recommendation is to become involved early and participate actively. In one respondent's words, "Link with the field quickly and frequently." Another person mentioned the importance of working hard at local and state levels.

Teacher Education

CRA members who would change their dissertation topics if entering the field initially at this point in time and who wanted to focus on teacher education said they would investigate the quality of the educational experiences students receive in their undergraduate programs. For example, one respondent would study whether or not more reading courses and higher standards in teacher education programs would lead to a higher quality of graduates. This person believed that "currently public schools seem to shoulder the responsibility of providing basic knowledge about reading instruction." Another respondent would investigate a similar topic—undergraduates' insecurity when it comes to providing reading instruction, while another would explore the impact of feedback on preservice teachers' ability to implement reading instruction. Only one individual expressed an interest in studying instruction cross-culturally.

Generally, respondents would like their former students to say that they felt prepared to teach reading as a result of having had their classes. In one respondent's words—"that they left our program with confidence." Another person wanted students to see a relationship between methods courses and field placement, while another wanted students to be able "to teach reading to every child and feel comfortable discussing methodologies with parents."

Looking into their crystal balls at CRA's role in teacher education in the first two decades of the next millennium, the respondents were in agreement that CRA will increase its focus on reading teacher education. The organization will do this by becoming "a strong and forceful voice for teacher educators," by "continuing to support the professional development of literacy educators through strong publications and annual meetings," and by "focusing on best practices." Although one respondent predicted that CRA will become increasingly influential in the field of reading teacher education, another person was not as optimistic about this possibility, noting that the only change she saw coming "is the unwillingness of younger people to become involved in professional organizations."

Technology

If respondents were to enter the literacy profession anew, a number of them would change their dissertation topics to reflect their current interests in technology. They listed topics that ranged from studying the impact of hypertext and hypermedia on literacy development and comprehension to looking for new ways that technology might be used to develop students' critical thinking. The rationale they gave for wanting to study technology in relation to literacy education was the sense they had of its potential impact on students' ability to meet the challenges of a highly technical world. One respondent, who had initially focused on technology as a dissertation topic, put it this way: "I'd still focus on technology because it represents the most significant change in literacy in several hundred years. Another person noted that she would study students' comprehension of multiple texts "because it's the kind of reading challenge that we're faced with increasingly as we become 'internet literate'."

By far, technology was the theme that surfaced most often in relation to CRA's status in the year 2020. Some individuals saw technology as a way to increase CRA's visibility in the field, while others believed it might lead to isolationism and a drop in conference attendance. A few wondered if CRA will become a "virtual" organization that conducts all its business (e.g., publishing and conferencing) on line. One respondent even posed the possibility that CRA may come to stand for "computer reading association." Generally speaking, respondents to the survey viewed technology as a tool to be used by teachers and a new generation of students who have grown up with the idea of a "virtual" world.

My Responses to the Survey Questions

If I were to begin my career anew, I would change my dissertation topic. This time around I would study some aspect of critical media literacy as it pertains to adolescents in non-school settings, such as public libraries, teen clubs, and so on. This topic interests me because I wonder to what extent teenagers, who are deemed at risk of dropping out of school, will engage in literacy activities involving print and nonprint popular culture texts. In terms of what I would like former students and advisees to say about me, it would be that we collaborated on projects of mutual interest, and that I helped them think critically about what is said and done in the name of literacy research and instruction. In a somewhat related vein, my advice to new assistant professors would be to turn a critical eye to what they otherwise might not question about their teaching and research. The very things we take for granted—the "just because they are" sort of phenomena—are what we need to question the hardest. Finally, what do I see in store for CRA by the year 2020? An organization that has changed considerably to keep pace with the changing technologies, and increasingly, an organization that addresses issues of vital importance if we are to grow as a profession—issues such as the politics of literacy and a more visible presence of underrepresented populations, both in the CRA membership and its publications.

Trend Spotters or Tale Spinners

This section of the paper was the most challenging to write. I relied on the current literature to gain a sense of whether or not the responses to the survey questions were more in the realm of trend spotting than tale spinning, or vice versa. In the end, of course, it was a judgment call, but I offer here some current thinking about the themes that I identified in the responses to the survey. This thinking is based on the work of numerous scholars who are writing in three general areas: the interface between literacy and social change, the critique of constructivist pedagogy, and the promises and dangers of new communication technologies. After considering what the literature has to say about issues that are presently on the minds of a number of CRA members, I conclude by answering the question, so, are we trend spotters or tale spinners?

Interface Between Literacy and Social Change

Currently, there is much attention given to the social character of reading and writing and to the embeddness of these literacy practices in the larger social milieu. Less than two decades ago, reading and writing were seen as psychologically motivated and largely cognitive in nature. Today, as Colin Lankshear and his colleagues (1997) have noted, literacy studies encompass far more than the private internal cognitive states and events that were the focus of reading researchers in the 1970s and '80s. In their assessment of where the field of literacy is on the eve of a new millennium, Lankshear et al. describe it as framed within a sociocultural perspective:

> Within this frame, questions of power and the role of literacies as social practices within social productions and distributions of power [are] foregrounded, and "the politics of literacy" has emerged as a well-subscribed focus of theoretical attention. . . . And most recently, those who adopt a sociocultural approach to literacy have begun to address in earnest the implications of current developments in electronic technologies, which threaten to move us from print to post-print text cultures. (p. 3)

Personally, I think it is important to bear in mind that conceptions of literacy as critical social practice do not deny the cognitive or behavioral aspects of reading and writing; instead, they portray them as attendant processes in a much larger social context, one that is institutionally located in the political structures of society where power is at stake in people's social interactions on a day-to-day basis. Issues of race, class, gender, age, sexual orientation, and other identity markers are historically part of these interactions (Luke & Freebody, 1997).

This change in the way literacy researchers and practitioners are thinking about print and nonprint text-mediated practices[3] is reflected in a number of recently published books, several of which have been edited by members of the College Reading Association—e.g., *Handbook of Literacy and Technology: Transformations in a Post-Typographic World* (Reinking, McKenna, Labbo, & Kieffer, 1998); *Learning from Text Across Conceptual Domains* (Hynd, 1998), and *Reconceptualizing the Literacies in Adolescents' Lives* (Alvermann, Hinchman, Moore, Phelps, & Waff, 1998). What each of these books has in common is a focus on changing literacies, and to varying degrees, the embeddedness of these literacies in a sociocultural framework.

Literacy educators are just beginning to make practical connections between popular culture texts of all types (e. g., print, CDs, videos) and students' motivations to read. Lorri Neilsen's (1998) and David O'Brien's (1998) chapters on how adolescents connect popular culture texts to the realities of their lives, Cynthia Lewis's (1998) article on horror fiction in the classroom, and Anne Haas Dyson's (1996) book on young children's writing about their superheroes are just a few of the recent publications by well-known literacy researchers. Although generally opposed to the mindless insertion of popular culture texts into school curricula, Michael Apple (1996) does acknowledge that such texts have a place if the intent is to teach toward a more socially just society by connecting students' real life experiences to school learning. What Apple (1996), writing as a critical theorist, and Neilsen (1998), O'Brien (1998), Lewis (1998), and Dyson (1996), writing as literacy educators, seem to agree on are the important social and political uses that can be made of popular culture in the curriculum. Teachers who neither disparage students' choices in reading materials nor look the other way when students bring their everyday life outside the classroom into school stand a good chance of helping them understand why reading is always a social practice.

Critique of Constructivist Pedagogy

A constructivist teacher is a facilitator, not a transmitter, of knowledge. That is what Mary Klein (1997), a preservice teacher educator at James Cook University in Australia, saw herself, as someone who helped undergraduates in mathematics education personally construct their own meanings of the content they would teach through problem solving, exploration, and collaboration.[4] Only after taking a hard look at what was largely unexamined about her constructivist practice was Klein able to understand how her modeling of preferred pedagogical methods served to maintain the status quo. This discovery about herself and the pitfalls associated with the rhetoric of constructivist pedagogy were made visible when Klein used Australian theorist Bronwyn Davies' (1994) notion of positioning.

Briefly, *positioning* is a poststructuralist term for describing how members of any discourse group (e.g., teachers, students, and so on) speak themselves and others into existence through everyday talk. This talk varies, of course, in relation to the discourses available to the group members, especially in terms of who is doing the speaking, from what position of authority (or lack of authority), in what context, and with what gain in mind. In Klein's (1997) case, she was speaking from her position as an adult, a teacher, a giver of grades, and an expert in her field. Klein's students, on the other hand, were speaking as novices, as undergraduates who depended on her to prepare them for the real world of primary school teaching.

What Klein (1997) discovered was that through her modeling of strategies in what she supposed was a supportive environment, she in fact was sending a message that there is really only one way to teach young children—and that is through modeling. In Klein's words:

Modelling may become a problem because every possibility cannot be modelled. I later realised that I was modelling not only authoritative and immutable content, but also a given and supposedly unquestionable process or method of teaching. . . . On occasion students would express some concerns they had with constructivist practice. This occurred most frequently when engaged in discussion with me on a one to one basis. One such encounter is produced [below]:

Student: This 'constructivism", that's just another angle isn't it, I mean it's not the way you've got to go?

Klein: Well it's not the way you've got to go . . . you have to decide which way you want to go. It's kind of the theory behind the sourcebooks and the syllabus. . . . But you've got to decide where you are going to fall between the traditional, which was how I was taught at school and the constructivist ideas . . . (pp. 280-282)

As Klein (1997) went on to note, by reminding the student of the theory and authority behind the constructivist approach, she left little room for experimenting with alternative methods. In her words:

There was little ambiguity concerning to which end of the continuum I felt this student should aspire in her teaching, and of course in any assessment connected with the subject. Thus the discourse becomes regulatory in that it sets up a discursive framework into which student talk and writing must be fitted if it is to be heard. (p. 282)

While it is certainly the case that not all constructivist teaching ends up positioning students in the manner just illustrated, the literature on modeling (especially when the modeling is done by a mentor teacher) suggests that it is the rare student who questions or resists what he or she sees being advocated.

Constructivist pedagogy has also come under critical scrutiny of late for its tendency to focus on the creation of activity-based, problem-solving contexts for students' learning rather than on the inquiry processes students actually use in thinking about course-specific content in new and meaningful ways (Ball, 1992; Bonnett, 1995). For example, the premise that literacy teacher educators will improve preservice and inservice teachers' instructional performance by helping them acquire research-based knowledge about print-rich environments is suspect. Instead, what the literature on the value of educational research for professional development suggests is that teacher educators are most effective when they support preservice and inservice teachers "in building relationships between research-based models of children's thinking, their own students' thinking, and how they can interpret the models in light of their own students and classrooms" (Rhine, 1998, p. 29). As Deborah Ball's work (cited in Rhine, 1998) has demonstrated,

> Teachers are usually not prepared to transform rich environments into rich learning. Activities can be devoid of meaning unless the teacher is capable of providing students with appropriate challenges and helping the learner bring the meaning out of the activity. (p. 27)

The implications of this critique of constructivist pedagogy for literacy teacher educators are perhaps best understood when considered in terms of professional development initiatives. For these initiatives to result in the changes envisioned, service providers will need to engage teachers in inquiry-oriented instruction that moves beyond increasing their knowledge base about strategy instruction to orienting them toward inquiring into their students' thinking about specific content.

Promises and Dangers of New Communication Technologies

One of the most intriguing questions educators are asking on the eve of the new millennium is whether or not technology is changing family, community, and workplace structures. David Hakken, a professor of anthropology and director of the Policy Center at the State University of New York Institute of Technology, believes the answer is no, or at least not to the degree that was predicted. Speaking at a special congressional seminar sponsored by the Consortium for Social Science Associations on social changes attributed to the new communication technologies, Hakken (cited in Sroufe, Wurtz, & Maher, 1998) contended that "despite the belief that we are currently in the midst of a profound transformation to a new way of life brought about by computer technology, many early predictions have not come about" (p. 11).

A second speaker, Jan English-Lueck, an associate professor of anthroplogy at San Jose State University, took a slightly different view. As a result of studying the impact of computer technology on family life in Silicon Valley, English-Lueck (cited in Sroufe, Wurtz, & Maher, 1998) concluded that while there have been no changes in basic family patterns, the new communication technologies have led to our spending "a great deal of supposedly free time . . . thinking about work-related issues" (p. 12). This change is reflected in the increased number of separate rooms set aside in people's homes for computers and work-related tasks. The intrusion of computer technology into nonwork settings, then, is currently the only major trend that has been spotted by scholars studying the social impact of communication technologies on families, communities, and the workplace.

An area that promises to be the site of several new trends in technology for the next decade or two is the school. In fact, studies of how the new communication technologies are being used to realize certain societal expectations in schools are already the focus of several international scholars' collective writings on language, literacy, and the new work order (e.g., Gee, Hull, & Lankshear, 1996; Lankshear & Knobel, 1998). Briefly, the *new work order* refers to a new form of capitalism—what some (e.g., Drucker, 1993; Peters, 1992) might call a kinder, gentler capitalism, at least rhetorically speaking.

However, as James Gee and Colin Lankshear (1997) have pointed out, the new work order and its attendant genre of "fast capitalist texts" are best understood in relation to how they are changing and shaping the face of education. Fast capitalist texts comprise an emerging genre of business texts that attempt to explain a global, hyper-competitive "new capitalism," which Gee (1998) describes as a "non-authoritarian hierarchy, a fitting oxymoron for our new age" (p.387). An example of a fast capitalist text is Peter's (1992) book, *Liberation Management,* in which he applies Bakhtin's notion of "carnival" to describe new capitalism and to call for business leaders who are adept at using new imagery—the language of which has often been used in the past to critique capitalism and Western hegemonic practices. According to Gee and Lankshear, this literature has helped to forge school reform movements organized around such motifs as preparing students to engage in "higher order thinking, real understanding, situated expertise . . . [and] learning to learn" (p. 86) activities. Spurred on by the highly competitive global economies of new capitalism, these fast capitalist texts have a darker side to them—a side which we, as educators, might want to investigate more thoroughly before endorsing wholesale their implications for school literacy reform.

What is important here is the connection between these new work order texts and the communication technologies on which they depend. As

Colin Lankshear and Michele Knobel (1998) have pointed out, "this 'new frontier' can be a dangerous space. . . . [Dangerous because] the issues attending the introduction of new technologies have far-reaching and often invisible implications, which present worthy subject matter for practices of critical literacy" (p. 5). As literacy educators we have the responsibility, then, of teaching our students how to read critically the texts of these new technologies so that they become opportunities for liberation rather than openings for oppression.

Conclusion

So, are we trend spotters or tale spinners? Judging from what I could find in the education research literature that was relevant to the survey themes described earlier, I tend to think we qualify more often as trend spotters than tale spinners, and for these reasons. First, those who responded to the survey indicated a substantial interest in the sociocultural, both in the changes they would make in their dissertation topics and in the issues they saw in store for CRA by the year 2020. This focus on the sociocultural is in line with the increased attention being paid to the interface between literacy and social change in the research literature.

Second, the constructivist model of teaching and learning seemed well ingrained in the survey respondents' written responses to the question, "What do you want the students whom you teach and advise to say about you after they have completed their programs?" Certainly, the research literature suggests that constructivist thinking is very much in vogue right now. However, the literature also suggests that there is a growing critique of certain aspects of constructivist pedagogy. Specifically, there is concern over how we position students in our classrooms and in our relationships with them as their advisors. There is also some question about the degree to which inquiry-oriented instruction actually takes into account preservice and inservice teachers' expertise in inquiring into their own students' thinking processes and linking that inquiry with what the research literature has to say about children's literacy acquisition and development.

Finally, the respondents to the CRA survey were definitely trend spotters when they consistently pointed out the need for balance. Whether describing how they would change their dissertation topics, how they want to be remembered by their students, what advice they would offer new assistant professors, or what they predict lies in store for CRA in the next millennium, the respondents were clear in their call for balance. The education research literature also reflects a field caught up in the balancing act. Even the critique of the constructivist model of teaching and learning could be viewed as one way of addressing the imbalance some scholars see in that model.

In terms of tale spinning, it occurs to me that the survey responses suggested far more radical changes in the structure of CRA as an organization than might be supported in the literature that I read. For instance, I did not locate any studies that predicted professional organizations, such as CRA, are on the road to becoming "virtual" organizations. In fact, the report recently issued by the Consortium for Social Science Associations (Sroufe, Wurtz, & Maher, 1998) would suggest just the opposite.

Finally, as an organization we seem pretty adept at offering practical advice when it comes to helping new assistant professors make their way up the career ladder. Whether this advice is more tale spinning than trend spotting is difficult to say. Although a relatively large body of research exists on mentoring in general, that which pertains to mentoring colleagues in our own field of literacy education, especially in the academy, is virtually unchartered territory (Alvermann & Hruby, 1998). And, interestingly enough, none of the survey respondents listed it as a possible dissertation topic. Perhaps this is an area that members of our profession might consider exploring in a collaborative project that involves cross-institutional participation.

Author Notes

[1]According to Mangione (1995), response rates on mail surveys that fall below 50% are not scientifically acceptable. In Mangione's words, "If the only thing you did was to put a questionnaire in an envelope and ask people to fill it out, it would be common to see response rates in the 20% range, and it would not be surprising to see them in the 5% range" (p. 62). To have obtained a higher response rate, I would have needed to supply potential respondents. with a self-addressed postage-paid envelope and to follow up with a second-wave mailing reminder. Due to time constraints and budgetary concerns, I did neither. Justifications aside, the 25% return rate was at the upper end of what Mangione (1995) would have predicted, and more importantly, it did provide me with some direction for the keynote talk that inspired the use of a survey in the first place.

[2]A complete listing of all themes with their supporter descriptors for questions one through four is available from the author at the University of Georgia, College of Education, 309 Aderhold Hall, Athens, GA 30602 or dalverma@arches.uga.edu

[3]The New London Group (1996) has also written extensively on the impact of digital texs on our thinking about text-mediated practices.

[4]An example from mathematics education is included here because little research has been conducted on modeling the constructivist approach in literacy teacher education. What has been conducted is typically presented

at annual meetings of various professional organizations but not written up for publication. Interestingly enough, even fewer studies have been published on the role of mentoring among literacy faculty.

References

Alvermann, D. E., Hinchman, K A., Moore, D. W., Phelps, S. F., & Waff, D. R. (Eds.). (1998). *Reconceptualizing the literacies in adolescents' lives.* Mahwah, NJ: Lawrence Erlbaum.

Alvermann, D. E., & Hruby, G. G. (1998, April). *A survey of literacy teacher educators' mentoring relationships.* Paper presented at the annual meeting of the American Educational Research Association, San Diego, CA.

Apple, M. W. (1996). *Cultural politics and education.* New York: Teachers College Press.

Bonnett, M. (1995). Teaching thinking, and the sanctity of content. *Journal of Philosophy of Education, 29,* 295-309.

Carr. D. (1995). Is understanding the professional knowledge of teachers a theory-practice problem? *Journal of Philosophy of Education, 29,* 311-331.

Davies, B. (1994). *Poststructural theory and classroom practice.* Geelong, Australia: Deakin University Press.

Drucker, P. F. (1993). *Post-capitalist society.* New York: Harper.

Gee, J. P. (1998). On mobots and classrooms: The converging languages of the new capitalism and schooling. *Organization, 3*(3), 385-407.

Gee, J. P., & Lankshear, C. (1997). Language, literacy and the new work order. In C. Lankshear (with J. P. Gee, M. Knobel, & C. Searle). (1997). *Changing literacies* (pp. 83-102). Buckingham, UK: Open University Press.

Gee, J., Hull, G., & Lankshear, C. (1996). *The new work order: Behind the language of the new capitalism.* Boulder, CO: Westview Press.

Hynd, C. R. (Ed.). (1998). *Learning from text across conceptual domains.* Mahwah, NJ: Lawrence Erlbaum.

Klein, M. (1997). Looking again at the "supportive" environment of constructivist pedagogy: An example from preservice teacher education in mathematics. *Journal of Education for Teaching, 23*(3), 277-292.

Lankshear, C. (with J. P. Gee, M. Knobel, & C. Searle). (1997). *Changing literacies.* Buckingham, UK: Open University Press.

Lankshear, C., & Knobel, M. (1998, April). *Critical literacy and new technologies.* Paper presented at the annual meeting of the American Educational Research Association, San Diego, CA.

Lewis, C. (1998). Rock 'n' roll and horror stories: Students, teachers, and popular culture. *Journal of Adolescent and Adult Literacy, 42,* 116-120.

Luke, A., & Freebody, P. (1997). Critical literacy and the question of normativity: An introduction. In S. Muspratt, A. Luke, & P. Freebody (Eds.), *Constructing critical literacies* (pp. 1-18). Cresskill, NJ: Hampton Press.

Mangione, T. W. (1995). *Mail surveys: Improving the quality.* Thousand Oaks, CA: Sage.

Neilsen, L. (1998). Playing for real: Performative texts and adolescent identities. In D. E Alvermann, J. P. Young, K. A Hinchman, D W. Moore, S. F. Phelps, & D. R. Waff (Eds.), *Reconceptualizing the literacies in adolescents' lives* (pp. 3-26). Mahwah, NJ: Lawrence Erlbaum.

New London Group (1996). A pedagogy of multiliteracies: Designing social futures. *Harvard Educational Review, 66,* 60-92.

O'Brien, D. G. (1998). Multiple literacies in a high-school program for "at-risk" adolescents. In D. E. Alvermann, J. P. Young, K. A. Hinchman, D. W. Moore, S. F. Phelps, & D. R. Waff (Eds.), *Reconceptualizing the literacies in adolescents' lives* (pp. 27-50). Mahwah, NJ: Lawrence Erlbaum.

Peters, T. (1992). *Liberation management: Necessary disorganization for the nanosecond nineties.* New York: Fawcett.

Reinking, D., McKenna, M. C., Labbo, L. D., & Kieffer, R. D. (Eds.), (1998). *Handbook of literacy and technology: Transformations in a post-typographic world.* Mahwah, NJ: Lawrence Erlbaum.

Rhine, S. (1998). The role of research and teachers' knowledge base in professional development. *Educational Researcher, 27*(5), 27-31.

Richards, C. (1998). Popular culture, politics, and the curriculum. *Educational Researcher, 27*(5), 32-34.

Sroufe, J., Wurtz, S., & Maher, B. (1998, August/September). Is technology changing society? *AERA Research Policy Notes (OIA Info Memo),* 11-12.

EARLY
LEADER

HOW THE SQ3R CAME TO BE

Walter Pauk

Professor Emeritus
Cornell University

Walter Pauk is a Professor Emeritus at Cornell University. Dr. Pauk holds a B.A. in Philosophy, awarded magna cum laude from the University of Connecticut. He earned his Ph.D. in Educational Psychology from Cornell University. Dr. Pauk was a Fulbright lecturer at the University of West Indies, Jamaica. He also taught for eighteen months at the University of Liberia, West Africa, under a United States State Department program. He served overseas as an artillery officer in both World War II and the Korean conflict.

Dr. Pauk continues to write. He has just finished revising two books, Study Skills for Athletes *and* Study Skill for Community and Junior Colleges. *Both are published by H&H Publishing of Clearwater, Florida. Currently, he is revising the 7th edition of* How to Study in College, *published by Houghton Mifflin. Dr. Pauk's books under the Jamestown label are now published by Contemporary Publishing of Chicago.*

Dr. Pauk's active hobbies are backpacking, mountain climbing, and canoeing. In addition, he jogs six miles every day.

The creation of the SQ3R Method is the Mount Everest of study skills. All of us who have stood on the firing line, facing class after class of students, teaching them how to gain academic success, have Professor Francis Robinson of Ohio State University to thank.

Has Professor Robinson ever been thanked or acknowledged? It may be too late to thank him, but it is not too late to honor him. Perhaps, the

CRA or the CRLA could start the ball rolling by awarding Francis Robinson its greatest award in remembrance. Perhaps, then, the International Reading Association might take notice and etch his name where it rightfully belongs, on its Hall of Fame scroll, just one notch below the innovative William S. Gray, the creator of the Dick and Jane series. What Professor Gray did for beginning reading, Professor Robinson did for college reading.

Professor Robinson laid out his SQ3R Method in a book, *Effective Study*, published in 1946, a full fifty-two years ago. Even after fifty-two years, his SQ3R Method is actively used. It has tremendous staying power. I suspect that the SQ3R Method is still taught in almost every college and university in the United States. I suspect, too, that it is taught in many secondary schools.

Why do instructors like the SQ3R Method? I believe instructors like it because it is neat, tidy, with a well-organized sequence of steps, and truly exciting to teach. You simply explain each step—Survey, Question, Read, Recall, and Review—one by one, and you end up feeling that you did a great job, and you really gave the students something tangible, realistic, and practical. So practical that they could use it when studying tonight.

What kind of reading instruction took place in the early 50's? This is an important question, as I will point out later. Instruction was almost all machine oriented. Tachistoscopes flashed to prove that the eyes could see a phrase of three words in one-hundredth of a second. Harvard Speed Reading films cascaded down a screen line by line at five or six hundred words per minute to prove that reading could be done at a break-neck speed (and the title of "Harvard" precluded doubt). Then, the shutters of reading accelerators zoomed down the pages of a book to show day-by-day improvement in speed. All this equipment viewed reading as a physical activity, not a mental or intellectual activity.

What else was taught in the old days? Vocalization! The attack on vocalization was intense. This was viewed as the culprit of the reading process. It was thought that the reading process could be carried out simply by moving the eyes over the lines of print without overt or covert vocalization. This is untrue. Even when valid research came out in the 60's, instructors still lambasted vocalization as the cause for slow and poor reading; yet, vocalization had nothing to do with poor reading in general. The new research showed that "silent speech" goes on in the brain during the reading process. Ake Edfeldt, of the University of Stockholm Institute of Reading Research, had studied vocalization with a team of medical doctors who used electrodes to detect movement in the lips, tongues, and vocal cords of volunteer readers. After exhaustive medical tests, Edfeldt (1960) concluded, "In any case, it seems quite clear that all kinds of training aimed at removing silent speech should be discarded" (p. 154).

While we are on the subject of vocalization, let me briefly quote a few lines by Robert A. Hall, Jr. (1966), an internationally famous linguist, who explains the "silent speech" process beautifully.

It is commonly thought that we can read and write in complete silence, without any speech taking place. True, many people learn to suppress the movements of their organs of speech when they read, so that no sound comes forth; but nevertheless, inside the brain, the impulses for speech are still being sent forth through the nerves, and only the actualization of these impulses is being inhibited on the muscular level, as has been shown by numerous experiments (p. 28-29).

In 1953, I was a graduate teaching assistant in the Speed Reading Program. I knew that the mechanical approach to reading was on the wrong track. I knew that vocalization, which sounded solid and good in a lecture, was a side issue without scientific basis. But, as a teaching assistant, I knew no alternative. Then, the critical incident took place in an Educational Psychology class. The professor routinely explained the SQ3R Method. Instantly, I could see through the open door that study skills, not speed reading, was the way to help students to help themselves. Then, as fast as I could prepare new materials, I changed the Speed Reading course into a Study Skills course, even without discussing the change with the professor in charge of the entire program. To teach otherwise would have been charlatinism.

Since I have established a "before SQ3R," I can now highlight the major points of the SQ3R Method and discuss an "after SQ3R." Let's start by asking these rhetorical questions: Why was and why is the SQ3R Method so popular and so well known? Why did Robinson's Method catch fire? Were his five steps of surveying the chapter, formulating questions based on titles and captions, reading with concentration, reciting for remembering, and reviewing for reinforcement of facts and ending up with an integrated view of the whole chapter brand new ideas? No! These five steps were well known.

How do I know? Well, I always wanted to know the history of the SQ3R Method. I wondered how Professor Robinson came up with the idea. As it happened, my first finding was through Professor Gordon Nelson who was teaching at Cornell University during World War II. During the war, many colleges and universities cooperated with the government to hold many special programs for both the Army and the Navy. Professor Nelson said that there was a very large program at Ohio State University, training and teaching soldiers and sailors to become officers. This training required a great deal of reading technical manuals, and the students were experiencing reading and learning difficulties. The administration at Ohio State University turned to the psychology department for help. Professor Robinson was selected to head this new Learning and Study Skills Program.

As a professor of psychology, Professor Robinson already knew a great deal about the general theories of forgetting, remembering, reciting, and recalling. But, he did not know of any method for teaching the process in reading a textbook. Based on my own research and speculation, I believe Dr. Robinson went to the library to find out what had been written on reading and study skills.

So, the next step in my research was to find out what books were in print and available to Professor Robinson at that time. To find out, I went to Cornell University's library in the Agriculture College. There in a remote corner of the basement, I found four shelves filled with books on reading and studying. Some books were written back in the late 1800's and early 1900's. I dipped only into books written before 1942, believing that such books had a good chance of being in the library at Ohio State University during the time when Professor Robinson was there.

There in the basement corner of the library, I felt like a medieval monk. No one ever came down there to disturb me. I spent a week of looking and reading book after book, page by page, searching for some method for reading a textbook. Finally, I found the nugget. I found the exact same nugget, I am sure, that Professor Robinson found.

I found Professor Charles Bird's book titled, *Effective Study Habits*, with a copyright date of 1931. Beginning on page sixty-eight, Professor Bird, in a scholarly prose, explained the five steps for mastering a textbook chapter. He called these steps the "Self-Recitation Study Methods." Here are the excerpts of his five steps.

Attempting to master an assignment, a student should first read it through rapidly without pausing to stress any particular topic or to underline points of apparent major importance. This preliminary survey helps in the formulation of a general idea of the content.

The next step is to read carefully the first section of the assignment. . . . It may be helpful to translate the topic headings into questions.

During the first reading, the serious student is assimilating his assignment, but this does not insure that details are completely mastered; only drill can fix them securely.

As soon as these become familiar, cover up the answers to the first questions, supply the answers from memory, then check the answers immediately against the written outline.

The final step in the self-recitation method takes little time, since it involves only a very rapid re-reading of the assignment. A pleasant surprise awaits the student in this final reading, for now his rich associations make lively the relationship of part to part and of details to the whole discussion (p. 69-71).

Now, for the first time, Professor Robinson had in his hands a logical sequence of steps to use in teaching the students in the Army and Navy programs at Ohio State University. Did these five steps bring fame to Professor Robinson? No, they did not! These five steps brought no more fame to Robinson than they did to Professor Bird, the originator of the five steps.

Well, then, what did bring fame to Professor Robinson? In his teaching, explaining, and mental handling of Professor Bird's five steps, Robinson somehow, with a flash of great insight, saw a mnemonic using the first five letters of the five steps: Survey—Question—Read—Recite—Review. These first five letters created a formula, the SQ3R Method.

This acronymic formula looked scientific, sounded scientific and implied precision. It looked as scientific as Einstein's $e=mc^2$ or the mundane formula for water, H_2O. We respect science. We believe in science. This one imaginative formula took study skills forever out of the misty realm of well-meaning, paternalistic advice and placed textbook reading and study skills into a sharp category where prescribed techniques are based on and backed by research and experimentation.

For the field of reading and study skills, the SQ3R Method was far more than another reading technique or study method. It was a major *breakthrough*. It was to reading and study skills what the breaking of the four-minute mile by the Englishman, Roger Bannister, was to track and athletics. It helped tremendously to sweep away to a large extent reliance on the mechanistic approach of tachistoscopes and reading accelerators. The SQ3R Method opened the way for instructors to devise their own special versions modeled after Robinson's systems. A rash of systems such as PQRST and OARQWET were put forth. These were just copycat systems. As I see it, none of these versions is an improvement over Robinson's SQ3R Method.

I once wrote and published an article, probably in Sam Zeman's fine *Reading World*, pointing out that none of the writers of these various versions gave credit to Robinson for pointing the way. Professor Robinson's colleagues showed him my article, and Professor Robinson wrote me a letter expressing appreciation. We, thereafter, corresponded lightly. I never met him, but I visualize him as a fine, thoughtful, sensitive man. His last days were spent in Florida.

After having said all these good and true words about the SQ3R Method, I am going to turn the page. I am going to show what I think are some of its shortcomings. First, though most instructors like the SQ3R Method, most students do not. Students say, "It takes too long, and after all, I have four other subjects to study." I can see a lot of merit in such opinions by the students. The alphabet soup of steps can schematize reading to such an extent that most of the life of a passage is squeezed out. Students get so caught up in moving from "S" to "Q" and figuring out which "R" is next, that they often lose sight of the very reason they are reading in the first place—to compre-hend.

The Surveying step, too, galls many students. I can see why. It promises much too much. Even Professor Charles Bird became rhapsodic. He writes:

> As the engineer first surveys the land upon which a structure is to be raised, and as the leader of an expedition gains information to aid in mapping routes, so the intelligent student will explore his assignment (p. 69).

And what does the good Professor tell the student on how to get all this wisdom? He writes as follows:

> First, read the chapter through rapidly without pausing to stress any particular topic or to underline points of apparent major importance. This preliminary survey helps in the formulation of a general idea of the content (p. 69).

I seriously wonder how all this information, knowledge, and wisdom can be gotten by the mere rolling of eyes over heading and subheading, without stopping to think and to reflect or even underline. This procedure is a perfect setting for massive and almost instantaneous forgetting. Can't you see what mayhem would be caused by the rapid succession of headings, subheadings, main ideas, sub-ideas, details, and transitions? We know about Proactive Inhibition and Retroactive Inhibition: the new information is trying to eject the old information already in the memory, and the old is fighting to stay there by pushing out the new information. It is like five or six big bas-ketball players under the basket pushing, shoving, and elbowing each other to get their hands on a rebound. Furthermore, there is no time at all for the short-term memory to transfer information to the long-term memory, as far as time for consolidation is concerned, forget it. The only good thing that I can say about surveying is that many students find it difficult to open a text-book and begin to study. If surveying, a non-demanding sort of step, will ease them into action, then I am all for it, but without any promises.

Without question, the Recitation step is an essential step to take; but to have something to recite, you better have the proper information to recite. If you picked details or even slightly erroneous impressions when you read, you will probably end up with the same details and off-center ideas. To be effective, you have to end up with the true salient points. How do you find these true salient points? You find them by asking the right question of *each* paragraph that you read.

Of course, the idea of using questions to aid reading comprehension is nothing new. It dates back to Socrates, 450 B.C. The Question step in the SQ3R Method says that you create your questions out of the textbook head-ings by prefacing them with a *Who, How* or *When*. The questions that result are designed to stimulate interest and increase comprehension. In theory, this idea is a good one; but, in practice, the SQ3R Method of questioning places an undue emphasis on chapter headings and sub-headings as the keys to comprehension, and in the process it makes some risky assumptions.

The first risky assumption is that the headings encapsulate the most important information in the section. Some headings simply clue you in the general subject matter, for example, "Human Memory." It is extremely difficult to formulate an intelligent question based on some of these bare-boned headings. Other headings function as tone setters. For example, "A Collison of Viewpoints," may create interest, but hardly provides the sort of raw material needed to come up with a specific, helpful, intelligent question.

The second risky assumption is that headings will occur often enough to allow students adequate opportunities to formulate questions. The number of paragraphs per textbook section can vary widely. A section with twenty paragraphs with only one heading theoretically poses twenty separate questions. The textbook heading provides only one. Not all of these paragraphs will be crucial, of course, but if the student is content to answer a single question for the entire twenty paragraphs, it is almost certain that important information will be lost.

Unlike the SQ3R Method and its imitators, I suggest that questions be formulated directly from textbook paragraphs instead of from chapter headings and subheadings. A textbook paragraph, after all, adheres to at least one standard; that is, every paragraph contains one main idea. If you look at it another way, every paragraph provides the answer to an unasked question. Find the question and you will find a way of getting to the heart of the paragraph. The new rule is: Extract a basic question from every paragraph you read.

Once you decide on a question, write it down in the margin; then, return to the textbook paragraph and underline the sentence or sentences that supply the answer. Then, move on to the next paragraph. As you read each paragraph, just keep in mind that you already know the answer; the answer is the information in the paragraph itself. Now, all you need to do is come up with the question.

Viewing the information in each paragraph as an answer to a question has a wonderful way of magnetizing that information. Suddenly, the relationship between the sentences in a paragraph becomes clearer. Students begin to develop an experiential understanding of the value of things like supporting materials, details, conclusions, and transitions.

Although it may appear that my system, which is called the Questions-in-the-Margin System, is missing most of the steps that comprise the SQ3R Method, it really does not. Actually, the Questions-in-the-Margin System eliminates only one step, the surveying step; yet, it manages to include the steps of reading, reciting, and reviewing within the single process of formulating questions. Out of this one-step system grow all the important elements of the other study systems. The fat is trimmed; but, no muscle is lost in the process.

The value of the Questions-in-the Margin System is that although it *has not* neglected the valuable techniques that made the SQ3R Method appealing to educators, it has consolidated three principles into a single step. The results are a system that is both teacher-friendly and student-friendly, not because it is ultra modern and full of gimmicks, but because it is scholarly and it gets back to the basics that count.

Scott Solomon, a medical student studying to become a neuro-surgeon, said that he always wanted to read Emmanuel Kant's *Critique of Pure Reason*, but was afraid that it was beyond his background and beyond his capabilities. Then, he ran across the Questions-in-the-Margin system. He tried it and was highly successful. He is able to explain Kant's work to others now.

Presently, Solomon is plowing through Bertrand Russell's *A History of Western Philosophy*. Here is what he says:

> It's been a sheer joy. There is nothing in the world I love more than going back and reviewing using the Questions-in-the-Margins. I simply can not express my gratitude to you for that technique. Reading your article again on the Questions-in-the-Margins technique got me really excited. To me, it's just amazing that since the time of Homer until now, no one ever came up with this omnipotent technique. Are you sure you didn't pirate the method from some 13th century Cathari tract?

The best way, perhaps the only way, for the reader to come to grips with the comprehension of a paragraph is the Questions-in-the-Margin way; that is, when you finish reading, take the next mental step and ask yourself out loud, "What question was answered?" You cannot formulate a question unless you understood the paragraph you just read. So, you, the reader, is forced *back* into the paragraph to re-read it. The reader realizes that on his first foray, he did not get it! This re-reading forces him to do it by himself and for himself. Doing it by yourself is the only way to become an INDEPENDENT LEARNER.

Epilogue

This article started out genuinely and sincerely as a tribute to Professor Francis Robinson and to establish a significant and permanent place for him in the annals of reading, learning, and study skills. This is as far as I had planned to go. But, as much as I embraced the SQ3R Method in the beginning for its innovative, original approach, I just could not leave the impression that the SQ3R Method is still the best way to teach students how to read a textbook chapter. Remember, the five steps go back to Professor Charles Bird's writings, which took place in 1931, a full sixty-eight years ago. Much has happened since and much has been gained through experience. So, I just had to present an alternative method, the Questions-in-the-Margins System. What I have said about this System, I would have still said if it were devised by someone else. I say this in the hope to foreclose any thought that these comments are simply "self-serving."

Let's end up the way we started—with a few more words about Professor Francis Robinson. What a wonderful and memorable event it would have been if we had as our keynote speaker at one of our annual conferences Professor Francis Robinson. Such an event would have been memorable to us in the audience, and with the ovation that we would have given, the event would have been forever memorable to him. This scene, of course, will not occur; but, the honoring can and I am sure, will.

References

Bird, C. (1931). *Effective study habits.* New York: The Century Company.

Edfeldt, A. W. (1960). *Silent speech and silent reading.* Chicago: University of Chicago Press.

Kant, E. (1990). *Critique of pure reason.* Amherst, NY: Prometheus Books.

Hall, R. A., Jr. (1966). *New ways to learn a foreign language.* New York: Bantam Books, Inc.

Russell, B. (1945). *A history of western philosophy.* New York: Simon & Schuster Trade.

RESEARCH
AWARDS

A CASE STUDY OF A LAST-TO-EMERGE-INTO-LITERACY FIRST GRADE READER AND THE INTERPLAY OF READER AND CONTEXTS

Dissertation Award

Linda S. Wold
The University of Chicago

Abstract

This paper provides a brief summary of a year-long case study (Stake, 1988) of a last-to-emerge-into-literacy first grade reader and his interplay within and among a range of reading contexts. The researcher designed this qualitative study to learn more about why some children, despite their participation and active engagement in literacy-rich contexts, seem less able to make sense of reading than their peers (Dyson, 1984; Wold, 1998). The inquiry focused on: (a) the verbal and nonverbal communications that an emergent first-grade reader experiences in the interplay of language arts, math, social studies, and reading intervention contexts, (b) the ways an emergent reader uses different verbal and nonverbal communications to negotiate reading understandings, and (c) how an emergent reader develops appropriate or inappropriate literacy behaviors.

This naturalistic study was conducted in a first grade classroom of a public elementary school in a Midwestern suburb near a large metropolitan city. The school was committed to students' learning, to small class sizes (20-25 students), and to providing early reading intervention services for developing readers. As an advocate for nonreaders, the first grade teacher was chosen for the study. She willingly provided classroom access to the researcher who serviced first graders receiving reading intervention support. Nicholas, the focal child, was selected for this study because his informal assessment rank indicated he was the last child in his first grade classroom to emerge into literacy. The case study allowed the researcher, as a "researcher partici- pant" (Merriam, 1988, p. 93), to scrutinize "the visible and unseen processes that account for pupils' learning" (Huberman, 1996, p. 138). Observations involved the emerging literacy development of the focal child and his lit- eracy contexts within the larger context of the first grade classroom.

Early reading research (Clay, 1966; Ferreiro & Teberosky, 1982; Teale & Sulzby, 1986), constructivist learning theory (Piaget, 1955; Vygotsky, 1978, 1986; Wells & Chang-Wells, 1992), and sociolinguistics (Hymes, 1974; Florio- Ruane, 1987) were important theoretical strands woven in this emergent lit- eracy case study. The research bases framed emergent literacy development within a sociocultural perspective. In such a perspective, the emergent reader was viewed as a thoughtful, communicative partner in the reading process while being socialized simultaneously in the cultural ways of knowing literacy in his classroom (Bloome, 1994). Verbal and nonverbal interactions (Rogoff, 1990; Kantor, Miller, & Fernie, 1992) helped the researcher more fully exam- ine the emergent reader as he explored literacy and acted on information while attending to the cultural dimensions of classroom learning. The researcher was interested in discovering how the interplay between the emergent reader and his different reading contexts affected others and how others affected him in his everyday literacy encounters.

Research Design

The theoretical framework connected emergent literacy development in sociocultural communications (Dyson, 1984, 1993) and school-specific literacy contexts (Bussis, Chittenden, Amarel, & Klausner, 1985; McIntyre, 1990; Richgels, 1995) to study the focal child's interactive behaviors among learners. Case study methodology was used to explore the interplay between an emergent first grade reader in a range of reading contexts to understand how the reader developed appropriate reading behaviors. Like other qualitative investigations informed by ethnographic methods (Harste, Woodward, & Burke, 1984; Nelson, 1992; Wolcott, 1988), this study included prolonged field work, re- search occurring in natural contexts (Spradley, 1979), data collections through "participant observation" routines (Merriam, 1988, p. 87), and "thick descrip- tions" (Geertz, 1973; Guba & Lincoln, 1981) of data to explain phenomena.

Data Collection

During the year-long case study, the researcher systematically observed an emergent reader in his school literacy contexts. In phase one of the study (August-December), the researcher selected a case study child and, for ap- proximately five hours weekly, informally observed language arts, math, social studies, and reading intervention contexts of the case study student and the classroom at large to become comfortable with the students and their routines. During phase two (January-June), formal observations occurred and documentary evidence was collected for each hour-long language arts, math, social studies, and some reading intervention contexts. These observations were audio and video recorded, and transcribed on the same day to insure accuracy of written reports. The researcher focused on the case study student's interactional behaviors with his immediate peers in order to document the focal contexts and the emergent reader's negotiations within those contexts.

Analysis

Miles and Huberman's (1994) three-part interactive model for qualitative analysis, including data reduction, data display, and conclusion drawing/verification, guided the data collection and analyses. The model provided a frame for coding and sorting data by clusters or themes, and for systematizing displays to organize cumbersome data. Written "documentary evidence" (Erickson, 1986), such as field notes, transcriptions of the reading contexts, and written documentation, were coded for instructional and affective behaviors of the case study student, classroom teacher, researcher, and parent. From more than 100 hours of coded, transcribed records of video taped sessions, the researcher triangulated evidence among the comprehensively coded events, student artifacts, parent-teacher-student interviews, and a teacher-researcher journal. The data collection of 1,206 independent, dependent, and negotiated literacy events became the source for conclusion drawing and verification (Miles & Huberman, 1994). Preliminary findings were used to develop matrices to chart the case study student's verbal and nonverbal communications and to interview or instruct the case study child on a daily basis. During the final phase of the project the researcher triangulated data to verify findings and to cross-check multiple contexts, informants, data collection procedures, and peer examiners (Mathison, 1988). Two qualitative researchers reviewed 15% of the data collection during the twenty-one weeks of formal observations. Interrater reliability on coded events was .96, and preliminary findings were corroborated.

Findings and Recommendations

Despite the emergent reader's more active engagement in literacy-rich contexts, he was less able to make reading sense than his peers because his verbal and nonverbal communications mainly involved assistance. Nicholas negotiated literacy patterns exhibited his reliance on others because he reproduced other students' responses/routines, and he exhibited consistent passive, dependent literacy patterns. These findings were verified in the documentary evidence. First, Nicholas resorted increasingly to more independent-active literacy patterns over the course of the research. Despite this, the second finding showed that Nicholas remained context-dependent approximately fifty percent of the time; he relied on literacy contexts and their participants to understand reading. Specifically, the case study student was not able to focus on literacy activities for important content learning, but rather for the task presentation (Alton-Lee, Nuthall, & Patrick, 1993; Freppon, 1991). He learned appropriate and inappropriate literacy patterns from his interpretations of the sociocultural classroom literacy contexts. The third finding verified the notion that Nicholas, a child who was last-to-emerge-into-literacy in his first grade classroom, was not able to unlearn some inappropriate reading knowledge that he interpreted as "unconditional truths" (Langer, 1997, p. 130) or facts. He understood reading as a "sounding out" process by which he copied and reproduced other students' spoken and written responses.

Major findings were verified by Nicholas' literacy patterns and his changing literacy interactions. This unique case study explains Nicholas' negotiations (Cannella, 1993) across a range of reading contexts and his interpretation of schooling as a passive, dependent learner, reliant on others to understand literacy processes. Although the findings are not generalizable to other populations of emergent readers, this study suggests important ways to use basic research to extend knowledge about emergent literacy development including the notion that:

1. Reading group format, size, scaffolding partners/support, and materials affect an emergent reader's verbal and nonverbal communications and how actively a less able reader responds to literacy contexts (Wold, 1998). This finding implies the need for creating scaffolded opportunities (Meyer, 1993) for active learning, including developmentally paced and instructionally appropriate literacy experiences for a last-to-emerge-into-literacy first grader.

2. The distinction between "doing school" routines and "doing literacy" routines provides an observable and useful way to examine literacy understandings of a child who is last-to-emerge-into-literacy. This finding implies the need for teachers to learn how active knowledge construction for early literacy learning is facilitated by reconstruction, the deep structure of "doing authentic literacy" routines, rather than by reproduction of the surface structure of "doing school" routines. Educational practice may benefit from future studies that address how children and teachers approach and value distinctions in classroom literacy learning routines.

3. Singular approaches to reading, such as reading as reproduction and aspectual reading (Sulzby, 1985), suggest the need for instruction based on emergent literacy theories. That is, teachers must use what is known

about emergent literacy development and teach accordingly to provide more mindful learning opportunities (Langer, 1997) for emerging readers.

Summary

The researcher discovered that the focal child "adopted different notions of the purpose and value of literacy" (Turner, 1997, p. 183). Conclusions from this study's findings were that the design of and materials for literacy activities and instruction in reading contexts create a distinction between "doing school" and "doing literacy" routines. The implication for teaching was that a last-to-emerge-into-literacy first grade student needs opportunities for active literacy involvement which is supported by literacy instruction and meets his developmental and sociocultural needs. School and home literacy contexts need to present options for learning about emerging literacy knowledge that provide increased interactions for spoken and written language learning routines in flexible, need-based instructional formats (Wold, 1998). Suggestions for future related research include studies about how to diagnose learning obstacles and to provide more accessible and equitable classroom literacy practices for a child such as Nicholas who was the last-to-emerge-into-literacy in his first grade classroom.

References

Alton-Lee, A., Nuthall, G., & Patrick, J. (1993). Reframing classroom research: A lesson from the private world of children. *Harvard Educational Review, 63*(1), 50-84.

Bloome, D. (1994). Reading as a social process in a middle school classroom. In D. Graddol, J. Maybin, & B. Stierer (Eds.), *Researching language and literacy in social contexts*, (pp. 100-130). Bristol, PA: The Open University.

Bussis, A. M., Chittenden, E., Amarel, M., & Klausner, E. (1985). *Inquiry into meaning: An investigation of learning to read.* Hillsdale, NJ: Erlbaum.

Cannella, G. (1993). Learning through social interaction: Shared cognitive experience, negotiation strategies, and joint concept construction for young children. *Early Childhood Research Quarterly, 8*(4), 427-444.

Clay, M. M. (1966). *Emergent reading behaviours.* Unpublished doctoral dissertation. University of Auckland, New Zealand.

Dyson, A. H. (1984). Learning to write/learning to do school: Emergent writers' interpretations of school literacy tasks. *Research in the Teaching of English, 18*(3), 233-264.

Dyson, A. H. (1993). *From invention to social action in early childhood literacy: A reconceptualization through dialogue about difference* (Report No. 67). Berkeley, CA: National Center for the Study of Writing.

Erickson, F. (1986). Qualitative methods in research on teaching. In M. C. Wittrock (Ed.), *Handbook of research on teaching* (3rd ed.). (pp. 119-161). New York: Macmillan.

Ferreiro, E., & Teberosky, A. (1982). *Literacy before schooling.* Portsmouth, NH: Heinemann.

Florio-Ruane, S. (1987). Sociolinguistics for educational researchers. *American Educational Research Journal, 24*(2), 185-197.

Freppon, P. A. (1991). Children's concepts of the nature and purpose of reading in different instructional settings. *Journal of Reading Behavior, 23*(2), 139-163.

Geertz, C. (1973). Thick description: Toward and interpretive theory of culture. In C. Geertz (Ed.) *The interpretation of cultures: Selected essays by Clifford Geertz.* New York: Basic Books, Inc.

Guba, E. G. & Lincoln, Y. S. (1981). *Effective evaluation: Improving the usefulness of evaluation results through responsive and naturalistic approaches.* San Francisco: Jossey-Bass.

Harste, J. C., Woodward, V. A., & Burke, C. L. (1984). Examining our assumptions: A transactional view of literacy and learning. *Research in the Teaching of English, 18*(1), 84-107.

Huberman, M. (1996). Moving mainstream: Taking a closer look at teacher research. *Language Arts, 73*(2), 124-140.

Hymes, D. (1974). Introduction. In C. B. Cazden, V. P. Jones, & D. Hymes (Eds.), *Foundations in sociolinguistics: An ethnographic approach* (pp. xi-lvii) Philadelphia: University of Pennsylvania Press.

Kantor, R., Miller, S., & Fernie, D. E. (1992). Diverse paths to literacy in a preschool classroom: A sociocultural perspective. *Reading Research Quarterly, 27*(3), 185-201.

Langer, E. (1997). *The power of mindful learning.* New York: Addison Wesley.

Mathison, S. (1988). Why triangulate? *Educational Researcher, 17*(2), 13-17.

McIntyre, E. (1990). *Young children's responses to various reading contexts in an urban traditional classroom.* Unpublished doctoral dissertation, University of Cincinnati, OH.

Merriam, S. B. (1988). *Case study research in education: A qualitative approach.* San Francisco, CA: Jossey-Bass.

Meyer, D. K. (1993). What is scaffolded instruction? Definitions, distinguishing features, and misnomers. In D. J. Leu & C. K. Kinzer (Eds.), *Examining central issues in literacy research, theory, and practice.* Forty-second yearbook of the National Reading Conference (pp. 41-53). Chicago: National Reading Conference.

Miles, M. B., & Huberman, A. M. (1994). *Qualitative Data Analysis.* Thousand Oaks, CA: Sage Publications.

Nelson, P. A. (1992). *Stories, memorials, and games: Fourth graders respond to history in classroom and museum contexts.* Unpublished doctoral dissertation, Northern Illinois University, DeKalb, IL.

Piaget, J. (1955). *The language and thought of the child.* Cleveland, OH: World.

Richgels, D. J. (1995). A kindergarten sign-in procedure: A routine in support of written language learning. *Forty-fourth Yearbook of The National Reading Conference* (pp. 243-254). Chicago: National Reading Conference, Inc.

Rogoff, B. (1990). *Apprenticeship in thinking.* New York: Oxford University Press.

Spradley, J. P. (1979). *Ethnographic interview.* New York: Holt, Rinehart, and Winston.

Stake, R. E. (1988). Case study methods in educational research: Seeking sweet water. In R. M. Jaeger (Ed.), *Complementary methods for research in education* (pp. 253-265). Washington, DC: American Educational Research Association.

Sulzby, E. (1985). Children's emergent reading of favorite storybooks: A developmental study. *Reading Research Quarterly, 20*(4), 458-481.

Teale, W. H., & Sulzby, E. (1986). Introduction: Emergent literacy as a perspective for examining how young children become writers and readers. In W. H. Teale and E. Sulzby (Eds.), *Emergent literacy: Writing and reading* (pp. vii-xxv). Norwood, NJ: Ablex.

Turner, J. C. (1997). Starting right: Strategies for engaging young literacy learners. In J. T. Guthrie & A. Wigfield (Eds.), *Reading engagement: Motivating readers through integration instruction* (pp. 183-204). Newark, DE: International Reading Association.

Wells, G. & Chang-Wells, L. (1992). *Constructing knowledge together: Classrooms as centers of inquiry and literacy.* Portsmouth, NH: Heinemann.

Vygotsky, L. S. (1978). *Mind in society: The development of higher psychological processes* (M. Cole, Ed.). Cambridge, MA: Harvard University Press. (Original work published in 1930)

Vygotsky, L. S. (1986). *Thought and language.* (Ed. and Trans. by A. Kozulin). Cambridge: MIT Press. (Original work published in 1934)

Wolcott, H. F. (1988). Ethnographic research in education. In R. M. Jaeger (Ed.), *Complementary methods for research in education* (pp. 187-206). Washington, DC: American Educational Research Association.

Wold, L. S. (1998). *Understanding emergent reading in grade one: An investigation of the interplay between reader and contexts.* Unpublished doctoral dissertation, Northern Illinois University, DeKalb.

EMERGENT READERS AND LITERATURE CIRCLE DISCUSSIONS

Thesis Award

Brenda Greene Williams

Warren City School District and
Kent State University

Abstract

The purpose of this teacher action research project was to implement Literature Circles with emergent readers in an all-day kindergarten classroom. Implementation proceeded in three phases. Through interactive read-aloud and direct teacher supervision, the Demonstration Phase modeled various groupings of books children could use, discussion techniques and listening skills. The Guided Phase allowed children limited autonomy in directing their own literature, discussions; the teacher was available to provide necessary support. The Extended Phase of the project began when students had sufficiently internalized the process to function independently. Upon completion of the project, it was found that kindergartners could function independently using a structured Literature Circle format. Their types of responses shifted over time to include more evaluative comments and greater ability to make personal and intertextual links between stories. Literature Circle discussion provided a forum for the practical application of shared activity as outlined in Vygotskian theory.

Introduction

Prior to beginning this project, I had become interested in the Vygotskian idea of shared activity as it supports learning. I had observed children as they supported one another in complex learning activities during center time and journal writing, as well as through the sharing of their independent work with an audience of their peers. I had found that student conversations and comments during interactive read aloud displayed higher levels of thinking with repeated readings of text. Together, these observations made me curious about the possibility of literature discussions with and between emergent readers.

In approaching this action research project, I suspected that even the youngest of school- age children could benefit from the use of literature circles in the classroom. Through this study, I implemented literature circles with my kindergarten students, asking them to share their reading, their re-tellings, and their conversation about quality children's literature.

Literature Review

Marie Clay (1991) defines reading as "a message gaining, problem solving activity that increases in power and flexibility the more it is practiced" (p. 6). Children learn to read by practicing within the social context of the learning environment; they also learn to gain the message of a text by "practicing this action alongside makers of meaning who are more experienced than they are" (Peterson and Eeds, 1990, p. 16). In the classroom environment, literacy learning is not only related to oral communication in the characteristics of the process that occurs. Oral communication facilitates literacy learning because children best learn this message-gaining, problem solving activity, called reading, through dialogue. "Talk helps us to construct ideas and represent experiences for ourselves and others" (Strickland, et. al., 1989, p. 193); it is the catalyst that allows problem solving to become a shared activity because "the give-and-take nature of the system depends on other participants to take up an idea, expand it, and add to it" (Peterson and Eeds, 1990, p. 21).

Chambers contends that dialogue surrounding books should approximate gossip in that participants share both positive and negative enthusiasm, puzzles or difficulties created by the text, and connections which are both "world-to-text" and inter-text. This deep understanding achieved through dialogue is the purpose for implementing literature circles in the classroom. Through the shared activity of conversation, readers of all ability levels, even young learners and emergent readers, can develop great insight (Kasten, 1997; Peterson and Eeds, 1990; Roser and Martinez, 1985). After all:

> Talking well about books is a high-value activity in itself. But talking well about books is also the best rehearsal there is for talking well about other things. So in helping children to talk about their reading, we help them to be articulate about the rest of their lives (Chambers, 1996, p. 2)

Proponents of Vygotskian theory explain that learning is a social process; people learn in community. According to Bodrova and Leong (1996), Vygotsky was unique in his approach to learning theory because he believed that higher mental processes can be shared. "Mental processes not only exist internally to the individual but can occur in an exchange between several people. . . .Shared activity is the means that facilitates a child's internalization of mental processes" (p. 11-12). The breadth and depth of learning are enhanced when rich interactions occur among people of varying degrees of expertise. Communication that facilitates learning and shared activity raises particular concern for educators in the area of literacy instruction.

If learning is a social process, as Vygotsky proposed, then *all* learning is social and the act of constructing meaning from a text can no more be separated from its social context than any other type of learning. "A traditional error of thinking about reading and writing [is] to see them as discrete subjects isolated from the world of language and spoken culture and then to teach them as if they [have] no relationship to listening and speaking" (Holdaway, 1979, p. 12). According to Holdaway (1979), the learning of written language, reading, writing, and spelling, must be intertwined; oral language must infuse the whole process in the same way that talking and listening are related to each other. Imaginative, quality literature is a rich source of instructional material which draws children into the reading experience. In the early stages of learning to read, children often rely on their ability to re-tell those stories found most enjoyable. In the re-telling, they begin to see themselves as readers. Fry (1985) explains that re-tellings are valuable in that they ". . . assist [children] in [their] own silent reading of the text, helping [them] to picture what [they] read and know what's coming next" (p. 23). The conversation that surrounds the development of a re-telling, makes it possible for the child to internalize the story and improve the ability to re-tell with accuracy. Fry further states that a child who re-tells differentiates between reading and other forms of spoken communication. Such a child "is learning about reading, as a skill, and as an experience" (Fry, 1985, p. 23).

Peterson and Eeds (1990) highlight the importance of growth toward more sophisticated re-telling when they discuss layers of story meaning: "Teachers of literature want children to be more than plot readers. They want them to get beyond book-jacket reporting to interpreting story at different levels of meaning" (p. 26). However, children do not begin as readers with the mature sense of awareness teachers want them to eventually achieve. "The complication that results from tracking story movement at various levels makes imaginative interpretation possible. [But] changes in perception take time" (Peterson & Eeds, 1990, p. 27). Conversation helps children to understand the meanings of a text, at various levels. When children begin to understand the story at various levels, their discussion will naturally include the world-to-text and inter-text connections mentioned by Chambers (1996), as well as increasingly complex re-tellings.

Children best learn the strategic act of making meaning from print in a supportive learning environment. Dialogue helps children to make ideas more accessible and thereby facilitates literacy learning; it changes a singular act into a shared activity allowing every member of the group to benefit from various degrees of expertise. The availability of high-interest, quality children's literature further supports literacy learning by providing motivation to read and a focus for conversation. As children hear stories and begin to re-tell them, they begin to define themselves as readers; they can convey the meaning of a familiar text and share understandings of its various layers of meaning. Literature circles are one means of structuring the classroom to provide opportunity for literary conversation.

Design
Subjects

The participants in this study were the children in my self-contained, full-day kindergarten classroom, which is located in an urban school district. My twenty seven students ranged in age from five to six years old. Approximately eighty two percent received free or reduced lunch; this percentage was consistent with the general school population and therefore helped our school to qualify for school-wide, Title I, federal funding. There were fourteen boys and thirteen girls in our class, of whom fifty nine percent were at least partially African-American and thirty seven percent were Caucasian. One child was of Hawaiian descent.

Setting

The classroom space was divided and furniture arranged to allow for various groupings of children and instructional settings. There was a carpet area for whole-class meetings and activities such as read aloud, shared reading, interactive writing, and content area discussions or demonstrations. Each student had an individual work space at one of the tables where school supplies were shared for journal or math work; they had individual book boxes and mailbox spaces for storing personal materials. The remaining sections of the room were divided into learning centers emphasizing literacy play. A management system had been implemented so that children were responsible for their own movement through the various centers during our daily, literacy block of time. They understood the boundaries of each center, appropriate activities, and limited the number of children at each area through the routines that had been established in the classroom.

The kindergarten curriculum at our building follows The Ohio State University LC (Literacy Collaborative) framework; it is a literacy-intense, child-centered program. We had a two and a half hour, uninterrupted block of time each morning for implementing the eight elements of the LC framework: read aloud, shared reading, guided reading, independent reading, shared writing, interactive writing, guided writing, and independent writing. In the afternoon, math, science and social studies theme activities, and special subjects (art, music, gym, etc.) took place.

Description

My action research project was comprised of three phases to implement the use of literature circles with my emergent readers. Phase one was the *Demonstration Phase*. It lasted for two weeks and included three sessions to identify types of book groupings that children might later choose in forming literature circles: multiple versions of the same title, titles by the same author, several versions of a familiar story, or more random groupings of favorite stories. The discussion following our rereadings was directly focused on modeling the use of higher order thinking skills in conversation. The objective was to have children internalize discussion procedures (e.g.: patterns of thinking, types of responses, listening skills). We also had some discussion about the discussion itself, to help the children understand the importance of listening, asking questions, sharing openly, and remaining on-task

The second phase of the project was the *Guided Phase*. Here the children were asked to "give it a try." This phase lasted about two weeks with at least two sessions per week. I planned to ask each child to choose a book first and then cooperatively decide on appropriate groupings. My instructional aide and I circulated to make observations, redirect children who seemed at an "impasse," and record snippets of conversation on audio or video tape. We were available to support children in their attempts, ensure on-task behaviors, interject appropriate comments, or instigate discussion when necessary.

The final phase of the project was the *Extended Phase*. By this time, the children had achieved a working knowledge of the desired procedures as well as a sense of ownership during literature circle discussions; they required less teacher-prompting and intervention. We had experimented with various structures outlined in the aforementioned phases and settled on one which seemed most comfortable for the students to use independently. Less direct supervision and guidance was necessary and therefore, more teacher time was spent on observation and data collection. I continued to record snippets of conversation and to make anecdotal notes for the purpose of analyzing student comments.

Changes in the Study

The Demonstration and Guided Phases of the project proceeded as planned. The children participated in the interactive read-aloud as anticipated. In the Extended Phase, several changes were addressed. It became apparent that children needed to have the books "in hand" in order to focus discussion; they also needed to have the story fresh in their minds, even if it was a favorite. The time factor was a problematic issue in scheduling literature circles since other reading activities already occupied at least an hour of our instructional day; it became necessary to allow literature circles to replace some pre-existing activities. Toward the end of the final phase, a first-grade element was introduced. The first graders helped to resolve the lack-of-time issue because the class divided into groups immediately and did not spend time determining roles, or re-reading stories as a whole group.

Because students in my classroom were accustomed to sharing in front of the group for various purposes, they were associating literature circle discussion with the "Comments and Questions" that usually followed sharing. A discussion structure helped to resolve this problem. The group members needed to take turns talking without one child being designated "leader"; so, we decided that the book under discussion would be passed around the circle to indicate turns. Furthermore, as a general rule, children were to begin by finding a favorite part of the story and explaining why they found it significant. Beginning with "I liked this part of the story because. . ." not only encouraged those children who would otherwise not have known how to join the discussion, but it also acted as a springboard for those who wished to contribute more.

Another problem we encountered was that once literature circles became separate from interactive read-aloud, the students seemed to lack ownership. I feared that instead of being child-centered, it would become a project-centered or curriculum-centered activity. My own tendency to "jump in and rescue" the children when discussion began to wane seemed an additional cause of their lack of ownership. In response, we returned to the Demonstration Phase of the project but had *students* conduct the interactive read-aloud. The purpose of this was to show the class that they were free to comment on the story, their own similar experiences, and ask questions about the plot when *another child* was reading or re-telling, just as when the teacher did the reading. During these demonstrations, I limited myself to comments along the order of "What do you think about what she said?" The children seemed to remain more on-task given this structure, and began to focus on re-telling and linking. We were able to add "That makes me think about. . ." to their repertoire of possible opening discussion phrases.

Results

The results of the study can best be analyzed in reference to the anticipated findings that initiated my desire to implement literature circles: that they would support development toward more detailed and in-depth retellings as well as insightful converstaion and evidence of higher order thinking skills. During the initial phase of the project, story discussion illustrated the children's ability to remember concrete story details and to quote the main characters. However, without teacher guidance, re-tellings lacked correct sequence and tended to leave significant gaps in the story. Children were satisfied to contribute random remembrances which conveyed no continuous sense of the story. During the Extended Phase of the project, in whole-group re-telling, the children remembered the sequence of the story and realized that they were recreating the story experience. They were able to assume and maintain roles, non-verbally prompt one another to maintain the flow of the story, and refrain from making "stray" comments. Though the latter example incorporated a more predictably patterned text with less complicated language than the former example, the children were more attentive and displayed greater ability to maintain the story without teacher assistance than they had prior to regularly participating in literature circles.

Similarly, when student comments from the initial and final stages of the project were compared, a shift became evident in their ability and to respond to one another. Early in the study, teacher comments accounted for 24% of the discussion; this was reduced to 5% near completion of the project. One of the reasons I felt able to withdraw my participation was that the children were less often giving one another "blank stares." The children had not only become proficient at responding to one another in agreement, but they could also disagree and clear up confusions for one another.

Near the end of the project's implementation, the children showed evidence of having learned to more critically evaluate the actions of characters in the story by making links to personal experiences. At the beginning, the children could understand and identify inappropriate behavior, but they did little to elaborate on their ideas. In the final phase, they were able to relate in detail about personal experiences, draw parallels to the story at hand, and come to conclusions that story characters "should have" behaved differently.

In carefully assessing the data collected during each phase of the project, several types of comments emerged. The categories were labelled: Linking Comments, Clarification Comments, Choral Comments, and Evaluative Comments. Linking comments were those referred to by Chambers (1996) as world-to-text and inter-text. These were the responses that reflected the children's ability to connect a story to their personal experiences, associate stories with background knowledge, and notice similarities and differences between stories. Clarification comments were those responses aimed at re-telling portions of the story, predicting what might come next, or asking questions to learn an unknown concept. Choral comments included opportunities for children to recite familiar parts of the story, or jump on the proverbial bandwagon when they liked a comment made by another participant. Finally, evaluative comments were those seeming to exhibit value judgements about things, for example, that "should" or "should not" happen. Choral and clarification comments generally demonstrated less depth of insight than linking or evaluative comments.

Sample conversations from each phase of the project were analyzed and percentages for each comment category were calculated. Though linking and clarification were predominant during each phase, linking comments (which exhibited higher levels of thinking) surpassed clarification by the end of the Extended Phase. From the Guided Phase on, data reflected a decrease in clarification comments (lower level thinking) and a general increase in evaluative comments (higher level thinking). Choral responses became largely nonexistent after the Demonstration Phase, except for a mild resurgence in the Extended Phase which took more the form of "band-wagon" agreements than actual choral recitation. The choral responses became unnecessary when discussion was removed from the interactive read-aloud setting.

Finally, there was a marked, steady decline in teacher prompting throughout the duration of the study which seemed to indicate that the students were able to assume responsibility for directing their own activity with autonomy. Student comments elicited by teacher prompts (which took the form of both questions and suggestive remarks leading children to predictable responses) dropped from approximately 40% during the demonstration phase to approximately 15% by the extended phase of the study, at which time the children were making evaluative comments in the complete absence of teacher prompts. They were also able to redirect their own off-task discussion.

Reflections

I was satisfied to view the results of implementing literature circles with my kindergarten students as successful. My favorite aspect of the project was actually hearing the children converse. Once we got past having the conversation stop when the teacher approached each group, it was exciting to observe the direction their conversations would take. Aside from any improvements evidenced by the tallies, percentages, and graphs, the increased ability of the students to monitor themselves in small groups alone was a valuable product of the endeavor. But far beyond that benefit, is the understanding of story and the motivation to learn to read precipitated by the opportunity for discussion.

For me, the idea of using literature circles with emergent readers has proven itself worthy of further experimentation. However, I would hope to approach such a project in future years with the benefit of hind-sight. Given the emphasis in our curriculum on early reading strategies, and the availability of leveled books, it would be appropriate to begin Literature Circles in the Guided Reading context. Guided Reading is an aspect of the instructional day which already incorporates small groups of children with knowledge of a common text. Guided reading groups are formed on the basis of instructional need and are, therefore, homogeneous. Placing the debate over homogeneous grouping versus heterogeneous grouping aside, we have found that flexible grouping on the basis of need is one necessary element of developing early literacy proficiency. I would not want to limit literature circles to this setting because of the need for diverse levels of ability in stimulating shared activity, but perhaps Guided Reading groups could provide a natural transition. Once routines were established, guidelines could be expanded to include interest-based grouping and the quality children's literature I want children to experience in a variety of settings throughout the day.

It would be valuable to consider more varied forms of student response. My particular students seemed to have difficulty understanding the task in the absence of some formulated structure for the conversation but this approach had its pros and cons. Though I believe providing them with routines for beginning discussion was beneficial, it was also a limiting factor in some respects. Given the somewhat brief duration of this project, I observed that having children begin discussion with a familiar phrase such as "I like this part of the story because. . ." or "This makes me think of. . ." helped to jump-start participation. However, I was beginning to see evidence that this could stilt conversation once children really understood the process. Perhaps the Demonstration Phase could return in cycles as children became increasingly proficient in order to model discussion of the parts of a story that dissatisfy a reader, make the reader wonder, or even anger the reader. I return to Chambers's (1996) assertion that the dialogue surrounding books should approximate gossip and am reminded that gossip can be either good-natured or disparaging, humorous or melancholy, positive or negative. L oiterature circle discussion should reflect both extremes of the emotional continuum.

Literature circles are a prime example of Vygotskian theory in practical application. Through demonstration, children begin to internalize the desired behavior or skill and they in turn become expert-demonstrators for lower functioning peers. The community of learners supports itself toward deeper understanding through shared activity; no one learns in isolation, but rather everyone benefits from each participant's strengths. In the context of literature circles, I observed increasing depth of insight from my *kindergartners* on a daily basis; they had relevant and wonderful things to say!

References

Bodrova, E. & Leong, D. J. (1996). *Tools of the mind: The Vygotskian approach to early childhood education.* Englewood Cliffs, NJ: Prentice Hall, Inc.

Cambourne, B. (1995). Toward an educationally relevant theory of literacy learning: Twenty years of inquiry. *The Reading Teacher, 49,* 182-190.

Chambers, A. (1996). *Tell me: Children, reading, and talk.* York, Maine: Stenhouse Publishers.

Clay, M. M. (1991). *Becoming literate: The construction of inner control.* Portsmouth, NH: Heinemann.

Fry, D. (1985). *Children talk about books: Seeing themselves as readers.* Philadelphia, PA: Open University Press.

Holdaway, D. (1979). *Foundations of literacy.* Gosford, N.S.W.: Ashton Scholastic.

Huck, C. (1977). Literature as the content of reading. *Theory into practice, 16,* 363-371.

Kasten, W. (1997). In Paratore, J. R. & McCormack, R. L. (eds.). *Peer talk in the classroom: Learning from research.* Newark, Delaware: International Reading Association.

Peterson, R. & Eeds, M. (1990). *Grand conversations: Literature groups in action.* New York: Scholastic Inc.

Roser, N., & Martinez, M. (1985). Roles adults play in preschoolers' response to literature. *Language Arts, 62,* 485-490.

Strickland, D. S., Dillon, R. M., Funkhouse, L., Glick, M., & Rogers, C. (1989). Research currents: Classroom dialogue during literature response groups. *Language Arts, 66,* 192-200.

THE IMPACT OF UNIVERSITY AND SCHOOL PARTNERSHIPS ON LITERACY LEARNING

Preservice Teachers Constructing Their Meanings of Literacy in a Field-Based Program

Michael A. Martin
Sarah H. Martin

The University of Southern Mississippi

Charles E. Martin

Georgia College & State University

Abstract

The purpose of this study was to provide a description of how preservice teachers enrolled in a field-based early childhood education program (P-5) constructed their own definitions of literacy and literacy instruction. Specifically, we developed descriptions to answer (1) What concepts of literacy are preservice teachers exposed to during their field placements? (2) How are preservice teachers' literacy concepts affected by the theories espoused by instructors in university classrooms? (3) What effect will their developing concepts of literacy have upon preservice teachers' literacy instruction?

Data from students' journals, field observations/notes, and conferences with students and their cooperating teachers revealed that the majority of students were (a) exposed to traditional teaching in their placements, (b) exposed primarily to constructivist approaches to literacy in university classes, (c) planning to use literature to teach literacy skills, vocabulary, and writing. Finally, it was concluded that the cooperating teachers were also learning from the program. Teachers reported that they were using strategies modeled by the students and were positive toward the field-based program.

The use of field experiences in preservice teacher education programs has become increasingly prevalent as educators turn to constructivist theories for explanations of learning (Fosnot, 1989). Schon (1987) stated that teacher education programs need to place more emphasis on the inclusion of practica so that students gain direct experiences in schools. However, Cochran, DeRuiter, and King (1993) noted that "careful attention must be paid to the context in which the development of understanding occurs, and learning must be situated in a context like the one in which these understandings are to be used" (p. 266).

Participation in field experiences will also have a significant impact upon students' beliefs specific to literacy instruction. Roehler, Duffy, Hermann, Conley and Johnson (1988) felt that a teacher's beliefs about literacy would influence their decisions and judgments about how literacy instruction took place in the classroom. Therefore, as students go into these experiences, a number of issues which impact their beliefs and performance need to be addressed. One such issue concerns the concepts of literacy that students see and develop as a result of their field placements. Kagan (1992) discovered that new teachers, as a result of their interactions with children, "may begin to stand back from their personal beliefs and images, acknowledging where they are incorrect or inappropriate. As the image of self as teacher is resolved, attention shifts to the design of instruction and finally to what pupils are learning from academic tasks" (p. 155).

Another issue relates to how students' concepts of literacy are affected by the theories espoused by instructors in their university classrooms. Newton (1997) stated that "students' knowledge construction is influenced not only by the students' continuous interaction with all members of the school community, but also by the university instructor" (p. 212). Additionally, Longerger (1992) discussed the notion that reading courses taken as a part of the perservice teacher education program influence the students' literacy beliefs. A final issue of concern is the effect students' concepts of literacy instruction will have on the literacy instruction they plan for their future as teachers. Duchein, Frazier, Konopak, and Palmer (1994) found that preservice teacher's experiences did have an impact upon their future instructional decisions. Additionally, Harste & Burke, (1977) and Hollingsworth (1989) have stated that a teacher's concept of literacy instruction will have a significant impact on how they teach literacy. Pajares (1992) concluded that "findings suggest a strong relationship between teachers' educational beliefs and their planning, instructional decisions, and classroom practices" (p. 326). The purpose of this study was to investigate the issues discussed above as they affected the students enrolled in their junior year of a teacher education program. Specifically, we developed descriptions to answer (1) What concepts of literacy are preservice teachers exposed to during their field placements? (2) How are preservice teachers' literacy concepts affected by the theories espoused by instructors in university classrooms? (3) What effect will their developing concepts of literacy have upon preservice teachers' literacy instruction?

Method

Participants

The participants involved in the study were 34 early childhood (P-5) education students. There were 32 white females, one black female, and one white male. Participants were beginning their junior year in a teacher education program at a small southern public university. Participants were judged to represent a variety of ability levels based on their undergraduate GPA's (2.5-3.8). The participants were members of a cohort group which remained together, both in the field work and university class-work, for the junior and senior years of their undergraduate program.

The Professional Education Program: Junior Year

The present study focused on the junior year, the first year in which the participants were in the professional education portion of their program. The professional education program under investigation is unique in that it provides extensive fieldwork, approximately 1000 hours, over the course of the junior and senior years. In addition, the course work offered the students was presented in an integrated fashion. The purpose of this integration was twofold. We wished to teach the students course content and methods for teaching the content, but we also wanted to stress the importance of integrating curriculum, so we modeled how to teach courses in an integrated fashion.

The program implements a constructivist philosophy. During the year of this study, students were involved in experiences which enabled them to construct their own meanings by direct experiences rather than by sitting in classrooms taking notes from learned instructors. Approximately two weeks into the first quarter, the students were placed in kindergarten through fifth-grade classrooms with volunteer teachers. The second and third quarters, students were involved in classrooms during every week of the quarters. Each week students spent three mornings and one full day per week in classrooms. In the afternoons, students took university classes. Students became an integral part of the classroom as quickly as possible. Initial requirements included observing children and assisting the teacher with various classroom duties; however, they were soon required to plan and teach daily lessons. Over the course of the year, in addition to their daily planning and teaching, the students were required to develop integrated instructional units in groups and individually which ranged from one to two weeks in duration. Each quarter students were placed with different teachers at different grade levels to allow them to see a variety of classrooms, children, and teachers. Friday mornings were reserved for special workshops, such as Project Wild; invovlement in professional teaching activities, such as the Very Special Arts Festival, and individual projects.

Literacy Course Content

Each quarter the students were enrolled in courses which contained a literacy component. As mentioned earlier, courses were integrated, so no course was unadulterated language arts. Fall quarter included a course of elementary reading/language arts and social studies. During winter quarter students took reading/language arts combined with educational psychology, and in spring, the reading/language arts topics were again taught with social studies. These courses exposed the students to a variety of philosophies about literacy using Gunning (1996) as the required textbook. Literacy topics covered in the courses included models of the reading process, stages of literacy development, phonics instruction, sight word/vocabulary development, comprehension instruction, literacy across the curriculum, children's literature, approaches to teaching reading, process writing instruction, evaluating literacy, and diversity issues in literacy. Course assignments required that students complete written quizzes on course content, collect literacy resources—especially surveying children's literature, evaluate informal and standardized tests, and respond in journals. Throughout the year students were guided through increasingly complex instructional planning tasks. During the fall quarter students were required to plan and teach individual integrated lessons and to begin the development of a resource file. In the winter quarter, students worked in small groups to develop one-week thematic units in which they were required to integrate literacy and content area instruction, incorporate children's literature, and use writing to learn. In the spring quarter, students were required to work in small groups to develop a one to two week unit which integrated a minimum of three content areas.

Data Collection and Analysis

The data for this study were collected over one year of the professional education program. Students kept journals in which they chronicled their experiences during the academic year and made personal reflective responses. These journals served as the primary data source for the study. Each student's journal was collected three times during each quarter. The concurrent analysis of this data was organized by question. Bogdan & Biklen (1992) describe the process of generating coding categories dependent upon the specific questions asked in the research. This process guided our analysis. The journals were read with the research questions in mind.

Students' responses were categorized as they contributed to answers regarding how students were conceptualizing what they saw in (1) their field placements, (2) their university classrooms, and (3) responses which described how they planned to teach. Students' entries which were pertinent to these questions were noted and categorized by separate researchers as contributing to answers. Consensus discussions were held to categorize responses which were coded differently by individual researchers. When ideas were difficult to categorize or understand, classroom discussions with the students sometimes helped to clarify meaning.

In addition, throughout the year, all students were visited weekly in their practicum placements by their university supervisor—one of the authors of this study. This totaled approximately twenty-five visits per student per year. Each visit lasted approximately thirty minutes per student. These multiple visits assisted in informing the data analysis. During these visits, the supervisor observed the student teaching in the classroom, conferenced with the student, and/or conferenced with the student and his/her teacher. The field notes collected from the observations and conferences during these visits served as a secondary data source and informed the development of answers. Responses that were most illustrative of various facets of the answers which developed were selected to be used as quotes.

Results/Discussion

The results of this study are limited by the sources of data collected. The primary data source, the students' journals, is self report data and subject to bias. Additionally, Hollingsworth (1989) discusses the influences which instructors have on the language and ideas expressed by preservice teachers. As the instructors were the researchers in this study and were data sources themselves, the researchers provided field observation data, the data is subject to researcher bias.

What Concepts of Literacy are Preservice Teachers Exposed to During Their Field Placements?

The majority of students stated in their journals and during supervisor conferences that their teachers were teaching "traditional lessons . . . emphasizing a skill of the day." Many of the lessons were centered around the use of the phonics program used in the district. "All kids do is worksheets!" was a common response from students. Otherwise, many said that "the teacher used some children's literature, but mostly used the basal readers." Much of the time spent using the basal readers involved "children taking turns reading aloud, followed by doing worksheets." On other occasions, students observed "teachers letting children take turns reading orally . . . going down each row."

Students also noted in their journals and during supervisor conferences a concern for the lack of pre-reading, reading, and post-reading activities. Students stated that they "never really saw the teacher activating children's prior knowledge before reading." A common observation was of "the teachers taking a few minutes to remind the children of what they did earlier or the day before." During reading, the teacher "mainly just read the book or story, or had the children read, and asked questions afterwards." The questions were usually in the form of "recall or inferencing." A number of students stated "seldom were [children] asked to apply the story to their own lives." Sometimes the teacher would "ask the children to write about their favorite part afterwards or something like that. . . ." These types of activities were observed during the supervisor observations and noted in the field notes.

Additionally, students were concerned by how little children were read to. On one occasion, a student was observed while reading to the children in her classroom. As she read the book, the children moved closer and closer towards her. The classroom teacher eventually interrupted the reading and told the children to remain in their seats while being read to. In her journal, the student noted, "When I read aloud to the kids, they moved their chairs closer and closer. The teacher got mad at them, but I felt like they were really involved. [The teacher] didn't understand how they were acting because she never reads to them."

How are Preservice Teachers' Literacy Concepts Affected by the Theories Espoused by Instructors in University Classrooms?

For our students, the university classes in literacy provided a framework for their literacy constructions and a catalyst for questioning both their preconceived ideas and the practices they saw in their field experiences (Newton 1997). The data answering the second question concerning what students saw in their university classrooms revealed that initially, the students found the major philosophies of literacy instruction: (1) bottom-up, (2) interactive, and (3) top-down useful for evaluating their pre-existing beliefs. Data from students' journals indicated that students applied these three philosophies as labels for their beliefs. "I have a name for what I think now. This helps me tell people what I think about how reading is done."

In the first journal responses collected after the class meeting which introduced students to these philosophies, most of the students identified themselves as bottom-up. Their journals supported this with responses like, "It is important to teach the basic skills and build upon those. This is the best way for students to learn to read and write." Students who found themselves being more interactive in their approach to literacy instruction/learning stated "you have to use what they know to help children get what they are reading." Course content helped them identify themselves as having a bottom-up or interactive philosophy toward literacy instruction/learning.

As the course work progressed, the students were introduced to a variety of teaching methods/strategies connected with the three major models mentioned above. The journals reflected students' responses to the new ideas and how the new ideas were influencing their thinking. "Before I had this class, I felt that you had to know letters to read words, words to read sentences, and so on. I can see now how some children can do this as they learn to read." Another student who identified herself as bottom-up in her thinking stated, "You have to know the alphabet, for example, before you can learn new words, but it's important to have students practice writing early and as often as possible. This can help them learn words too."

Coursework emphasized the use of literature, the writing process, and the incorporation of writing across the curriculum to help children become strategic readers who were actively involved in their own literacy learning. Eventually, the majority of students responded positively toward these ideas in their journals. They appreciated the child centered approach. "Children come to school with such different backgrounds, but each child is interested and excited about things. If I can connect the interest and excitement to what I'm teaching, the child will learn better." As students began to see new teaching strategies and were required to use them in their field experiences, they questioned, "These strategies are good, but how much can we really do them when we have to get through the basal and prepare students for the ITBS?" Students also reported conversations with their cooperating teachers where they were told that the "real world is a lot different than what they tell you in college." The new ideas presented in class were causing students to question their original concepts about literacy as well as what they were seeing in their field placements.

What Effect Will Their Developing Concepts of Literacy Have Upon Preservice Teachers' Literacy Instruction?

By the end of the first year in the program, most students stated that they "understood why teachers are teaching skills in a traditional manner. Teaching this way fits in well with the programs they use for teaching, and the standardized tests they have to administer." Many students also stated that they "plan on teaching differently" than what they saw their teachers doing. "I should be able to do some of the things my university instructors are asking me to do and still prepare the children for the standardized tests."

Data suggested that the majority of the students "plan to use a lot of children's literature" in their teaching both of reading and various subject areas. The students stated that they "still planned to teach skills," but that they wanted to do it as much as they could "in the context of actual reading and strategy usage." An example of this related to a common approach to vocabulary instruction. Many students stated that "the teachers give out a vocabulary list each week. The children are asked to spell the words a number of times, create sentences with the words, and use the words in their journal writing." Students stated that they would "still have word lists for the students, but that a lot of the words would come from their books." Additionally, students stated that they planned "to use strategies to teach vocabulary words . . . not just spelling them and writing sentences with them." Almost all students stated that they felt that "writing had an important place" in the teaching they did in their classrooms. Students also felt that teachers "need to provide more hands-on experiences which relate to the stories that children are reading. This would make learning more fun, and interesting." Finally, a number of students stated that teachers "need to try to teach the children on their own level."

The fact that the university students saw classroom teachers using classroom practices which were contradictory to what they were learning in the university setting caused some concern among the students. However, this concern did not often cause them to change what they had planned to do. They often asked, "Why aren't the teachers doing any of this stuff? Don't they see that this is more interesting?" Additionally, because the students believed in what they were doing, and because the classroom teachers had agreed to let them use their classrooms for the practicum requirements, the students still planned their instruction using the classroom practices they were exposed to in their university classrooms. Therefore, when the students were observed by the supervisor, the lessons they had planned and what they actually taught were usually consistent.

The students did occasionally make adjustments to their lessons as they interacted with the children. Sometimes they should have made adjustments and did not. During observations, the supervisor had a copy of the intended lesson plan. As the teaching was occurring, students were able to adjust a strategy to better teach the lesson. At other times, they were too focused on teaching their lesson and not the children. In conferences after the teaching had occurred, the supervisor and student discussed these situations. One student explained, "I changed the plan. Instead of having everyone doing the activity, some did it on their own while I worked with the ones who did not understand." Illustrating the lack of adjustment, another student bemoaned, "I don't know why they did not get it. We had done some of this before, so I figured they understood." The outcome of these conferences was often an understanding by the students of what they could have done differently and what they did well. Something that was stressed in these conferences and throughout the year was the need to develop plans with the children in mind, and the need to be flexible in one's implementation of plans .

Finally, some interesting additional information surfaced during conferences with the classroom teachers. Some of the teachers mentioned that they were learning about and "using some of the new teaching strategies modeled by the preservice teachers." The teachers stated that learning these new approaches gave them "some new perspectives on their children." Many of the teachers stated that they "wished that they had gone through a program which provided for so much field experience before they student taught and graduated."

Conclusions/Implications

One major conclusion we draw from this investigation is that it is essential that university education faculty examine and take into account the constructs of teaching and learning that our preservice teachers bring with them. "Links may exist between the contexts under which preservice teachers acquire literacy and the beliefs about literacy learning they come to hold" (Roe & Vukelich, 1998, p. 281). Students come into preservice teaching programs with years of experience in traditional school settings which have developed their concepts of literacy and literacy instruction (Gray, 1984). "Teacher education programs cannot ignore the power of the understandings its preservice teachers hold and how these beliefs might shape their candidates' intended teaching practices" (Roe & Vukelich, 1998, p. 282). We must be constantly aware of these existing constructs and base our instruction on that knowledge. We found, as did Lonberger (1992) and Newton (1997), that students' beliefs are influenced by their university classroom experiences. The classes required of students inform preservice teachers of new descriptions of literacy and approaches to literacy instruction and help them to integrate this new information into their personal concepts of literacy. However, if we fail to guide preservice teachers to an understanding or realization of their personal beliefs, we might reduce the impact of the teacher education program (Roe & Vukelich, 1998). The students in our study were able examine their preexisting beliefs and to attach labels to them as they entered the program and were introduced to various philosophies of reading in their university classes. These labels helped to objectify their beliefs. Class discussions and journal responses allowed students to talk about them and adjust them as they were introduced to new methods.

Schon (1987) stated that "a reflective practicum could serve as a bridge between the worlds of the university and practice" (p. 309). The field-based program described in this study, with its intensive field component, is one such "practicum" for preservice teachers which allows for in-depth learning experiences. However, preservice teacher preparation must go further than simply including field experiences. Field experiences must be conducted in tandem with classes which introduce new literacy methods, and reflective activities must integrate learning class concepts and interpreting the field experiences. An aggregate of new concepts and practice cemented by critical thinking through guided reflection can bring about changed conceptions that lead to changed practice. In this study, the development of students' literacy concepts was affected not only by university classroom experiences but also by the field experiences. When students reflected on their experiences in traditional settings, we realized that teachers and their teaching were supporting our students' preexisting concepts rather than the new methods presented in class. Kagan's (1992) review noted that preservice teachers need "to study pupils in systematic ways" (p. 142), and Newton's (1997) data illustrate how preservice teachers learn to focus on their students in field experiences. We found that what our students saw in the field experiences was as influential for them as what they saw teachers doing. What our students perceived as being best for the children they saw in the field experiences was influencing them along with what they saw teachers doing. Reflection and discussion of these experiences allowed students to use their own literacy processes to continue the adjustment of their beliefs.

It is clear that what preservice teachers see in field experiences and what they hear in university classes do not always match. The field placement may be providing them with direct experience in the context in which they will be using their teaching skills as Schon (1987) suggested, but it does not always provide a context which supports our students' implementation of university course concepts. Classroom teachers told our students that the university is not educating future teachers to deal with the realities of the public schools. We must think carefully about this situation. We need to create teachers who feel confident as agents of change in elementary schools, and we must forge partnerships with the school personnel who provide the field experiences our students need. To facilitate this end, university personnel must understand current practices in the schools and that school communities deserve input into the teacher education programs that utilize their facilities and personnel. Just as importantly, we need to help school personnel understand the concepts taught in the university. Therefore, our teacher preparation programs must not isolate the stakeholders in the process; rather we should capitalize on the expertise available. A social constructivist (Fosnot, 1996; Vygotsky, 1978) view of learning can provide a foundation for the use of this expertise as well as it does for the preparation of students in professional education programs. We should understand that not only are the students constructing their concepts of literacy instruction, but so are the university personnel and classroom teachers. We are all involved in an ongoing conversation about what works, what is important, and what needs improvement. We all can grow from the perspectives of the others present in this endeavor (Stephens, 1998).

Everyone concerned must be willing to examine the traditions which exist, respect them, and participate in ongoing conversations about growth. Preservice teachers, public school personnel, and university faculty involved in teacher education programs can then assume that teachers' concepts of literacy education may not coalesce during the time they are in our programs. It will, in all probability, take a number of years of teaching for new teachers to feel comfortable with their concepts of literacy instruction. While their concepts develop, field experience programs in the schools can continue to affect their development. Additionally, although teachers may develop a set of beliefs about literacy education during their preservice program which matures in their first years of teaching, we can also assume that these beliefs remain mutable. Conceptions of literacy change as teachers gain more experience and as the field of literacy education grows. Teacher education programs which support collaboration between inservice teachers and university personnel in the preparation of new teachers seem to provide an environment that supports the growth and the development of literacy education (Hermann & Sarracino, 1993; Mosenthal, 1996; Roskos & Walker, 1994).

In our interaction with our students and the teachers in the field, we saw that all members were being affected by the experiences. The effect on students is described in this study, but we observed effects on teachers, as well. Some practicing teachers were impressed by the methods used by our students in their classrooms and were able to adopt some of these methods as their own. Some teachers were reminded by our students of the importance of a child centered focus. They were able to de-emphasize some of the demands of textbooks and standardized tests as they saw their own students' responses to different teaching methods. They praised the intensive field experiences in our program to some extent because the program respects the real context of teaching. Newton (1997) discussed the impact that ongoing interactions with children in the schools had on her as a university instructor. We found this affecting us as well. Daily observations in classrooms and interactions with school personnel kept us aware of the many pressures teachers endure. Our university classes were enriched by contemporary cases to discuss as exemplars of concepts being taught. Our own beliefs were tested daily. We are convinced that teacher education programs which carefully integrate coursework with extensive field experiences through critical reflection benefit preservice teachers, inservice teachers, university professors and, logically, school children.

References

Bogdan, R.C., & Biklen, S.K. (1992). *Qualitative research for education: An introduction to theory and methods (2nd ed.)*. Boston, MA: Allyn and Bacon.

Cochran, K.F., DeRuiter, J.A., & King, R.A. (1993). Pedagogical content knowing: An integrative model for teacher preparation. *Journal of Teacher Education, 44,* (4), 263-272.

Duchein, M.A., Frazier, D.W., Konopak, B.C., & Palmer, P. (1994, December). *Preservice teachers' literacy life histories: Exploring the influence of personal experience on beliefs about reading and instruction.* Paper presented at the Annual Meeting of the National Reading Conference, Coronado, CA.

Fosnot, C.T. (1989). *Inquiring teachers, inquiring learners: A constructivist approach for teaching.* New York: Teachers College.

Fosnot, C.T. (1996). *Constructivism: Theory, perspectives, and practice.* New York: Teachers College.

Gray, M.J. (1984). Is the influence of phycholinguistic research evident in preservice teachers' view of the reading process? *Reading Horizons, 24,* 253-258.

Gunning, T. G. (1996). *Creating reading instruction for all children (2nd ed.).* Needham Heights, MA: Simon & Schuster.

Harste, J.C., & Burke, C.L. (1977). A new hypothesis for reading teacher research: Both the teaching and learning of reading is theoretically based. In P.D. Pearson (Ed.), *Reading: Theory, research, and practice* (pp. 32-40). New York: Mason.

Hermann, B.A., & Sarracino, J. (1993). Restructuring a preservice literacy methods course: Dilemmas and lessons learned. *Journal of Teacher Education, 44,* 96-106.

Hollingsworth, S. (1989). Prior beliefs and cognitive change in learning to teach. *American Educational Research Journal, 2,* 160-189.

Kagan, D. (1992). Professional growth among preservice and beginning teachers. *Review of Educational Research, 62,* 129-169.

Lonberger, R.B. (1992). Belief systems and instructional choices of preservice teachers. In N.D. Padak, T.V. Rasinski, & J.Logan (Eds.), *Literacy research and practice: Foundations for the year 2000* (pp. 71-78). Commerce, TX: College Reading Association.

Mosenthal, J. (1996). Situated learning and methods coursework in the teaching of literacy. *Journal of Literacy Research, 28,* 379-403.

Newton, E.V. (1997). Learning to teach in the "real world": Reflections on field-based reading instruction. In W.M. Linek & E.G. Sturtevant (Eds.). *Exploring literacy* (pp. 207-219). Commerce, TX: College Reading Association.

Pajares, M.F. (1992). Teachers' beliefs and educational research: Cleaning up a messy construct. *Review of Educational Research, 62,* 307-332.

Roe, M.F., & Vukelich, C. (1998). Literacy histories: Categories of influence. *Reading Research and Instruction, 37*(4), 281-295.

Roehler, L.R., Duffy, G.G., Hermann, B.A., Conley, M., & Johnson, J. (1988). Knowledge structures as evidence of the personal: Bridging the gap from thought to practice. *Journal of Curriculum Studies, 20,* 159-165.

Roskos, K., & Walker, B.J. (1994). Learning to teach problem readers: Instructional influences on preservice teachers' practical knowledge. *Journal of Teacher Education, 45,* 279-288.

Schon, D.A. (1987). *Educating the reflective practitioner.* San Francisco: Jossey-Bass.

Stephens, D. (1998). An agenda for teacher educators. In T. E. Raphael & K. H. Au (Eds.), *Literature-based instruction: Reshaping the curriculum* (pp. 371-378). Norwood, MA: Christopher-Gordon.

Vygotsky, L.S. (1978). *Mind in society: The development of higher phychological processes.* Cambridge, MA: Harvard University.

Collaborative Research, Reflection and Refinement: The Evolution of Literacy Coursework in a Professional Development Center

Mary Beth Sampson
Carole Walker
Michelle Fazio

Texas A&M University-Commerce

Abstract

While two studies examining the perceptions of both preservice teachers and public school mentor (cooperating) teachers regarding literacy coursework, integrated course content, and field experiences in a professional development center are briefly described in this article the primary focus is a discussion of the collaborative use of the data. University faculty, public school mentors (cooperating teachers) and university students enrolled in teacher education courses collaboratively examined the data from the two studies, reflected upon the information gleaned from the research, and utilized the information to inform and refine instructional practices in a professional development center.

The research literature documents numerous obstacles to collaboration between public schools and universities (Winitzky, Stoddart, & O'Keefe, 1992). It also presents compelling evidence that collaboration in professional development schools does not often provide equal voice and responsibility for all participants (Dixon & Ishler, 1992; Roemer, 1991; Sarason, 1982). However, the shared responsibility for educating preservice teachers can be enhanced when partners jointly ask questions, analyze responses, and make lessons learned visible (Foote, Walker, and Zeek, 1997).

In this article, two studies examining the perceptions of both preservice teachers and public school mentor (cooperating) teachers regarding literacy coursework, integrated course content, and field experiences in a professional development center are briefly described. However, the primary focus of the article is a discussion of the process that occurred when partners collaboratively examined the data from the two studies, reflected upon the information gleaned from the research, and utilized the information to inform and refine instructional practices in a professional development center.

Theoretical Framework

The two studies were conducted within a professional development school at a southwestern state university that strives to follow the model of organic collaboration (Dixon & Isher, 1992) in which university and public school partners mutually redefine their roles and responsibilities. When the program was initiated in 1992, the following vision for the professional development center was jointly developed by public school and university partners: "[Our center will be] designed, implemented, delivered, monitored, evaluated, and modified by a collaboration of partners with representation from all constituents of the program, i. e., teacher educators, university students, public school classroom teachers" (Governing Board of the NETCPDT, 1994, p. 1).

Public school and university partners view the field-based program as an opportunity to weave together theory and practice. Their collaborative program design places preservice teachers who are in the final two semesters of their undergraduate university experience in a public school setting for an entire year. During the first semester of this final year of preparation, the preservice teachers are referred to as *interns* and are in the public school two days each week. One day per week, the interns participate in an integrated seminar. A major design challenge in the seminars is curriculum integration. In striving to meet this challenge, literacy theory and strategies are meshed throughout the content areas as interns connect content and pedagogy within and across five courses: content reading, math, science, and social studies methods, and working with diverse learners.

The second semester, the preservice teachers or *residents* are in the public school five days per week with the exception of nine daylong integrated seminars interspersed throughout the semester. Residents earn nine hours credit for three practical courses centered around the classroom challenges experienced during residency: classroom management, technology, and inclusion in field-based settings. Residents also earn an additional six hours credit for student teaching, which provides the opportunity for them to apply knowledge and strategies gleaned from seminar experiences as they teach in their mentors' classrooms in public schools.

Both intern and resident seminars are designed and taught by a team of two to five university faculty members with public school mentor participation and input. Constructivist approaches (Brooks and Brooks, 1993) such as problem solving and action research are used so that these preservice teachers gain practical, theoretical, and content knowledge.

In line with the initial mission of our professional development center, expanded opportunities for reflection for both inservice and preservice partners have remained a goal in order to extend collaboration beyond initial implementation (Olson, 1990) and to allow reflection to guide future action (Killion & Todhem, 1991). As literacy educators within the centers, we engaged in ongoing collaborative research to determine the perceptions of all partners and to refine our program. We were concerned that the "reflections" of all partners could be analyzed, yet the full impact of the research not be realized unless the findings were shared with all partners. The professional growth in both partners and the program was our goal. While we believe that research should help educators understand, monitor, refine and solidify rationales for instructional actions, studies have found that often research does not impact practice (Sarason, 1982; Fenstermacher, 1986; Barth, 1990).

The reasons for this lack of impact are varied. Conducting and writing research are often seen as roles of the university academician; consequently, the primary audience for written research is often other academicians (Sarason, 1982; Barth, 1990). Thus, the notion persists that the research community operates in the world of "theory," while the public school focuses on "practice." Separating these worlds is counterproductive to the development of "reflective practitioners"— professionals who engage in reflective thought about both current practices and research which leads to reflective action (Olson & Singer, 1994; Smyth, 1989; Van Manen, 1990).

Several researchers have identified promising practices which allow these worlds to overlap if not merge. Santa and Santa (1995) found that teachers given opportunities to explore the research process demonstrated reflective behavior by thinking about instructional experiences, locating and describing problem areas, and trying and testing options. The importance of literacy teachers engaging in collaborative research with university partners is described by Ayers and Schubert (1994) as an opportunity for "collective reflection" (p. 108) which will "perhaps reconstruct their own teaching and conception of teaching . . . what teachers have learned, or what they think they have learned" (p. 114). Our intent, as literacy educators, must not only be to examine instructional situations to determine what is effective, but also to utilize research to refine the instruction (Kamil, 1984). Therefore, while this article includes information from two collaborative research studies, it focuses on efforts to include all partners in the processes of thoughtfully reflecting on and utilizing the feedback from preservice and inservice teachers to enhance growth in all partners—and refine the professional development center

The Initial Studies

Mentors in Study A and interns in Study B responded to a survey consisting of open-ended questions designed to determine their perceptions concerning skills, experiences, and knowledge needed upon the beginning of internship. In addition, the interns in Study B were asked to respond to an open-ended question concerning the most important things they had learned during their internship.

In Study A, interns in two of the professional development school centers interviewed public school mentors using the survey. The interviews occurred toward the end of the Fall 1996 semester. The interns asked mentors the following questions:

1. What should interns know and be able to do upon entering the public school classroom?

2. Why is this important to you?

The interns recorded the mentors' responses on the "Survey of Mentor Teachers" form. Forty-five mentor teachers from two centers working in seven independent school districts—about half of those eligible—completed the survey.

Data in Study B were collected over two semesters (Fall 1997 and Spring 1998) from interns who completed their internship in ten public schools in two public school districts. Both districts were partners in the initial design of the professional development school program. At the conclusion of internship, interns were asked to complete an open-ended written survey consisting of the following prompts:

1. An intern should know and/or be able to do the important things listed below when she/he arrives at the beginning of the intern semester. . .

2. The most important things I learned in internship were. . .

Responses were received from 98% of the interns.

In Study A, a team consisting of three public school mentor teachers expressing interest in the research process and one university liaison who was a member of the university research team which had designed the study utilized constant comparative analysis (Glaser & Strauss, 1967; Strauss & Corbin, 1990) to identify categories of mentor responses. The three mentors and the liaison/researcher each has at least four years experience working in the field-based collaborative. The mentors and university liaison/researcher compared the categories and through discussion and joint recursive analysis reached consensus on refined categories (Glaser & Strauss, 1967; Glaser, 1992). During this process, no attempt was made to suggest a priority order for the items on the list. After the categories were determined, two members of the university research team sorted the responses into various categories. The two university researchers again utilized discussion and joint recursive analysis in order to reach consensus concerning the sorting of the responses. After consensus was reached, the responses in each category were tallied using a frequency count, and percentages were computed.

Researchers in Study B analyzed the interns' responses to the prompts separately. Two university researchers who also served as university liaisons in the field-based program examined the data and utilized constant comparative analysis to identify categories (Glaser & Strauss, 1967; Strauss & Corbin, 1990). As in Study A, discussion and joint recursive analysis were utilized to reach consensus in the sorting of responses. Responses in each category were then tallied using a frequency count and percentages were calculated. A third university researcher (a research assistant) examined the data, and through discussion and joint recursive analysis consensus was reached on both the categories and the sorting of the responses into the various categories.

Results of Initial Studies

Table 1 summarizes the findings in Study A giving the five highest categories of mentors' responses, examples within each category, the frequency with which these items appeared on the mentors' lists and the percentage of mentors whose responses fit that category. The majority of the mentors' responses were grouped within four categories. The categories reflected the mentors' concerns about the basics of teaching school such as being a professional with a frequency of 21 (47% of mentors listed this as important), planning (21, 47%), classroom management (20, 44%) and delivering effective lessons in an environment where learning is the focus (18, 40%).

Tables 2 and 3 display the results of Study B. As can be seen, "Classroom Management/ Organization" with a frequency of 52 (83% of interns cited this as important) was by far the most frequent response to both prompts. "Professionalism" was the second most frequently listed item (26) with 41% of the interns citing this as an important attribute for interns to demonstrate upon arrival in the field. Thirty-five percent of the interns noted "Professionalism" on their surveys making it the third item (22) in the listing of the most important things learned. In contrast, "Strategies"—the second most frequent response to the most important things learned—was not listed as a response in the first survey.

Table 1. Mentor Teachers Beliefs About What an Intern Should Know and/or be Able to do at Beginning of the Semester (N = 45) (Frequency ≥10)

CATEGORY	FREQUENCY	PERCENTAGE
Professionalism: (demonstrate initiative; see what needs to be done in the classroom; communicate with the mentor and students; ask questions; have a positive attitude; smile; bring something to share—books, etc.; be prompt and willing to spend extra time; avoid absences; be on campus more; show enthusiasm; do not get friendly with students)	21	47%
Lesson Cycle: (how to write lesson plans; familiar with the lesson cycle; Bloom's Taxonomy; present/evaluate lessons; importance of questioning for understanding; monitor and assist children; higher level thinking skills)	21	47%
Classroom Management: (return classroom items to their proper place; plan; do paperwork; be familiar with state-adopted texts; have organization skills; listen to children and record what they know; have research skills; be flexible; be confident; know discipline management strategies; understand the age group; be independent; complete lesson plans by end of week)	20	44%
How to Teach and Content Knowledge/Strategies: (have content knowledge; be familiar with the "Essential Elements;" have science and social studies classes before interning; observe and utilize classroom procedures; know practical approaches for reading instruction; recognize strategies in use; know research-based practices.)	18	40%

Table 2. Interns Beliefs about What an Intern Should Know and/or be Able to do at Beginning of the Semester (N = 63) (Frequency ≥9)

Category	Frequency	Percentage
Classroom Management/Organization: (school rules; time management; routine; teacher duties; praise; how to plan lessons; knowing what lesson plan terms mean; locating resources; respecting students and commanding respect from students; being in charge; behavior management; structure and consistency)	52	83%
Professionalism: (dress; being courteous; conduct; confidentiality; integrity; ethics; ITEPs; familiarity with portfolios; teamwork; educational philosophies; accepting constructive criticism; preparation for interviews; educational goals; flexibility regarding planning, time, and lessons)	26	41%
University Requirements: (awareness of assignments; due dates; amount of time needed; when courses are offered; meeting dates; classes needed; schedules; grading systems for seminars; rubric requirements; requirements for reflection journals; whom to contact for questions)	14	22%
The Five Proficiencies: (how to align lessons/proficiencies; understanding how they help with the portfolio; prior knowledge)	12	19%
Communication Skills: (diction; communicating with students, mentors, liaisons, and parents; listening skills; social skills; asking questions)	9	14%

Table 3. The Three Most Important Things I Learned in Internship (N=63) (Frequency ≥10)

CATEGORY	FREQUENCY	PERCENTAGE
Classroom management/organization (high expectations of students; time management; being efficient; have an activity for them to do when they come in; lesson planning; importance of objectives; importance of first two weeks; classroom discipline; praising students; respect; being in charge; locating resources; variety of roles teachers play)	55	87%
Strategies/Activities (mini-lessons; adapting strategies to various content areas; cooperative groups; bubbles; paper towel experiments; tournament; 12 Important Ways to Become a Better Math Teacher; fine arts; music and arts; physical activity; how to vary reading; instructional learning)	27	43%
Professionalism (not to panic over portfolios; using ITEPs as a communication tool; portfolios; team work; being reflective; recognizing improvement needs; accepting constructive criticism; flexibility concerning paradigm shifts; understanding the dynamics of education; expectations; the desire to learn; ask questions; participate; observe; willingness to help)	22	35%
Recognizing Diversity (teaching/learning styles; how to adapt to/deal with diversity; knowing not all students have adequate resources at home; importance of cultural sensitivity; understanding students' needs)	20	32%
Integration (integrating many disciplines/curricular areas into one lesson, thematic units; integrating literature into science, social studies, math)	16	25%

What Happened as We Engaged in Collaborative Research—and Reflection

Mentor Reflections and Actions

While the research design in Study A called for a frequency count of the responses after generating the categories, the mentors chose other ways of examining the data. After mentors generated categories for the data in Study A, they decided to compare the categories to the 15 competencies which comprise the Professional Development Examination for the Certification of Educators in Texas (ExCET). Then, they made the comparison to the 19 competencies in the English Language Arts Domain of the Elementary Comprehensive ExCET. The mentor teachers were interested in conducting this comparison between the categories they had generated and these 34 competencies because preservice teachers must demonstrate knowledge of the competencies by passing the ExCET in order to receive teacher certification in Texas. In addition, the competencies are also aligned with objectives of four core courses completed prior to the beginning of internship. While mastery of these competencies is not required within these pre-internship courses, the experiences in the university classrooms are expected to hasten their accomplishment during the semester and a half in the field prior to the administration of the ExCETs.

As the mentor teachers engaged in discussion concerning their mentoring experiences, they reached consensus regarding the preparation of most of the preservice teachers. They decided that most began internship with sufficient expertise in 11 of the 13 categories so that they could be coached to mastery during their year in the field. However, they determined that two categories were inadequately developed in many beginning interns: 1) Professionalism and 2) Grammar. The mentors then explored attributes of those two items and concluded it was the university's responsibility to certify the applicant's basic proficiency in these areas prior to internship.

Student Reflections and Actions

The feedback from mentors was shared with students in some of the pre-internship courses to enhance students' awareness of the qualities mentors view as "prerequisites" to a successful internship experience. In one class, 34 students analyzed the mentors' lists in small groups to make "top 10" lists of their own and then compiled a composite list. Then they compared their work with that of the mentor/liaison researchers. Following this, the students listed positive, negative, and interesting features of the process. To conclude the process, they used Venn Diagrams to compare and contrast their composite chart with the researchers' chart and write a summary statement about their comparison.

Summary statements from the Venn Diagrams revealed that students were impressed that their work had many things in common with the responses of the mentor teachers: "[It is interesting] how we (the students) basically listed the same things that they (the teachers) felt were important." The students expressed surprise that some of the items were on the list: "Most (not all) of these things should already be second nature to the biggest majority of us going into the field." However, some students felt that "fledgling" teachers should not have to know so much: "Isn't this what we are to be gaining from the field-based [program]?"

Other positive items were noted. The emphasis mentor teachers placed on professionalism pleased the students: "It is interesting to see that some teachers still care about these things." They made "connections" between the mentors' responses and the content of their campus-based courses: "[It is interesting] that they relate so much to all we have been learning." They affirmed that sharing the mentors' lists was helpful: "They really gave us a good idea what they expected from us, and what we should know before we even set foot in their classroom."

Perhaps most importantly, the process made developmental needs apparent: "There are many things that I was not aware I would be held accountable for. Now that I've finished the Venn Diagram I know that I should worry less about my image and more about the way I teach. Their ideas challenge us . . . [to think about] . . . where we should be going in our growth."

The process caused an issue to surface that has not been resolved. Even though "grammar" was not listed frequently in the responses, during ensuing discussions, mentors cited this area as a significant area of concern. In contrast, when interns were asked what they needed to know upon entering the field, they did not list "grammar" as a response to either prompt. When mentor feedback was shared in pre-internship classes, students expressed surprise at the mentors' concerns addressing this area. Grammar was seldom mentioned in the pre-interns' summary statements following their analyses of the mentors' responses. However, one pre-intern did write, "[It] seems unusual that good grammar is listed. I would have thought it would already be a 'common sense' expectation."

University Faculty Reflections and Actions

Intern seminar faculty teams examined the results and engaged in discussions concerning the implications and impact on pre-internship coursework and internship seminars. These teams were encouraged that the five most common responses ("Classroom Management/Organization," "Strategies," "Professionalism," "Recognizing Diversity," and "Integration") to the "most important things learned" prompt focused on items which impacted the learning of the public school students.

Faculty found it intriguing that "Strategies" was not identified as an item that interns felt they needed to know upon entering their internship, yet it was the second most frequently cited item (27, 43%) to the "most important thing I learned" prompt. Many of the seminar team members also teach the pre-internship reading courses and were surprised—and slightly disturbed—by the indication that the internship experience was where the "learning" of strategies occurred. Instructors noted that a major portion of the instruction in their courses is focused on the use of instructional strategies for effective learning. During discussion, they speculated that lack of opportunity to implement the strategies with public school students during pre-internship coursework may result in students not understanding the classroom applications of the strategies. Consequently, pre-internship courses were examined in order to make the connection more explicit. Changes have included implementing "Strategy Logs" to take into internship, additional "hands-on" experiences with strategies, and continual discussion of "connections" to the upcoming field experience. Intern seminar instruction has been adjusted to attempt to "activate" and "access" knowledge of strategies early in the seminar in order to scaffold students to an awareness of the knowledge base of instructional strategies they have upon entering the field.

Instructors also were concerned that students perceived they did not have a basic knowledge of "classroom management/organization" upon entering the field. Pre-internship course instructors explored methods to make the connections more explicit. Upon reflection these responses have strengthened the instructors' belief that the field experiences appear to create a "need to know" for students when addressing items such as strategies and classroom management/organization. As a result, "classroom management/organization" is interwoven into each intern seminar early in the semester.

"Professionalism" was another item in the top three most common responses to both prompts, and also a major concern of the mentors. Hence, professionalism was added as a component to pre-internship course syllabi and a process was instituted to give students feedback concerning professional behavior in campus courses. In addition, feedback from mentors has been shared with students in pre-internship courses to enhance students' awareness of the qualities mentors view as "prerequisites" to a successful internship experience. From the beginning of the field-based program, internship seminars have had a strong emphasis on professional behavior. In addition, during the intern experience preservice teachers experience both formative and summative self-assessment, liaison assessment and mentor assessment on their professionalism. Therefore, it is not expected that this item will "shift" in subsequent surveys of our preservice teachers. Perhaps with the increased emphasis on professionalism in pre-internship experiences, mentors will begin to observe an increased level of professionalism among beginning interns. Still worth pondering is the question of a pre-intern who after thirty hours of observation in the public school classroom and careful consideration of the mentors' expectations wrote: "While our mentor teachers will expect professionals, will they respect and treat us like we are professionals?"

"[University] Requirements" was the third most frequently cited item in the intern responses. Consequently, information about the program and its requirements has been disseminated earlier in the pre-internship courses and during intern orientations.

Conclusion

Even though refinements in seminars focusing on literacy instruction have been implemented, concerns remain. Both mentors and preservice teachers felt that professionalism should be at a proficient level before entry into the field, and professional requirements have been added to pre-internship coursework. However, is demonstration of professionalism in pre-internship coursework a reliable indicator of what the preservice teacher will demonstrate in the public school?

It was obvious students viewed the discussion of the mentors' concerns about grammar as valuable. While some instructors have noted students demonstrating an increased awareness of the necessity of monitoring their language, will this awareness impact interns' performance when they are undergoing the "stress" of the public school classroom?

The emphasis on literacy strategies and classroom management and organization has been increased in pre-internship coursework. Yet, will students in pre-internship courses internalize these concepts without the opportunity to "try them out" with public school students?

These are just a few of the questions that surfaced as partners "reflected" on the data. All partners concurred that there is a need to continue to examine the perceptions of mentors and interns to determine if any shifts in responses occur. The information will be shared with all partners in the field-based program, and program refinements will continue.

Educational research "should not be conducted in the absence of consideration of two questions: Who owns the knowledge on teaching practice? and Who benefits from the research?" (Richardson, 1994, p. 8). We hope that the collaborative processes being used in this project will result in all partners feeling "ownership" of the knowledge. Even more importantly, since reflective thinking prompts growth in both in-service and preservice teachers, the worth of this research in stimulating reflective thought and discussion is as valuable—if not more so—than the findings. Reflective thinking "makes possible action with a conscious aim" (Dewey, 1964, p.212). Our shared and mutual ability to act purposely after reflection and then reflect some more has grown, and as a result all have benefited.

References

Ayers, W. & Schubert, W. H. (1994). Examining the "Teacher Lore" project. In Shanahan, T. (Ed.), *Teachers knowing: Reflections on literacy and language education.* (pp. 106-117). Urbana, IL: National Conference on Research in English/National Council of Teachers of English.

Barth, R. S. (1990). *Improving schools from within.* San Francisco: Jossey-Bass.

Bogdan, R. C. & Biklen, S. K. (1992). *Qualitative research for education: An introduction to theory and methods.* Boston: Allyn and Bacon.

Brooks, J. B. & Brooks, M. G. (1993). *In search of understanding: The case for constructivist classrooms.* Alexandria, VA: Association for Supervision and Curriculum Development.

Dewey, J. (1964). *John Dewey on education: Selected writings.* (R. D. Archambault, Ed.). New York: The Modern Library.

Dixson, P. N. & Ishler, R. E. (1992). Professional development schools: Stages in collaboration. *Journal of Teacher Education (43)*, 28-34.

Fenstermacher, G. D. (1986). Philosophy of research on teaching: Three aspects. In M. C. Wittrock (Ed.), *Handbook of research on teaching* (3rd ed., pp. 37-49). New York: Macmillan.

Foote, M., Walker, C., & Zeek, C. (1997, February). Leadership development through mentoring: Professional development with—not for—mentor teachers. Paper presented at the annual meeting of the American Association for Teacher Education. Phoenix, AZ.

Glaser, B. G. (1992). *Basics of grounded theory analysis.* Mill Valley, CA: Sociology Press.

Glaser, B. G. & Strauss, A. L. (1967). *The discovery of grounded theory: Strategies for qualitative research.* Chicago: Aldine.

Governing Board of the Northeast Texas Center for Professional Development and Technology. (1994, April). Northeast Texas Center for Professional Development and Technology field-based teacher education programs: Criteria for participation. Paper presented at the Northeast Texas Center for Professional Development and Technology Teacher Education Planning Retreat, Sulphur Springs, TX.

Kamil, M. L. (1984). Current traditions of reading research. In P. D. Pearson, R. Barr, M. L. Kamil & P. Mosenthal (Eds.), *Handbook of Reading Research,* (pp. 39-62). New York: Longman.

Killion, J. P. & Todnem, G. (1991). A process for personal theory building. *Educational Leadership, 48*(6), 14-16.

Olson, G. (1990). The nature of collaboration. In H. S. Swartz (Ed.) *Collaboration: Building Common Agendas* (Teacher Education Monograph No. 10), (pp. 11-15). Washington, DC: ERIC Clearinghouse on Teacher Education.

Olson, J. R., & Singer, M. (1994). Examining teachers beliefs, reflective change, and the teaching of reading. *Reading Research and Instruction 34*(2), 97-110.

Richardson, V. (1994). Conducting research on practice. *Educational Researcher, 23*(5), 5-10.

Roemer, M. (1991). What we talk about when we talk about school reform. *Harvard Educational Review, 61,* 434-448.

Santa, C. M. & Santa, J. L. (1995). Teacher as researcher. *Journal of Reading Behavior, 27*(3), 439-451.

Sarason, S. (1982). *The culture of the school and the problem of change* (2nd ed.). Boston: Allyn & Bacon.

Smyth, J. (1989). Developing and sustaining critical reflection in teacher education. *Journal of Teacher Education, 40*(2), 2-9.

Strauss, A. L. & Corbin, J. (1990). *Basics of qualitative research: Grounded theory procedures and techniques.* Newbury Park, CA: Sage.

Van Manen, M. (1990). *Researching lived experience: Human science for an action sensitive pedagogy.* London: State University of New York Press.

Winitzky, N., Stoddart, T., & O'Keefe. P. (1992). Great expectations: Emergent Professional Development Schools. *Journal of Teacher Education, 43,* 3-18.

The Impact of School-University Partnerships on Reading Teacher Educators: Important Conversations We Must Have

Donna L. Wiseman

Northern Illinois University

Abstract

The efforts of many universities to link closer with schools suggest important conversations that reading teacher educators must have amongst themselves and with others. Involvement in school-university partnerships potentially impacts the very nature of educational professionals' teaching, research, and service. The implications of school-university endeavors provide a backdrop for conversations needed to clarify the roles of the reading education professorate as adjustments are made to recent reforms.

A first grade teacher entered the school office with a flurry of paper and a familiar story. Her young, preservice reading intern's philosophy of reading was in direct conflict with the language arts practices in her first-grade classroom. Frustrated by the emphasis on whole language reading methods at the local university, several teachers at the nearby elementary school were concerned that new teachers were entering the classroom unprepared for the "real world" of reading instruction. This was not a new complaint, but the friction was becoming more frequent as the neighboring university relied on the local schools more and more to provide critical teaching experiences for the growing number of undergraduate students.

At the same time, the conflict was brewing at the university as well. Preservice teachers at the university were frustrated to find that the classroom settings they encountered were not mirror images of the holistic classrooms of their textbooks. They believed today's school teachers were not innovative and were not aware of the current methods being discussed in their university classes. They often complained that professors were not realistic and did not understand what made a successful teacher in the "real world" of the classroom.

For a variety of reasons, including the national trend toward school-university collaboration, events resulting from the mutual dissatisfaction of teachers and teacher educators took a decidedly different direction than one might expect. The conflict between theory and practice at this elementary school was used as a starting point for teachers and university professors to ask the question, "How much whole language is too much?" and to find an acceptable approach together. The ramifications of their discussion went beyond the focus of reading and language arts instruction and began a dialogue that is still dynamic several years later. (Wiseman & Cooner, 1996, p 18-19)

In the past, higher education and public schools have traditionally stayed on their own turf—each doing common, overlapping jobs, with results that impact each other. However, over the last decade, collaboration between schools and universities has been seen as one way to do things differently (Book, 1996)—to bring the best research and practice together and impact teaching and learning processes for all involved. Teacher education programs across the nation have used school-university partnerships to make their programs more relevant, feeling that involvement with experienced school teachers benefits, future teachers, teachers in the field, programs in higher education and ultimately teaching and learning in the schools.

There are many ways for school-university educators to collaborate. Most of the school-university partnerships attempt to nestle—or connect the initial preparation of new teachers with the continuing professional development of experienced teachers (Abdal-Haqq, 1998). At its best, this close linkage between teacher educators and public school professionals produces new teachers who are more able to teach in the modern schools and equips experienced teachers with new skills and confidence. In addition, it provides university faculty with the credibility they need to continue their work in teacher preparation.

This paper will discuss how effective collaboration and partnerships can change the roles of reading teachers in the schools and universities—and what these new roles might mean for reading and language arts educators. This will be accomplished by describing the partnership that evolved as a result of the conflict described in the introduction and framing several important conversations we must have if we are to expand the understanding of the new roles that emerge in school-university partnerships.

The Potential of Collaboration

Typically, universities aren't places where collaboration is encouraged (Sarason, 1993). Traditional work often imposes a life of isolation on the researchers and instructors. The exhaustive work of collaboration is just now beginning to gain acceptance as relevant in some tenure and promotion policies. Most reward systems continue to focus on individual work and encourage competition. The organizational structure of colleges and departments manages to fragment collective thinking and often discourages collaborative efforts that might provide different perspectives or assist in viewing the profession with a new light (Boyer, 1990). Worse yet, many studies emerging from school-university partnerships indicate marginal support in terms of resources and personal involvement of the faculty in school-university collaboration (Book, 1996).

It is still possible for reading educators to close office doors, teach classes, and never interact with colleagues—particularly those in other departments or colleges—much less those in elementary and secondary schools. In fact, it is possible for educators to work in absolute isolation and be greatly rewarded for their good work (Howey, 1998). The isolating behavior still displayed by a great proportion of our colleagues will not allow the profession to incorporate the changes brought on by the needs of society, technological initiatives, changing educational contexts, and the complexities of diversity. While isolation has been accepted in the past and considered a way that one could join the "club" of academia, if reform is to come to teacher education, collaboration rather than isolation may have to become the norm.

When my grandfather taught in 1897 in a one-room schoolhouse in the territory of Oklahoma, he was very much alone. He taught all his students by himself, covered all subjects, maintained the buildings, and took part in community events. But, teaching has changed in the last 100 years and requires collaboration and connecting with other teachers and professionals. There is a big contrast between my grandfather's teaching situation with my daughter's who has taught for four years. From the beginning of her preparation to become a teacher she was encouraged to work with others. During her college training, she was a member of a planning team and worked collaboratively with teachers in the field. This year her classroom is large and she and a colleague teach forty second graders in the same room. She has regular planning periods with the six other second grade teachers. There is a steady stream of aids, parent volunteers, older students in the school, the PE, art, and music teachers, and university students—all coming to work with her. She is definitely not alone when she teaches.

If teachers in the field are collaborating in various ways, then teacher education should model what teachers must do. Even if one accepts the premise that there is more educational collaboration, there are times that university faculty are nearly as isolated as my grandfather was in his one room school house in the territory of Oklahoma. This isolation and individualism is troublesome, because colleges of education have a great potential to model the collaborative problem solving, so necessary for success in today's schools.

Partnership and collaboration between schools and universities makes a lot of sense. But, partnerships are not without dilemmas and as John Goodlad

(1994) often says, there is no blueprint or map to do the work. It's not easy and it does not just happen. It requires serious review of current practices and commitment to growth and change from all involved. But, if and when we are successful, these partnerships could change the way we do things in the university setting and some public school environments. What do these partnerships look like? How do they affect our work? A description of the teaching and inquiry activities that took place in one school-university partnership will provide some answers to these questions.

One Partnership: One Example

One outcome of the conflict surrounding reading methods described earlier was for teachers and university faculty to work together and plan for integrated methodology instruction. As a result of extended conversations with the teachers, several of my colleagues and I began a long-term partnership by teaching collaboratively with the teachers at the school. Our work started with the planning and implementation of language arts methods courses and quickly expanded to other methods courses and professional development experiences. During the first semester of planning, we developed a model for teacher preparation that became the hallmark of the partnership (Wiseman & Cooner, 1996). I presented traditional lectures that were accompanied by assigned textbook readings. I met with the class regularly on campus in a traditional university lecture hall. My students were divided into smaller discussion groups scheduled to meet once a week with elementary teachers in the elementary school and participate in activities that paralleled the lecture topics. The teachers and I planned the activities together.

In addition to the three hours of lecture and discussion groups, university students were assigned one additional hour a week with a small group of elementary students. Teachers provided guidance to my students for work with their elementary students who demonstrated a need for individual attention in writing. The teachers planned activities that used the extra hands in ways that increased adult-student ratios in the classrooms. In one fourth grade, for example, five of my students worked with small groups of four or five elementary students each Friday, implementing plans designed by the fourth grade teacher. The focus at that time was on writing and the small group and individual interactions between preservice teachers and elementary students was referred to as the Writing Buddies Program (Wiseman & Cooner, 1996). There were many benefits. Writing Buddies provided elementary students a great deal of attention through the practicum associated with the university methodology course, the university students had real-life experiences with children and teachers in classrooms, and the elementary teachers had adults in the classroom who could deliver extra attention to students.

Participatory Research Process

The partnership expanded and eventually focused on another important aspect of teacher education. The school's professional development plan included the participatory research process in which teacher practitioners, with the support of their university partners, asked questions, designed methods for finding answers, and analyzed and reported the data. The teacher research teams worked with university partners to evaluate teacher and student learning within the collaborative model during a two year period.

A three phase participatory research format (Knight, 1993; Knight, Wiseman, & Cooner, 1998) was used to delineate and guide research activities. During the first phase of the research format, a Partnership Steering Committee was formed and consisted of teacher representatives from each grade level selected by a vote of their peers, school administrators including the principal and assistant principal, and three university faculty who worked with teacher education. Members discussed two general questions posed by the university facilitator: (1) What outcomes do we want for students (preK-4 and university preservice) and staff (school and university) as a result of participation in the partnership? and (2) How will we know when we've achieved these outcomes?

The second phase focused on the development of the research questions. The committee first generated 20 expectations for students and staff which were categorized later into four areas: (1) improvement of student (preK-4 and preservice) learning and skills, (2) professional development for university and school faculty, (3) increased collaboration among various participants for the improvement of teaching and learning, and (4) increased opportunities for field-based experiences for preservice teachers. The committee prioritized specific focus areas within each of the four categories and stated the focus in the form of a preliminary research question.

The third phase focused on the development and implementation of the research plan. Teachers and university representatives volunteered to participate on one or more research teams which refined the questions, determined methods to answer the questions, developed instruments where necessary, and collected and analyzed the data. Over the next two years, the university and the school implemented the research plan. Teachers assisted university researchers in formulating meaningful questions and interpreting outcomes. Summer workshops provided extended time to learn about research processes, to discuss how the research process could be implemented into their classroom settings, and to analyze and discuss findings. As teachers learned more about the research processes and became familiar with methodologies, their input began to directly impact all areas of the research.

Can Partnerships Make a Difference?

An example of one area the research team explored was the Writing Outcomes Study (Knight, Wiseman, & Cooner, 1998) which examined improvement in student writing skills as a result of individual and small group tutoring occurring in the Writing Buddies Program. The most tangible result of our collaboration was the immediate improvement of writing scores of the elementary students. When the partnership began, only 69% of the students at the elementary school were passing the writing portion of the state achievement test. The scores dramatically increased after the first year of collaboration to 82% passing and to 92% the third year. While I would never guarantee these dramatic results had come about as a result of collaborative work, the principal directly attributed the partnership for helping to increase the achievement of the children. Three years into the research plan, we shifted the focus to technology and math. Not surprisingly, the writing scores fell and the math scores went up.

Elementary students were not the only ones who were impacted by the collaboration. Veteran teachers began to change their classroom instruction based on university course content. Some teachers made major turn arounds in their classrooms and it soon became evident that the teachers, by their own admissions, were growing in self confidence, becoming more professional, and developing abilities to collaborate with teacher education programs and each other.

My own teaching was also transformed. I spent of a great deal of time in the school, talking to principals, teachers, and children. The teachers and I had long conversations about reading instruction and learning strategies. The experiences began to be reflected in changes to my own teaching of reading/language arts methods courses.

Defining Reading Teacher Educator Roles

Efforts to connect school-university educators require clarification and definition of new roles. The clarification of roles suggests some conversations that we must have amongst and between ourselves and with others. These conversations are crucial for the maintenance of necessary relationships and collaborative efforts. I would like to share three critical incidents (two of which came out of the partnership I just described) which suggest some of the needed conversations that might help us create a clearer professional identity. Each story introduces a series of difficult and complex questions that are crucial to the success of understanding the evolving roles in our collaborative endeavors.

Critical Incident #1: In the school-university partnership that I described above, I planned my language arts methods class to focus on the context of my partner school. Teachers in the school became my colleagues and we worked together to plan and deliver the language arts class. As I described, two days a week, I met with the class on campus in a traditional university lecture hall, presented lectures, and assigned regular textbook readings. In addition, my students took part in small discussion groups which met once a week on Wednesday afternoons with teachers on the elementary school campus. The university students participated in planned activities and clinical experiences that paralleled the lecture topics. The discussion sessions, planned jointly by the teachers and myself, provided opportunities for university students and practicing elementary teachers to discuss topics which had been presented in my university classroom.

As those of you who teach this way know, this arrangement takes a lot of work and commitment. I was very proud of how I had changed my content and my approach and the teachers and I were excited about the results. Even so, I will never forget when at the end of the semester one of my students wrote in her journal and described her experiences in my language arts methods course by commenting, "If you think that I learned about reading/language arts in the hallowed halls of the university, think again—it was sitting in the desks of the third graders watching the teacher in the school where I really learned how to teach." She had completely dismissed my role in the class. And this was a class where I had gone to great effort to connect between the practice and the theory—changing my lectures and activities to reflect what was happening in the classroom of the teachers who were my partners.

My student's attitude is an example from my own experience and it has been duplicated in other partnerships where I have worked. Future and experienced teachers will often comment on how it is so much more important to present the practical side of teaching at the expense of considering the theory (Howey, 1998). There seems to be general criticism of the university theoretical approach. Teachers and preservice teachers are often bothered by the theoretical content that many university professors present in their methods courses. They suggest that there should be less theory and more practical application in teacher preparation programs.

School-university partnerships offer us a situation in which the bounds of both theory and practice should be questioned, debated, and discussed. The "hallowed halls" remark from my student illustrates the tensions that will constantly exist between theory and practice. There will be times in our work that theory and practice collide (Garan, 1998). It happens each time that a future teacher plans a lesson as a result of a university course and then delivers that lesson in the classroom. Anything could happen. If the world was predictable, we wouldn't need professionals; we would only need robots. If children and young people were predictable, teachers wouldn't need theory to make decisions, we would only need technicians. But, theory is necessary in any profession. Theory is the foundation. Practice is the end to which theory is directed. The delicate balance will ultimately result in the theoretical grounding of the practice of teaching and the interpretations will have an impact on the way that teachers and professors practice (Zeichner, 1992). The linkages between theory and practice are an important feature of school-university partnerships. We use the phrase "theory and practice" almost as a cliché. But, the linkage is not necessarily clear to our students, elementary and secondary teachers, or even those of us who are university professors. The way we make the connections between theory and practice will define our roles in the partnerships.

How do we connect theory and practice in school-university partnerships? What does it look like, how is it delivered, and what must each partner contribute? **These are important conversations we must have.**

Critical Incident #2: When planning to conduct research related to the Writing Buddies Project in our school-university partnership, university researchers designed a research project that would measure the writing, reading and math achievement of the third grade children who were impacted by their partnerships. They decided that the ultimate impact on student achievement could best be discovered by identifying control groups, collecting and analyzing data, and comparing outcomes—fairly traditional processes. When the university researchers shared this idea with the teacher researchers in the school, there was a great concern over how the process would impact the school as a whole. The teacher researchers pointed out that using a control group design would exclude some teachers and students from participation in desirable school-university activities. This was completely unacceptable to the teachers. As a result of the teachers' voiced concerns, the research project was re-designed. The decision was made to abandon the traditional control group design and to lend support to cause and effect by using multiple data sources and other methods to establish a pattern of relationships. Ultimately, the teachers helped ask the questions, determine methods of data collection, and analyze the data. The study became much more credible to the school-based faculty because of the teachers' input into the methodology.

This scenario suggests the need to understand the impact of collaboration on what has been the university's trademark—the research process. Traditionally university faculty collect data and analyze and report findings with little interaction with colleagues, much less with the teachers and students who are located where the data was collected. It is viewed as an isolated endeavor in which the proverbial professor completes the research and writing behind closed doors in a university setting.

The incident illustrates the benefits of combining the technical expertise of university faculty who contribute their knowledge of alternative and traditional modes of research and the knowledge of the teachers who understand their students and how the research processes can best be applied in the school setting. When the two are combined, it is possible to create innovative research and inquiry strategies. And serendipitously, the partners learn a great deal from each other. Teachers begin to understand and feel more comfortable with research techniques and university faculty learn to adapt methods so that issues meaningful to classroom teachers are reflected in the inquiry process. Research processes in school-university partnerships should and will impact our roles. From the beginning, the Holmes Partnership (1986) has encouraged school-university collaborations to conduct research that grows out of the daily work of teachers, uses strategies that match the complexity of schools and teaching, and values the intellectual activity of teachers. The goal of school-based inquiry should not be merely the improvement of the teaching of reading, but also the improvement of reading/language arts research (Ducharme & Ducharme, 1996).

What are the contributions of public school teachers to reading research and inquiry? How must university researchers change their roles when conducting research in school-university partnerships? How is the role of traditional academic researcher different from the successful inquirer in school-university research? **These are important conversations we must have.**

Critical Incident # 3: Recently a colleague of mine was asked to write an outside letter of support for a faculty member who was being considered for promotion and tenure at another university. This was a young professional who had spent many hours in school-university work. Her papers indicated that she had helped a school turn around their reading test scores and as a result they were removed from the state list of schools in trouble. She had also done a considerable amount of work with a group of immigrants who had settled locally. She had meshed her professional service with the needs of the community and had received a great deal of recognition outside the university for her efforts. However, her publication record included six journal articles—a bit light for safe sailing through the tenure and promotion process. My colleague, a scholar with a national reputation and a long list of publications, and I talked for a long time about what to write in this letter of support. Fortunately, the directions from the department head requesting the letter were very clear in indicating that partnerships were a strong part of the departmental mission. My colleague was able to use the language of the mission and write a strong letter of support based on the commitment and effort that this young professional had demonstrated. The letter approached the issue of the number of publications in the following way:

"If I were to second guess the tenure and promotion process in your department, I would say that Dr. Jones' research and scholarship will be subjected to great scrutiny. Individuals who are comfortable with traditional measures of success in the university setting will focus on the number of publications and question if she has published enough to receive tenure and promotion. I have had the opportunity to sit on tenure and review committees at two universities and provide external evaluations for numerous colleagues seeking promotion and tenure at other universities. It is clear to me that faculty members active in school-university partnerships maintain different publications records than do their more campus-bound colleagues. I considered the goals of your department regarding the maintenance of field-based programs when reviewing Dr. Jones' research record. Her research is focused, she has demonstrated that she is capable of producing publishable manuscripts, and she has been able to write several successful grants. She has an extensive presentation record indicating her involvement in active scholarship. Her record indicates that she has contributed to the knowledge base while maintaining the demanding schedule of a field-based teacher educator."

Dr. Jones was awarded tenure and promotion the following spring.

This letter could not have been written had there not been a policy within the department that could be used to evaluate this teacher educators' contributions. Some colleges and schools of education, such as Montclair State University and others, may be involved in wide sweeping changes of the tenure and promotion process. Other institutions are making more subtle changes which support collaborative work. North Carolina at Greensboro, for example, has allowed teacher educators, who are heavily involved in school university partnership work, to reduce the number of expected yearly publications by one. Other institutions are reducing teaching loads for teacher educators in the field so they will have time to publish. Schools and colleges are adding language in documents that change policy and can support the non-traditional work associated with partnerships. Nowhere do we need the redefinition and description of the many facets of the work of teacher education, than in the tenure and promotion processes.

How do we reward reading educators who chose to work in the schools? How can tenure and promotion processes reflect the collaborative work of reading educators who work in partnerships and value the more traditional research at the same time? Do we honor collaborative and single authorship in the same way? **These are important conversations we must have.**

These three critical incidents only begin the needed conversations. But, if we face some of the issues head on, we will be clearer about our roles as reading teacher educators in school-university partnerships. Being explicit about our profession will force us to face many hard dilemmas. Some of them are at the foundation of academia. I am occasionally a bit frustrated at what I perceive as a hesitancy and reluctance to reflect upon our own practice as we go about attempting to change the culture where we do our work. I know why we resist these conversations. This is very hard work; it takes major risks and requires that we re-think how we talk, teach and research. Defining teacher education in new frameworks requires serious review of current practices and commitment to growth and change from all involved. And if we are successful in redefining and re-characterizing our roles, reading educators will teach collaboratively, write and research with elementary and secondary school colleagues; and spend more time in the schools.

A Changing Profession

Some of the redefinition in the roles of teacher education will occur with an influx of new faculty. Consider this contrast provided by Ed and Mary Ducharme (1996) in a recent evaluation of the teacher education professoriate: Currently, the average teacher education faculty member is a white male in his late forties or early fifties, tenured at either the full or associate professor level; he acquired his doctorate while studying part-time, has been at his current place of employment for more than fifteen years, and has published six or seven articles as refereed publications. Prior to going on for further graduate study, he taught for a minimum of three years in either an elementary or secondary school.

If the demographics continue as current trends indicate, future reading education faculty members are more likely to be female and possibly from a minority group; she will be in her mid-thirties, tenured as an associate professor; she acquired her doctorate while studying full time, supported by a foundation fellowship promoting educational excellence and equity and has been at the university for seven years with one of those years spent in an exchange program in another country (Ducharme & Ducharme, 1996). She has authored four articles, co-authored six more with teachers from the schools, has developed five media productions on teaching and spends two days a week at a local middle school working with teachers and children. Prior to working on her doctorate, she taught in a rural youth center for two years and in an inner city school for three years.

We study teaching and learning—we understand the role of the teachers in elementary and secondary schools—we look at the development of preservice teachers—but what do we know about our roles as teacher educators? While it is known that a teacher educator is one who teaches teachers, the composite of those who teach teachers is loosely defined (Lanier & Little, 1986, p. 528). Aside from some of the work of Ed and Mary Ducharme (1996), Donna Kagen (1996), and John Goodlad (1990) in his "Teachers for

Our Nations School" study, very few of us have contributed to descriptions and definitions related to teacher education (Widen, Mayer-Smith, & Moon, 1998). There is very little in the data explaining the roles of teacher educators in research related to school-university partnerships. Some of our conversations and reflections must consider how our roles are changing and expanding and what that means for day-to-day activities.

Many of us believe that we will obtain better answers for improving the teaching and learning of the future if educators in schools and universities continue to work together. It is imperative that we take responsibility for clarifying the identity of educators who work in school-university partnerships. It should be a high priority that teacher educators define the profession. The variety and potential within the teacher education profession are vast. We are talented intelligent people and in the next years we must show more unity, more understanding of the problems and issues of modern American society, more demonstrated effectiveness in bringing about desired outcomes in teacher education graduates, and more imagination in bridging the world of today's youth. It is time to participate in important conversations about our roles.

References

Abdal-Haqq, I. (1998). *Professional development schools: Weighing the evidence.* Thousand Oaks, CA: Corwin Press.

Book, C.L. (1996). Professional development schools. In J. Sikula, T.J. Buttery, & E. Guyton (Eds.), *Handbook of research on teacher education* (2nd ed., pp. 194-210). New York: Simon & Schuster Macmillan.

Boyer, E. L. (1990). *Scholarship reconsidered: Priorities of the professoriate.* The Carnegie Foundation for the Advancement of Teaching. San Francisco: Jossey-Bass.

Ducharme, E. R. & Ducharme, M. K. (1996). Development of the teacher education professoriate. In F. B. Murray (Ed.) *The teacher educator's handbook: Building a knowledge base for the preparation of teachers.* (pp. 691-714). San Francisco: Jossey Bass.

Garan, E. (1998). Getting off my high horse: A whole language missionary gets her comeuppance. *Language Arts, 76*(1), 36-39.

Goodlad, J. I. (1994). *Educational renewal: Better teachers, better schools.* San Francisco: Jossey Bass.

Goodlad, J. I. (1997). *In praise of education.* New York: Teachers College Press.

Goodlad, J. I. (1990). *Teachers for our nation's schools.* San Francisco: Jossey Bass.

The Holmes Group (1986). *Tomorrow's teachers: A report of the Holmes Group.* East Lansing, MI: Author.

Howey, K. R. (1998). The Context for leadership and the reform of teacher education in schools and colleges of education. In D. Thiessen & K.R. Howey (Eds.), *Agents, provocateurs: Reform minded leaders for schools of education,* (pp. 9-27). Washington, DC: AACTE.

Kagen, D. (1990). Teachers' workplace meets the professors of teaching: A chance encounter at 30,000 feet. *Journal of Teacher Education, 41*(5), 46-53.

Knight, S. (1993). *Implementing a model for participatory evaluation: Findings from three studies.* Paper presented at the 1996 American Educational Research Association, New York.

Knight, S. L., Wiseman, D. L., & Cooner, D. (1998). *Investigating the impact of school-university collaboration on elementary students' math and reading outcomes.* Paper presented at the 1998 Annual Meeting of the American Educational Research Association. San Diego, CA.

Lanier, J. E., and Little, J. W. (1986). Research in teacher education. In M.C. Wittrock (Ed). *Handbook of research on teaching* (3rd ed.). New York: Macmillan.

Sarason, S. B. (1993). *The case for change.* San Francisco: Jossey Bass.

Widen, M., Mayer-Smith, J. & Moon, B. (1998). A critical analysis of research on learning to teach: Making the case for an ecological perspective on inquiry. *Review of Educational Research, 68*(2), 130-178.

Wiseman, D.L. & Cooner, D. (1996). Discovering the power of collaboration: The impact of school-university partnership on teaching. *Teacher Education and Practice, 12*(1), 18-28.

Zeichner, K. (1992). Rethinking the practicum in the professional development school partnership. *Journal of Teacher Education, 43*(4), 296-307.

Professional Development to Promote Early Literacy Achievement

Rita M. Bean
R. Tony Eichelberger
Allison Swan
Rae Tucker

University of Pittsburgh

Abstract

An early literacy intervention program, Project SOAR*, was developed as a means of improving student literacy achievement by providing professional development to teachers. In this paper, Project SOAR* is described and the process used to implement Project SOAR* discussed. The paper concludes with a discussion of what was learned from the project about implementing effective professional development. Also, data about student achievement are described.

It is well established that students' experiences in the elementary grades have a profound impact on their futures. According to Juel (1988), children who are not adequate readers by the time they leave the primary grades, are less likely to succeed at middle or high school levels. In fact, success or failure in elementary school, especially in the early grades, may be far more important than socio-economic factors in predicting ultimate success in the educational system. In the actual experience of a child progressing through school, factors such as socio-economic status, race/ethnicity, language background, family structure, parents' education, and school resources are intertwined in a complex web of forces, events, and relationships that severely restrain a student's potential to learn (Natriello, McDill, & Pallas, 1990; Slavin, 1994; Snow, Burns, Griffin, 1998). Natriello, McDill and Pallas (1990) estimate that 40% of the school-age population under 18 is at risk of failure in school on the basis of at least one of the following five indicators: race/

ethnicity, poverty status, family structure, mother's education, and limited English proficiency.

According to research, early intervention programs are more effective and more cost efficient than remedial programs later in a student's schooling (Kennedy, Birman, & Demaline, 1986; Slavin, Karweit & Wasik, 1994; Snow, et al. 1998). Early school intervention programs are often designed to prevent literacy problems from developing or to catch potential problems before they become established. These programs address the needs of children in the first through the third grades and have been quite effective when compared to remedial programs (Pikulski, 1994). The evidence about learning and teaching of early reading has been accumulating over the past 25 years. Reports such as *Becoming a Nation of Readers* (Anderson, Hiebert, Scott, & Wilkinson, 1984), *Beginning to Read: Thinking and Learning About Print* (Adams, 1990), as well as the recent report by the National Research Council (Snow, et al. 1998) have much to say to school communities. Unfortunately, this information is not always available to schools in ways that promote program development.

In order to implement such literacy programs, stable, high-quality sources of professional development are needed (National Commission on Teaching and America's Future, 1996). In this project, one of the key elements in a larger school restructuring project was the implementation of a professional development program that was focused on helping teachers implement an early intervention, literacy based program for children in grades 1-3. The purpose of this paper is to describe (a) the context in which the intervention was implemented, (b) the intervention, (c) the process used to provide professional development as a means of implementing the intervention, and (d) some initial evaluation data collected during the first year of the project.

Context

This program took place in a small urban school district that has been heavily impacted by poverty. According to statistics from the Aid to Families with Dependent Children, 30% of the families received aid, and 75% of the children received free or reduced lunches. There were over 700 federal low-income housing units in 4 separate projects within the 2.9 square mile community. The district's elderly population was 35% greater than the county average and single parent households exceeded the county average by 45 percent. At the same time, the district just built a new elementary school that placed all children (formerly in 3 separate and very old schools) in one location.

The teachers in the school were experienced, the majority of them having taught for 20 years or more. Indeed, the last new classroom teacher hired at the elementary level was 15 years ago. Approximately 65% of the children in the school district scored below average on standardized tests in reading.

Administrators in the school were well aware of the need for school restructuring and renewal. Thus, in 1996, the Assistant Superintendent and the Title 1 Coordinator of the school district worked with the first author of this paper to prepare a proposal for local foundations proposing a large school restructuring project. Included in this large-scale proposal was a plan for professional development for primary grade teachers. This intervention, Project SOAR* (Success of All in Reading), emphasized the importance of early instruction and the need for professional development that would enable primary grade teachers to implement effective strategies for literacy achievement. The plan called for identifying a cohort of teachers to participate in a year-long project; two other groups of teachers would be identified for the second and third years.

Project SOAR*

The intervention was built on the abundant literature and research that emphasizes the importance of a well developed literacy program (Cunningham, 1975-76; Hiebert, 1996; Hiebert & Taylor, 1994; Juel, 1988), especially for children who come to school without the extensive background needed to be successful. Project SOAR* is based upon the following principles of early literacy instruction. Literacy instruction is effective when:

> There are high expectations for all students and respect and appreciation for what they bring to the classroom.
>
> Students are provided with instruction that is based upon up-to-date information about their literacy strengths and needs.
>
> Students learn skills necessary to master the alphabetic principle, an essential aspect of learning to read.
>
> Students are given opportunities to practice and apply what they are learning, that is, they read and write on a daily basis.
>
> Students think about the materials they read and make connections with what they know.
>
> Parents are involved in the literacy process of their children.
>
> Students are actively involved and engaged in their learning.

Six components of Project SOAR* were developed as a means of helping teachers visualize key aspects for literacy success (Figure 1). Each of these six components is described below.

Setting a Tone promotes the setting of high expectations for children. Teachers are encouraged to reinforce positive behaviors and to highlight progress and success. Moreover, the emphasis is one of promoting the belief that all students can learn. In SOAR* classrooms, teachers identify a long-

Figure 1. Project SOAR*: An Early Literacy Intervention Program

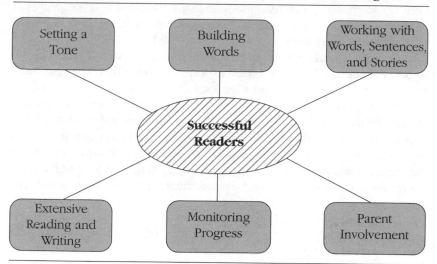

term project that involves children in sharing their own experiences and writing about them. For example, the first grade teachers had children work on a book describing some aspect of their lives each week. This autobiography then was sent home in May. The walls in the hallways exhibited lists of children who have perfect attendance and examples of children's best work.

Building Words promotes the development of phonemic awareness and decoding skills in a systematic fashion. This component was developed to help teachers understand the importance of phonics instruction as an aspect of effective reading instruction. Teachers in first grade use activities to promote phonemic awareness (Yopp, 1992; O'Connor, Notari-Syverson, & Vadasy, 1998). Activities developed by Beck and Hamilton (in press) and Cunningham and Cunningham (1992) also are incorporated into the weekly activities of teachers as part of the overall literacy program.

Working with Words, Sentences, and Stories provides teachers with many different strategies to develop vocabulary and comprehension skills of students as they are introduced to stories in their anthologies. The focus is twofold: heightening the conceptual knowledge needed by students so that they are successful when listening to or reading stories and helping students to think about the stories after they have read them. Because there are excellent activities in the anthology available at the school, teachers are encouraged to select those that would be most helpful to their students.

The fourth component, *Extensive Reading and Writing*, emphasizes the importance of daily reading and writing and especially the need for integrated, authentic literacy experiences. In Project SOAR*, students read daily from books that they can read independently. Students also are provided with opportunities to write on a daily basis. At the same time, teachers read to students each day from a wide variety of children's literature. As part of this component, authors have been invited into the school to talk with the students about their books and their experiences as a writer. Last year, Sally Alexander, author of *Mom, Can't See Me*, came to talk with the students.

Monitoring Progress provides teachers with guidelines for assessing and monitoring the work of the students in their classrooms and emphasizes the importance of using these results for classroom decision making. Various authentic measures are identified that enable teachers to learn more about the strengths and needs of their students. Teachers administer and interpret the results of these measures and discuss the implications of the results for instruction.

The sixth dimension, *Parental Involvement*, focuses on the need to involve parents in the schooling of their children. In this component, teachers are encouraged to communicate with parents about what they are doing in the classroom to promote literacy instruction and to send home ideas about how parents can help their children. Also, parents are invited to become partners in the classroom. For example, each classroom identified a "Mom" who, each month, read a book to the class and then conducted a followup activity with the children.

Project SOAR* is driven by the principles identified previously, but it is not a prescriptive or prepackaged program. It is a process by which teachers and University personnel together discuss what the school is doing to implement these principles and how they can be operationalized in the classroom. For example, assessment measures may differ from school to school, or activities developed to "Set the Tone" may vary. The school described in this study focused on thematic units that highlighted students' personal experiences while in another SOAR* school, teachers identified an "I Can" approach. Students placed a card in a large can in the classroom indicating a specific achievement, e.g., "I can read my sight words". Each day, some of these cards were drawn and the students demonstrated his/her accomplishment. In the Building Words component, teachers are introduced to specific activities, but they are also encouraged to use other activities that they have found successful. The focus is on increasing teachers' knowledge and creating an environment that requires teachers to become reflective decision makers.

Process for Professional Development

As critical as the intervention was, the process used for professional development was equally as important. The history of school restructuring is not a good one—reforms have come and gone, and the attitude of many teachers tends to be "We'll outlast this one too!" Too often they are right. Thus, the process that was used to implement this professional development program was carefully developed to promote success—and the essential pieces are described below.

Involve Teachers in the Decision

School administrators invited a cohort of primary teachers to participate in the year's project, with parameters carefully delineated. Teachers were required to attend the summer workshop and regularly scheduled meetings during the school year, document their efforts, and work with the site facilitator to implement SOAR*. They were reimbursed for time spent beyond the school day and also participated in personalized professional development (e.g., attended workshops in the area, purchased teaching materials). The selection of teachers was carefully made; teachers who were more receptive to change were identified. Teachers who might be quite resistant were not invited to be part of the first year's cohort group. The plan, using the words of a former superintendent of schools, was to "start with the horses who were on the track—not those in the barn." We invited six of the eighteen teachers to participate, two each from grades 1-3. All agreed to participate, knowing in advance the expectations for the project.

Provide Initial Knowledge in a Non-Threatening Environment

The initial 3-day workshop, held in the summer at the University, consisted of many hands-on experiences and activities for teachers. For example, to highlight the importance of Setting the Tone, a faculty member who has worked extensively with helping teachers respond positively to the cultural diversity of their classrooms, engaged the group in an experience he calls "Moving Through the World." Participants are asked to move from group to group, depending upon various characteristics, including age, gender, race, religion, college experience, etc. Teachers then discuss traditions and rituals that, although different from group to group, are similar in many ways (how we celebrate holidays, for example). This activity is designed to create awareness of cultural differences and similarities.

As the group was introduced to each component, strategies were demonstrated and then practiced. For example, Building Words (Beck & Hamilton, in press) was demonstrated, ways in which it could be used was discussed, and then teachers practiced using it with each other. On the final day of the workshop, teachers were encouraged to develop their own goals. Moreover, they were provided with a comprehensive manual that described the fundamental aspects of Project SOAR* and described specific strategies that could be used with children.

On-Going Support and Guidance

A site facilitator with experience in supervision and early childhood education was hired to work with teachers in implementing the program. There is much support for having personnel available in the school who can "remind" teachers about an intervention (Slavin, Madden, Dolan, & Wasik, 1996) and assist them when they are having difficulties with any of the procedures or approaches. Fullan (1991) discussed what he called the "implementation dip," a period during which teachers are likely to return to former practices when new strategies and approaches tend to be difficult to implement. With the presence of the site facilitator, teachers had more support for continuing with the new approaches. Further, the teachers, site facilitator, Title 1 coordinator, and the first author of this paper met on a monthly basis to discuss various dimensions of SOAR* and how it was being implemented. These meetings were important ones that provided time for team planning and teacher feedback.

Focus on the Students

By focusing on the needs of students, we believed we had a better chance of promoting change in teacher instructional practice. Therefore, the results of authentic assessments of students were shared with individual classroom teachers. Each teacher was asked to identify (1) the needs of the students, (2) how those needs could be met, and (3) goals that they set for students in their classroom. We also asked teachers to identify how the various resources (site facilitator, reading specialists) could help them implement strategies in their classroom

Teacher Involvement in Building the Program

At each of the monthly meetings, teachers were involved in deciding what they would like to include as part of the SOAR* project. As a result, teachers invited a children's author to speak to their students and they identified a year-long "literacy celebration" project in which their students were involved (e.g., first grade teachers produced personal books that included children's writing from September through May). Teachers also identified workshops that they wanted to attend and shared what they learned at those workshops.

Evaluation

The evaluation plan is focused on two dimensions of the professional development program: the impact of Project SOAR* on the students and the effect on classroom practices and teacher attitudes towards literacy instruction. Since we just completed the first year of the project, much of the evaluation work is ongoing. In the following sections, we discuss what we learned as a result of this year's efforts.

Effect on Classroom Practices/Teacher Attitudes

The information in this section came from our documentation of meetings, informal interactions with teachers, formal teacher interviews, teacher logs, and classroom observations. What follows are some conclusions drawn from the first year's efforts and critical to success of the project.

Gaining Trust and Credibility. Two key ingredients to any successful intervention that involves professional development are building trust and credibility with the teachers. Teachers were much more willing to invest in the project when they believed that they were working with individuals who were there for an extended period and who were willing to respect teachers' judgments and ideas. The more outside personnel become "insiders," the more teachers invested in the project. This was especially important for this partnership between university and school district. The monthly meetings were important ones for establishing this relationship, as were the weekly classroom visits from one of our university liaisons.

The Site Facilitator. As anticipated, the site facilitator was an important resource to the teachers, for providing encouragement, extending understanding, and assisting in the implementation of various strategies. Teachers valued the presence of this individual, especially since she was willing to work in the classrooms with the teacher, in assessing students and working with small groups so that individual needs of students could be met. Because of the importance of this individual, the district agreed to assign this role to one of its own teachers, releasing her from classroom responsibilities during the next school year.

Willingness to Accept Small Successes. As has been stated time and time again, change takes time. Conley (1993), for example, states, "it takes time to implement most new practices, usually several years, and that during the implementation phase there may be a time when efficiency and performance actually decrease" (p. 376). The logs that teachers kept provided much information about teacher implementation of Project SOAR* (see Table 1). In their weekly logs, teachers indicated when and how they implemented various components. The analysis of the logs, which covered between 7 and 14 weeks of instruction, revealed that teachers most frequently used the following components: Reading Words, Sentences, and Stories (91%), Monitor-

Table 1. Implementation of SOAR* Components by Grade 1-3 Teachers

Grd.	Teach.	Setting Tone		Build Words		Words Sentences Stories		Extensive Reading/ Writing		Monitor Progress		Parent Involve		Reported Weeks	Mean Percen.
		n	(%)	n	(%)	n	(%)	n	(%)	n	(%)	n	(%)		
1	1	13	(93)	14	(100)	14	(100)	14	(100)	13	(93)	2	(14)	14	85%
1	2	13	(100)	12	(92)	13	(100)	13	(100)	13	(100)	0	(0)	13	82%
2	3	0	(0)	7	(100)	7	(100)	7	(100)	7	(71)	7	(100)	7	79%
2	4	0	(0)	7	(50)	11	(79)	14	(100)	14	(100)	1	(7)	14	56%
3	5	1	(11)	4	(44)	6	(66)	9	(100)	8	(88)	0	(0)	9	52%
3	6	6	(55)	8	(73)	11	(100)	9	(82)	10	(91)	0	(0)	11	69%
Mean Percentage		43%		77%		91%		97%		91%		20%			

ing Progress (91%), Extensive Reading and Writing (77%), and Building Words (77%). The two components used least frequently were Setting the Tone (43%) and Parental Involvement (20%). Classroom observations revealed examples of specific practices that teachers readily accepted and implemented: graphics/visuals and retell protocols for building comprehension; strategies for building words; activities that encourage extensive reading and writing and a celebration of literacy; attention to individual needs of students through the analysis of assessment data; and use of learning centers and grouping strategies for meeting the needs of children.

The logs also indicated that the greatest degree of implementation occurred in first grade where the greatest achievement gains also occurred. However, although teachers seemed to react positively to the instructional ideas promoted in SOAR*, there is still work to be done relative to building a climate that is more positive and wholesome for children—one that shows respect for each child. This attitudinal change is probably the most difficult to affect, and only through demonstration and continued attention to the goals of the project will such change occur.

Support of All Involved. One of the major reasons that this restructuring effort had some potential for success is that it is built on a vision of what an effective elementary school should be. That vision is shared by the school board, administrators, and many different agencies in the community, including foundations who have funded the project and University personnel working with the district. Teachers in the cohort group, as a whole, shared this vision, although they were not directly involved in the conceptualization of it. It seems apparent that more has to be done to involve teachers in the ongoing development of the vision so that there is ownership and a belief that excellence can be achieved in this school district.

Student Achievement

To assess the effectiveness of Project SOAR*, we compared the reading performance on the California Achievement test of children in SOAR* classrooms to those in the other classrooms. The percentage of SOAR* and non-SOAR* students falling into each quarter (using test norms) was calculated. Then the percentage of students falling above the 50th percentile was calculated (see Table 2). The percentage of students above the 50th percentile was higher for students in SOAR* classrooms than non-SOAR* classrooms in all three grades (grade 1, +13.4%; grade 2, +4.1%; and grade 3, +3.0%). Although chi-square results did not indicate any significant differences at any grade level, the overall pattern of results was obvious. In SOAR* classrooms at all grades, there was a smaller percentage of students in the lowest quarter (1-25%ile) and a greater percentage of students in the highest quarter (76-99%ile). In fact, results of the chi-square test on differences between groups at lowest and highest quartiles indicated a significant difference at grade 1 (x^2 = 5.27, p<.05). Specifically, students with both high and low abilities benefited from the project. A graphic representation of student distribution is provided in Figure 2.

Table 2. Percentages of students in each quarter on CAT Total Reading: Grades 1 – 3

Grade 1

Group	N	1-25%ile	26-50%ile	51-75%ile	76-99%ile	Above 50th percentile
SOAR Students	47	19.1	29.8	27.7	23.4	51.1
Non-SOAR Students	122	32.0	30.3	26.2	11.5	37.7

Grade 2

Group	N	1-25%ile	26-50%ile	51-75%ile	76-99%ile	Above 50th percentile
SOAR Students	42	19.1	31.0	33.3	16.7	50.0
Non-SOAR Students	85	21.2	32.9	31.8	14.1	45.9

Grade 3

Group	N	1-25%ile	26-50%ile	51-75%ile	76-99%ile	Above 50th percentile
SOAR Students	58	17.2	25.9	27.6	29.3	56.9
Non-SOAR Students	89	24.7	21.4	29.2	24.7	53.9

Figure 2. Early Literacy Achievement

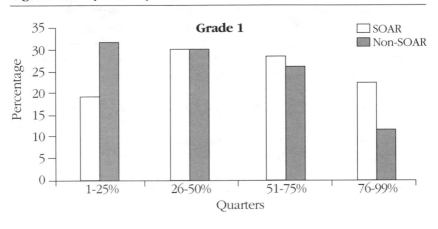

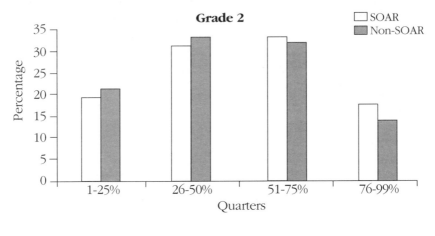

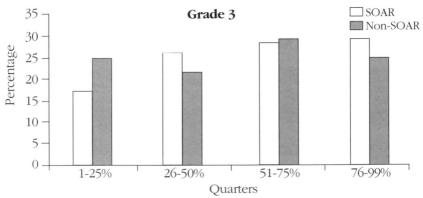

In summary, with the commitment of all involved in this project, the first year was one of small steps toward improving the educational experience for students in this district. The project created a dissonance for teachers that forced them to rethink and reflect on their classroom practices. Will this intervention continue in such a way that it will become part of the infrastructure of this school district? Those involved in the project have taken appropriate "first steps" towards this goal.

References

Adams, M. J. (1990). *Beginning to read: Thinking and learning about print.* Cambridge, MA: MIT Press.

Anderson, R. C., Hiebert, E. H., Scott, J. A., & Wilkinson, I. A. G. (1984). *Becoming a nation of readers: The report of the Commission on Reading.* Champaign-Urbana, IL: Center for the Study of Reading.

Beck, I. L. & Hamilton, R. (in press). *Beginning reading module.* Washington: The American Federation of Teachers.

Conley, D. T. (1993). *Roadmap to restructuring policies, practices, and the emerging visions of schooling.* Eugene, OR: Eric Clearinghouse on Educational Management. (ERIC Document Reproduction Service No. ED 359 593)

Cunningham, P. M. (1975-76). Investigating a synthesized theory of mediated word identification. *Reading Research Quarterly, 11,* 127-143.

Cunningham, P. M., & Cunningham, J. W. (1992). Making words: Enhancing the invented spelling-decoding connection. *The Reading Teacher, 46,* (2), 106-115.

Fullan, M. G. with Stiegelbauer, S. (1991). *The new meaning of educational change.* New York: Teachers College Press.

Hiebert, E. H. (1996). Creating and sustaining a love of literature . . . And the ability to read it. In Graves, van den Brock, & B. Taylor (Eds.). *The first R every child's right to read.* New York: Teachers College Press.

Hiebert, E. H. & Taylor, B. M. (Eds.). (1994). *Getting reading right from the start: Effective early literacy interventions.* Boston: Allyn & Bacon.

Juel, C. (1988). Learning to read and write: A longitudinal study of fifty-four children from first through fourth grades. *Journal of Educational Psychology, 80,* 437-447.

Kennedy, M., Birman, B. F., & Demaline, R. E. (1986). *The effectiveness of Chapter 1 services. Second Interim Report for the National Assessment of Chapter 1.* Washington, D.C.: Office of Educational Research and Improvement. (ERIC Document Reproduction Service No. ED281 919)

National Commission on Teaching and America's Future. (1996). *What matters most: Teaching for America's future.* New York: National Commission on Teaching and America's Future. (ERIC Document Reproduction Service No. ED 395 931)

Natriello, G, McDill, E.L., & Pallas, A.M. (1990). *Schooling disadvantaged children: Racing against catastrophe.* New York: Teachers College Press.

O'Connor, R. E., Notari-Syverson, A., & Vadasy, P.F. (1998). *Ladders to literacy: A kindergarten activity book.* Baltimore: Paul Brookes.

Pikulski, J. J. (1994). Preventing reading failure: A review of five effective programs. *The Reading Teacher, 48,* (1), 30-39.

Slavin, R. E. (1994). School and classroom organization in beginning reading: Class size, aides, and instructional grouping. In R. E. Slavin, N. L. Karweit, B. A., Wasik, & N. A. Madden (Eds.). *Preventing early school failure: Research on effective strategies.* Boston: Allyn & Bacon.

Slavin, R., Karweit, N. L., & Wasik, B. A. (1994). *Preventing early school failure: Research on effective strategies.* Boston: Allyn & Bacon.

Slavin, R. E., Madden, N. A., Dolan, L. J., & Wasik, B. A. (1996). *Every child, every school: Success for all.* Thousand Oaks, CA: Corwin Press.

Snow, C. E., Burns, M. S., & Griffin, P. (Eds.). (1998). *Preventing reding difficulties in young children.* Washington, D.C.: National Academy Press.

Yopp, H. K. (1992). Developing phonemic awareness in young children. *The Reading Teacher, 45,* (9), 696-703.

CREATING EFFECTIVE
LITERACY LEARNING
ENVIRONMENTS

'I JUST LOVED THOSE PROJECTS!' CHOICE AND VOICE IN STUDENTS' COMPUTER-BASED LANGUAGE ARTS ACTIVITIES: A CASE STUDY

Sarah Nixon-Ponder

Southwest Missouri State University

Abstract

The purpose of this case study was to explore students' perceptions of computer-based activities in their language arts classes. The teacher of these sixth graders was a constructivist who integrated computer technology into her lessons and curriculum. Data analysis revealed that the students believed computers helped them to improve their work and create interest and motivation in school. Students enjoyed participating in computer-based activities and took ownership and pride in their work.

Children in the United Stated are growing up in a technologically-advanced world with television, Nintendo, PlayStation, videotapes, CDs, music videos, cellular phones, and home computers hooked to the Internet. Yet many schools cannot afford and consequently lack the types of modern technologies that children are surrounded by outside of school. As a result, many students find school static, boring, and even alienating. Thus, children of today are caught in a precarious situation: They need to be prepared for the future, but to them, many schools represent the past.

Today's emerging technologies offer enormous potential for changing this scenario. These new technologies are creating different paths to reach learners and improve their abilities, as well as offering new ways for administrators and instructors to communicate. Furthermore, computer technology can be used to motivate and encourage students to work in groups collaboratively, thus changing instructional methods as well as the role of the teacher. Fiske

(1991) states that a "technological revolution now is totally transforming the role of learning and teaching in the modern economy" (p. 146).

McDonald and Ingvarson (1995) state, "It's not having computers that is important, it is how they are used" (p. 3). Skill and drill practices on the computer will not help to make school a more inviting atmosphere; instead, these practices may only further alienate children from school. Previous studies investigating computer use in the classroom and students' perceptions have reported that students enjoyed writing more when they used a computer for word processing (Baer, 1988; Mackinson & Peyton, 1993). Other studies noted how students were excited about working on computer-based projects (Chisholm, 1995; St. Pierre-Hirtle, 1996). Teachers have also reported their students' excitement and motivation to participate in computer-based activities (Davis, 1995; Noden, 1995).

Constructivism in the classroom leads to the discovery of knowledge by the learner, and a key component of constructivism is that students begin to take responsibility for their learning (Brooks, 1990). Both researchers and teachers (Brooks & Brooks, 1993; Kinzer & Leu, 1997; Noden, 1995) have reported changes in the classroom community that have resulted from students taking control of their learning. Adding the use of computer technology to a constructivist classroom can further enhance students' desire and ability to expand their knowledge base.

Several researchers have investigated various constructivist uses of computers where literacy is the instrument that makes it all possible—as the means toward the end. The following studies briefly outline computer-based activities in a constructivist learning environment. Anderson and Lee (1995) investigated the use of e-mail as an instructional tool in a graduate reading class and found that e-mail played a major role in building a sense of community within the class. Chisholm (1995) explored how a constructivist teacher in an urban, multicultural elementary school used computers in her multiage classroom. Students were required to share the computers and help each other when computer-related problems arose; they were responsible for their learning and were expected to work together collaboratively and amicably. Kinzer and Leu's study (1997) in a large urban elementary school outlined changes that occurred in classroom communities due to the implementation of various learner-centered computer software programs. Findings noted that students interacted and collaborated with each other to use technology to locate information that could be used in their reports. Keeler (1996) investigated the use of networked PCs and various learner-centered software programs in several classrooms in a large urban elementary school. Data revealed changes in teachers' attitudes, teaching strategies, classroom management, classroom climate, the community of learners, and teacher's role in the classroom. Noden (1995), a middle school teacher, described several projects which involved his students in a form of electronic globe trotting. In what Noden referred to as "global explorations" (p. 26), his students joined listservs on various topics and swapped ideas with other students around the world.

Purpose of the Study

The research presented in this paper is part of a larger study that explored the ways two constructivist teachers used computer technology in their language arts classrooms and how computer use impacted their students. This paper will address the third question of the larger study: What are students' perceptions of computer-based activities in language arts classes?

For the purpose of this study, computer-based activities are defined as student-generated or teacher-generated activities that use the computer as a means for gathering, clarifying, creating, and presenting information. Computer-based activities enhance the classroom lesson by incorporating critical as well as creative thinking and problem-solving skills; these activities are not skill and drill computer activities. Additionally, computer-based activities are congruent with a constructivist philosophy. When computer-based activities are integrated into a constructivist learning environment, the responsibility of learning shifts from the teacher to the learners, and students have the opportunity to work together to expand their knowledge base.

Methodology

Since one aspect of this research study focused on students' perceptions of the implementation of computer-based language arts activities in two constructivist classrooms, a naturalistic, descriptive research paradigm was an appropriate framework. Case study research is a means of understanding, informing, and improving practice and holistically describes and explains a specific event or phenomena (Merriam, 1988).

The Setting

The larger context for this study was a suburban school district that served four communities located between two large midwestern cities. The socio-economic make up ranged from middle to upper income; ten percent of the school district were eligible for free/reduced price lunches.

The Teachers, the Class, and the Projects

Since the larger study examined how constructivist teachers integrated computer-based activities into their language arts lessons, it was essential that the two teachers selected for this study follow a constructivist philosophy of teaching and learning. Eight teachers were interviewed about a) instructional philosophy, b) experience and level of comfort with computers,

c) beliefs about integrating computer technology into their language arts lessons, and d) how they integrate computer-based activities into literacy lessons. A sixth grade teacher in a self-contained classroom and a high school language arts teacher were selected for case study. For the purpose of this paper the investigator focused on Ms. Claire Rice's sixth-grade classroom. Names of participants in this case study are pseudonyms.

Ms. Rice. Ms. Rice's classroom had five computers and 26 students; the computers were located in the back of the room in what used to be the coat closet. Her room had six tables, no desks. Ms. Rice taught an integrated curriculum that was focused around six-week thematic units such as changes, cultures, systems, economics. Each six weeks, students chose a topic in which they were interested, researched it, and presented it to the class. These I-Search projects (Macrorie, 1980) were woven into the curriculum and played a critical role in the daily classroom operations.

The Projects. For the purpose of this paper, computer-based projects are defined as in-depth, multi-step assignments that usually (though not always) include research and a presentation to the class. These projects also utilized different computer applications and software other than or in addition to a word processing program.

Ms. Rice believed that I-Search projects were the key to helping her students "see meaningful connections. They're taking their ideas and expanding them beyond the classroom." The I-Search time was incorporated into the thematic units. "That's what they want to learn about that unit." They began by spending time brainstorming ideas about what they could do, and thinking and re-thinking through their topics. "It's got to be something they're passionate about because if not, it doesn't fly."

Students' I-Search projects were quite varied in topic, execution, and presentation. Students chose topics such as recycling, hurricanes, Mercury, and forest fires. They used both Encarta '95 and '97 electronic encyclopedias as well as the Internet to locate information. Students gathered material from websites such as the National Weather Service Center and NASA. Students worked in pairs or independently. Many students used HyperStudio to turn their projects into presentations and even ran their HyperStudio work through the television for easier viewing. Some students made PowerPoint slide shows to highlight their projects. A few used Quick Take digital cameras to import pictures into their projects and presentations; others created their own drawings using the software Paint Brush. Some students used Print Shop Deluxe II to make question and answer cards for their presentations. Their work was impressive and professional.

Most of the projects in Ms. Rice's classroom revolved around the I-Search; however, students also participated in other projects such as a newspaper on a famous person and mystery stories. Students participated in the creation of a newspaper on a famous person such as Golda Mier, Gandhi, and Nelson Mandela. Students chose their person and found information from the Internet, Encarta, and books in their library. They located maps and photos from various sources and scanned them into their newspapers. Students used Print Shop Deluxe II and Microsoft Works to add columns, headlines, and dates. The students' newspapers were very creative and individual.

Another computer-based project was the creation of their mystery stories. Students worked on this project in pairs. These projects were quite varied in their style, format, execution, and presentation. While some of the students chose to only word process their stories, most used multimedia programs such as HyperStudio, Media Weaver, Hollywood, and Hollywood High to "bring their mysteries to life." Hollywood and Hollywood High are learner-centered software programs that allow students to create scenes, sets, characters with various expressions, and sound effects.

The Students

Four students were selected to be case study participants. Both teachers were asked to identify four to six students for case study, and the investigator added two additional students to the pool. Complete data were collected on eleven students; all were interviewed in depth regarding their experience with computers, observed while working on the computer, and contributed documents that were products of computer-based activities. Two focal students from each classroom were selected so that the investigator could conduct a cross-case comparison between the students within each classroom. The four students chosen as key informants for this study were talkative, exhibited high levels of experience with computers, and had good literacy skills.

For the purpose of this paper the investigator will focus on the two sixth grade students, Jay and Star. Jay believed that computers should be used in all classes and subject areas, especially "if the kids know how to use them and if they're taught how to use them." Jay was "wild about computers." He stated, "I don't know how people got along without computers—I really don't." Star found using the computer fun and exciting and made school more interesting for her. She had an interesting outlook on computers at school.

> By using computers for the projects we do, people can see that sixth graders can do really good things on the computer, and they can see what we should get off the computer. And I think that helps because they can see we just aren't little kids, but like, "Hey, look what we can do!"

Data Collection and Analysis

Data for this study was collected until "successive examination of sources yields redundancy" (Glesne & Peshkin, 1992, p. 132). In other words, when the investigator found that there was no new circumstances occurring, interviews and conversations with teachers and students were not revealing any new information, and no new documents had been generated, data collection ceased. Glaser and Strauss (1967) refer to this as theoretical saturation. Redundancy was reached in six weeks.

The data was collected in three primary ways: a) formal interviews with teachers and students at the beginning and end of the study. The semi-structured interview questions are presented in the Appendix; b) field notes from classroom observations of students working on computer-based activities and informal conversations; and c) document collection such as student-produced reports, stories, plays, journal reflections, newsletters, articles, presentations, and portfolios.

Actual classroom use of computers was observed and field notes were recorded on an AlphaSmart Keys. Behaviors and verbal remarks of the case study participants were recorded as accurately as possible. "Observation makes it possible to record behavior as it is happening" (Merriam, 1988, p. 88). The investigator recorded a) classroom observations on the teachers' integration of computer-based activities with literacy lessons; b) the students' responses to the activities and interaction with the computer; and c) informal conversations with students and teachers. Both classrooms were observed every day for six weeks.

The principal method for data analysis was studying the multiple data gathered from interviews, classroom observation, and student-produced documents for emerging categories related to the questions that guided the study. This process was both deductive and inductive (Guba & Lincoln, 1981). Through the simultaneous process of collecting, coding, and analyzing data, findings began to emerge and cross paths, thus revealing the major domains. "The use of multiple-data-collection methods contributes to the trustworthiness of the data" (Glesne & Peshkin, 1992, p. 24). In addition, qualified colleagues were asked to examine the categories for discrepancies. A handout explaining the categories and definitions was provided for reference, and the raters were presented with several sample data that represented the connection between the data to the categories. There was an inter-rater reliability of 92%.

Findings

The analysis of data revealed two major categories regarding students' perceptions. Students believed that computer-based activities improve work and create interest.

Improves Work

The category "improves work" was divided into three subcategories: a) the computer made it easier for students to do their work; b) the computer made their work look better and more professional; and c) the computer helped them learn more and expand their skill base.

Makes Work Easier To Do. Jay believed that using the computer was just an easier way to do anything. He stated, "If you edit someone's work or your own stuff, it's just much easier to do on a computer." He thought that computers and research were the perfect match, and he couldn't imagine doing research without a computer. "I do almost all of my research and stuff on the computer because it's easier than looking it up in a book. If I have to do pictures for a project, I get them off the computer, too." When asked what he would have done with his I-Search projects on Pluto and the Big Bang if he had not had Internet access, he replied, "I would have had to call NASA and that would have taken way too long. The Internet is just so much faster."

Star also believed that using a computer made it easier to do her work. She stated, "I think it's easier using the computer. If you know how to type, it's easier. If you know how to type fast, it's faster." Star also found it easier and faster to do research on the computer. "The Internet and Encarta are like so much faster and easier than looking stuff up in books and magazines. Sometimes the books are old and the information is not as new as it is on the Internet."

Looks More Professional. Jay used the computer to improve the looks of his work. "Whenever I want to change something to make it look better, I just get on the computer and mess with the fonts." He was very conscious of his handwriting and stated: "It's neat if you do it on the computer. I think it's neater, it's better. It just looks nicer to do them on the computer with a fancy font than to write it all out."

Star found the computer helped her to make her work look neater and more professional. "It just wouldn't look as good because the computer is neat. It just looks a lot neater." For one of Star's projects, she created a newspaper on Nelson Mandela. She stated:

> I tried to make it look real professional by using columns, making a title, and adding the date. I also got pictures from Encarta and put them in with captions under the picture. {Big smile} I think it makes it like look more like a real newspaper.

Expands Skills. Jay believed that using the computer has greatly expanded his skills in many different areas. Having had a computer since he was in kindergarten, he reflected: "If you're learning how to use a computer when you're growing up, it can help you." He stated that using computers at school has helped him to become better at typing and using different software programs. "I think the ability to use computers has helped me {to} be better at typing. I'm getting faster at typing, and I've learned how to use things like Encarta, Print Shop, HyperStudio, and Correl." Jay believed that the new electronic encyclopedias like Encarta "are more up-to-date with facts and keeps kids more current."

Jay also saw the computer as a challenge. "It's a big step. I learn something new about them and from them every day. You can do anything you want to with a computer; you're only limited by what you don't know." He believed that computers helped build his problem-solving skills. "Like if you don't have a lot on your computer, you have to substitute. Just thinking about how to substitute what to get what I want is problem-solving in action."

Star believed that she learned a lot from her computer-based I-Search projects. "I feel if you just have regular resources on paper, then it's not as broad as it is on the computer because, like, well on the Internet you can get anything." She thought that using the computer to work on her projects made her a better thinker.

> You have to really think about what you're going to use in your reports and where you're going to get it from. I use a lot of different sources so it helps me understand how to get things on the Internet and how to get things in Encarta and . . . um . . . it's just that . . . I think I learn more from making a newspaper or something than just doing a regular report because I can get different pictures to go along with it. It's harder to make but that means you have to understand it more.

Creates Interest

The category "creates interest" was divided into four subcategories: a) students saw the computer as a resource that created more interest and motivation in school; b) students found computer-based activities fun and exciting; c) students found that they became more personally involved in computer-based activities, allowing them to take ownership and pride in their work; and d) computer-based activities allowed students to express their creativity.

Interest and Motivation in School. Being able to use the computer for his class projects kept Jay from getting bored with school. "I just think it's boring when you don't get to use the computer, and you have to write everything out by hand." Jay's favorite thing to do on the computer was to "get on the Internet and research because I know how to use it." Jay stated that for him, the best thing about his projects on Pluto and the Big Bang was that he got to use the computer.

> Computers just make school more interesting. Like you can get on the Internet to research, and you can go almost any place in the world at the click of a button. It's just so much more interesting than books, and you can use it to find a bunch of stuff.

Star stated that being able to participate in computer-based activities kept school interesting for her. "There's a lot of things you can do with a computer, and it was boring last year without them. It's just more interesting with computers."

Star not only found it interesting and motivational to "look for things for my papers and reports" on the Internet and Encarta; she also found her peers' presentations quite interesting. "I think it's more interesting to look at people's work, like when they've done it on the computer, because there's just more things you can do on a computer than you can do with just pencil and paper."

Fun and Exciting. Jay really enjoyed using the computer for his I-Search projects. It not only made school more interesting for him, but he found it fun and exciting to create his projects on the computer and use different software programs to do so.

> The report I did on the Big Bang was not too hard except for the pictures I drew on Paint Brush. Even though it was really hard to do, it was fun. Maybe that's because it's something I'm really interested in but I also think the Big Bang is just a fun topic.

Jay's report and presentation on Pluto was a totally computerized project. He described what aspects of it he thought were fun and exciting.

> Just using the computer is fun, well at least for me. But I thought watching it when it was all done was real exciting and so was the music I put in it—it was from Star Wars. There were also a whole bunch of other sound effects in it. I got to tape my voice and put that in it, and I got to use the computer to do the work. I also got to set up the TV with the computer, and that was fun.

More than anything else, Star had lots of fun working on the computer. "It just doesn't seem like work," she said. For Star, it was all fun, whether she was researching information on the Internet or Encarta, typing a paper, or cutting and pasting pictures from Encarta into her reports. "If you just take books and copy them, that's not as fun as going on the Internet and looking up information on it. And it's just a lot more interesting than going into books." Putting together a HyperStudio multimedia presentation was what she liked doing the most. "I just *love* making like presentations on HyperStudio and getting things off the Internet for it. It's just *so* much fun! I think it's fun because it's like realistic work."

Personal Involvement, Ownership, and Pride. Jay took great pride in his computer-based I-Search projects. He became very involved in each one and thought about them constantly. For his report on Pluto, Jay searched for weeks for the perfect pictures to use. When he couldn't find what he was looking for, he created his own.

> Making them took a really long time for just one of the pictures. I had to do it three times because I accidentally erased it, so it took me a couple of hours to do just one. But they turned out really nice. Some people were really surprised that I did that because I did this 3-D effect with them.

Jay's pride and ownership in his completed projects and presentations was quite evident. He stated:

> That was the best report I've ever done. I got 200 out of 200! {The teacher} is going to take it to Hudson with her for the exhibition of student computer work. I think that's good! I hope I get to go with her; that would be even better!

Star was very proud of her computer-based projects, and she loved showing her work to anyone who would appear interested. Her very favorite project was the family history project which she spent weeks interviewing, photographing, and putting together.

> I *really* liked the one that I did with the poster with all the pictures of my family because it was fun talking to all of them and asking them questions and hearing their answers. I really liked using the Snappy computer camera that puts them in different places anywhere in the world. Then I like pasted their pictures on a big poster board and typed up the interviews with them. I just really loved that project. {Big smile} My mom like has it hanging on her wall at home; I think she really liked it too.

Creativity. Jay believed that creativity and computer use went hand in hand. "They're just a tool, and you have to remember that so you have to be creative." He stated that the more experienced he became on the computer, the more creative he became on them also.

> You have to think, "How can I use these other things to make it work better?" or "How can I substitute these for this?" You're limited so you have to be creative to get past that. You *have* to be creative with it; it's the only way you can use it.

Star was a very creative young woman. She loved writing plays on the software Hollywood and Hollywood High; at the time of this study she had composed over 38 plays! Additionally, Star was always trying to find different ways to pull together different uses for multiple software programs. "I like putting it together a lot." She described several of her projects and how she pulled pictures and information from different sources.

> I like to do like HyperStudio at school and make presentations on it because there's a lot of pictures you can put in it, and you can put a lot of information into different cards, and you can do sound effects. But I also like to do reports where I like get things off of the computer and then like put them into whatever I'm making. Like sometimes I'll use Print Shop for part of my report, and I'll get a picture or two from Encarta, and then I'll get on the Internet and find some information to type in and stuff. I just like being creative and putting it all together.

Limitations

There are several limitations to this study. The case study presented in this paper reported on information regarding two students and their teacher. This information cannot be generalized to the whole population. Another limitation involved interview procedure to collect data for this study; classroom observation and document analysis as other means of collecting data attempted to minimize this limitation. A third limitation is that this study focused on students who were computer literate and had access to computers in their homes.

Conclusions

Several conclusions can be derived from the findings of this study. These students enjoyed participating in computer-based activities in a constructivist learning environment. They believed that computer-based activities improved their work and created interest in school and school work. Students found the computer easy to use for research. One student summed it up: "It's so easy! It's just quicker. You can find anything. There's nowhere else you can find that much information, and it's so quick." Students commented that computer-based activities were the key to interest and motivation. "Just being able to do it on the computer keeps them interested because it's something different. It helps *so much* and just gets the students motivated and keeps us interested in what we're doing," one student reflected. One student stated, "Computers just make school more interesting!" Students also found activities fun and exciting. "There's nothing better than a fun project that you're doing and you *know* you're doing it well," one young woman commented. One student summed up the beliefs of many of her peers when she stated, "It just doesn't seem like work."

Implementing computer-based activities in a constructivist learning environment encouraged a sense of ownership. The students were proud of their work; they wanted to show their work to others and talk about their projects. Students became very involved in their projects and spent time working on them during lunch and after school. They were also involved in their peers' projects, and they helped each other with various aspects of their work.

A constructivist learning environment where "students' freedom to chase their own ideas is abundant" (Brooks & Brooks, 1993, p. 10) motivates and excites students about what they are learning in school. They are able to see meaningful connections beyond the classroom. The students involved in this research study were given the freedom to "chase their own ideas" and this freedom helped them to see school in a different perspective.

References

Anderson, J., & Lee, A. (1995). Literacy teachers learning a new literacy: A study of the use of electronic mail in a reading education class. *Reading Research and Instruction, 34*(3), 222-238.

Baer, V. (1988). Computers as composition tools: A case study of student attitudes. *Journal of Computer-Based Instruction, 15*(4), 144-148.

Brooks, J. G. (1990). Teachers and students: Constructivists forging new connections. *Educational Leadership, 47*(5), 68-71.

Brooks, J. G., & Brooks, M. G. (1993). *In search of understanding: The case for constructivist classrooms*. Alexandria, VA: Association for Supervision and Curriculum Development.

Chisholm, I. M. (1995). Computer use in a multicultural classroom. *Journal of Research in Computing Education, 28*(2), 162-174.

Davis, C. (1995). The I-search paper goes global: Using the Internet as a research tool. *English Journal, 84*(6), 27-33.

Fiske, E. B. (1991). *Smart schools, smart kids*. New York: Simon & Schuster.

Glaser, G. G., & Strauss, A. L. (1967). *The discovery of grounded theory*. Chicago: Aldine

Glesne, C., & Peshkin, A. (1992). *Becoming qualitative researchers: An introduction*. White Plains, NY: Longman.

Guba, E. G., & Lincoln, Y. S. (1981). *Effective evaluation*. San Francisco: Jossey-Bass Publishers.

Keeler, C. M. (1996). Networked instructional computers in the elementary classroom and their effect on the learning environment: A qualitative evaluation. *Journal of Research in Computers in Education, 28*(3), 329-345.

Kinzer, C., & Leu, D. J. (1997). The challenge of change: Exploring literacy and learning in electronic environments. *Language Arts, 74*, 126-136.

Mackinson, J. A., & Peyton, J. K. (1993). Interactive writing on a computer network: A teacher/researcher collaboration. In S. J. Hudelson & J. W. Lindfors (Eds.), *Delicate balances: Collaborative research in language education* (pp. 21-36). Urbana, IL: National Council of Teachers of English.

Macrorie, K. (1980). *Searching writing*. Rochelle, NJ: Hayden Books.

McDonald, H., & Ingvarson, L. (1995). *Free at last? Teachers, computers and independent learning*. Paper presented at the annual meeting of the American Educational Research Association, San Francisco, CA. (ERIC Document Reproduction Service No. ED 389 278)

Merriam, S. B. (1988). *Case study research in education*. San Francisco: Jossey-Bass Publishers.

Noden, H. R. (1995). A journey through cyberspace: Reading and writing in a virtual school. *English Journal, 84*(6), 19-26.

St. Pierre-Hirtle, J. (1996). Technology and reflection: Knowing our world and our work. In Z. Donoahue, M. A. Van Tassell, & L. Patterson (Eds.), *Research in the classroom: Talk, texts, and inquiry* (pp. 81-90). Newark, DE: International Reading Association.

Appendix A. Interview with Teachers

Initial Interview with Teachers

1. Describe your instructional philosophy regarding teaching and learning.
2. Tell me about your experiences with computers.
3. How do you integrate computer technology into your language arts lessons?
4. What are some different types of projects you have had your students work on that incorporated computer-based activities?
5. What kinds of activities would you like to do with your students that you haven't been able to do so yet?

Second Interview with Teachers

1. Do you belong to any professional organizations?
2. Have you given workshops or staff development on computers?
3. As I see it now, how you use computers are in these ways: as research tool; for word processing; for projects and presentations; for communication; for student creativity; to do old things in new ways. Do you agree? Are there any other ways you can see how you use them?
4. How do you think your students perceive computer-based projects? Why do you think so? What do the student say about these projects? What are their reactions to them?
5. What types of literacy behaviors do you observe them using when they are involved in computer-based activities?
6. What types of changes, if any, have you observed in their attitudes about working on language arts lessons when they are tied to computer use? How do you know their attitudes have changed?
7. What else would you like to add to this?

Appendix B. Interview with Students

Initial Interview with Students
1. Tell me about your experiences with computers.
2. Tell me about some projects that you have done for school in which you used a computer.
3. What types of computer-based activities do you like doing the best?
4. What are your perceptions of these types of activities?
5. How do these differ from traditional pen-and-paper activities?
6. What do you like about computer-based activities? What do you dislike about them?
7. Do you think computers should be used in all Language Arts classrooms? Why? Why not?

Second Interview with Students
1. What do you think about using computers to do old things—like reports and presentations and writing—in a new way?
2. How else do you think a computer can be used in class?
3. What is the piece of work you have done on the computer for class that you liked the best? Why?
4. What do you think was your teacher's favorite piece of work from you? Why?
5. What types of computer work do you like doing best at school? Why?
6. What do you think you have gained from doing these?
7. What did you like about doing them? What did you dislike?
8. Do you think computers should be used in all classes? Why?

Using Literacy Play Centers to Engage Middle Grade Students in Content Area Learning

Lynn Romeo
Susan A. Young

Monmouth University

Abstract

This paper investigated fifth grade students' perceptions about their interactions while using a Literacy Play Center that was designed to promote social studies content learning. Groups of four or five students worked in the Literacy Play Center for forty-minute periods, five times per week for seven weeks. The methods employed in the study were surveys, interviews, and analysis of artifacts from the center. The categories that emerged from the data focused on the physical environment, the social interaction, and the motivation of the students. The results suggest that middle elementary age students benefit from a comfortable, contained classroom environment that allows students to socially interact while exploring a wide array of authentic, literacy enriched activities.

Background

Educators have been interested in the effects of student motivation on learning for decades (Dillon & al, 1992; Weiner,1990). Currently, "educators recognize that motivation is at the heart of many of the pervasive problems we face in educating today's youth" (Gambrell & Morrow, 1996 p. 115). It has been found that there is a strong relationship between motivation and achievement (Gambrell, 1996; Guthrie, Schafer, Wang & Afflerbach, 1993). Most developing readers tend to have strong motivation during the early grades. Children who have difficulty learning to read and write, however, begin to believe as they advance in grades that they do not have the ability to be successful readers and writers (Pressley, 1998).

It also appears that students' motivation may decline as they advance in grades, begin to value reading less (Eccles, Wigfield, & Midgley, 1993; Gambrell, 1996; Wigfield, 1997) and are frequently immersed in a competitive classroom environment. In fact, when Gambrell, Codling, & Palmer (1996) investigated the reading motivation of third through fifth grade students via an inventory, the fifth graders valued reading a lot less than the third grade subjects did. Seventeen percent of the sample indicated that they would rather clean their rooms than read a book and fourteen percent revealed that they do not intend to spend time reading when they become adults. The diminished motivation in older students is even more apparent when dealing with the at-risk population (Dillon & al, 1996; McKenna, 1995). In the Gambrell and et al. study (1996), low scores on the self-concept component of the instrument were associated with low reading achievement. Forty-five percent of the students indicated that they worry almost daily about what their peers think about their ability to read well.

Therefore, it is of paramount importance that teachers determine effective methods for increasing students' interest and motivation for reading and writing. We need to create authentic tasks that have personal value for the students and foster the development of intrinsic motivation for literacy activities (Gambrell & al, 1996; Guthrie, 1996; Oldfather, 1993; Turner, 1995). Further, students respond favorably to appropriate, challenging tasks that are not too simple or too difficult. It appears that engagement is also enhanced when the students are provided with choice in selecting materials and feel that they have some control in regard to their own learning (Oldfather, 1993; Gambrell & Morrow, 1996). Finally, opportunities for social interaction and collaboration have been found to enhance motivation for literacy tasks and peer learning (Almasi, McKeown, & Beck, 1996; Turner, 1997). The need for social interaction and collaboration becomes even more pronounced when learners are approaching middle school age. During this period of their development, students are striving to determine their place in their environment and how well they are accepted by their peers (Preisser, Anders, & Glider, 1990).

Many researchers have promoted the integration of literacy and content area subjects (Pressley, 1998; Guthrie & Mc Cann, 1997). This thematic instruction helps students build connections between the various disciplines, such as social studies and literacy. It supports the balanced literacy model that focuses on the development of self-directed, motivated, strategic learners (Guthrie & Mc Cann, 1997). Isolated instruction, on the other hand, makes it difficult for students, especially at-risk learners to make meaningful connections. Social studies instruction that consists of the use of a traditional textbook, with a lot of condensed facts is frequently viewed by the students as boring, and does not allow for higher level thinking and understanding (Dixon-Kraus, 1996; Beck & McKeown, 1988). In a study by Murden and Gillespie (1997) that involved middle and high school students and teachers, it was found that teachers relied heavily on one textbook for delivering content information. However, students frequently did not read the textbooks prior to class and believed that the teachers were attempting to teach them only the information that they would need to acquire to pass tests. Although it is important for students to learn historical information, it should be presented in a manner that allows for schema building as well as critical thinking and analysis (Stahl, Hynd, Glynn & Carr, 1996).

Reading and writing can be successfully integrated into the teaching of social studies to promote thinking skills and cognitive development. McGuire (1996) capitalized on Bloom's taxonomy when she developed an integrated model for social studies instruction the storypath method. This method integrates the content area topic, discussion, collaboration, and literature. Project-based instruction, that includes role playing, cooperative learning, and computers, has been used successfully with learning disabled students to increase their knowledge about historical concepts (Okolo & Ferretti, 1996). In a recent study, (Sternberg, Torff, & Grigorenko, 1998), third and fifth grade students who received social studies instruction via a triarchic method (analytical, creative, and practical tasks) learned more content information than groups of students whose instruction was either memory-based or analytically based.

Physical environment is an important component to consider when providing engaging, literacy experiences (Morrow, 1989,1990; Strickland & Morrow, 1989). Frequently, however, teachers do not consider the arrangement of the classroom when planning instruction. It has been found that altering the physical arrangement of the classroom can change the behavior patterns of the students (Weinstein, 1977). Classrooms that have been partitioned into smaller, more intimate spaces with engaging materials and comfortable furniture can captivate student interest and inspire learning (Morrow, 1997).

Literacy Play Centers, sometimes referred to as dramatic play areas, have been used with young children for many years. When props that focus on reading and writing are placed in a typical preschool center such as a kitchen, writing area, or block area, young children's voluntary use of literacy activities and materials have increased (Morrow & Rand, 1991; Neuman & Roskos, 1993; Vukelich, 1991; Young & Romeo, 1998). The areas are transformed into restaurants, post offices, doctor or veterinarian offices, and construction sites. Props can include writing utensils, books, magazines, pads, letters, puppets, and charts. When using Literacy Play Centers, children learn about literacy because it is integrated into an authentic context that is a familiar component of their environment (Pellegrini & Galda, 1993; Neuman & Roskos, 1997; Roskos, 1995; Walker, Allen & Glines, 1997; Labbo, 1998).

Although Literacy Play Centers have been utilized effectively with young children to promote interest in literacy and to increase print awareness (Campbell & Foster, 1993; Neuman & Roskos, 1991, 1992), their use with older students has only recently been explored (Stone & Christie, 1996; Jarrett, 1997). Although Jarrett focused on enhancing math and science concepts via play, there appear to be no investigations of Literacy Play Centers that target social studies and literacy via play-like activities.

To fulfill one of the requirements for a graduate course in literacy, students designed and constructed Literacy Play Centers in grades two through five classrooms for two years. The data collected thus far through surveys and conversations with classroom teachers suggests that these middle elementary students have been very motivated when using the centers in their classrooms and are actively engaged in meaningful literacy activities while playing and collaborating in various centers.

Methodology

The purpose of this qualitative pilot study was to investigate students' perceptions and feelings about their interactions while using a Literacy Play Center that was designed to promote content learning. More specifically, we wanted to explore their active involvement when using the materials, their choice of activities, and their social collaboration with other students.

Fifth grade students from one class in a suburban elementary school (grades three through six) in central New Jersey were the subjects for our study. There were nineteen Caucasian students in the class, ten girls and nine boys.

Five graduate pre-service students enrolled in a literacy course collaborated with the elementary students and classroom teachers to decide what type of Literacy Play Center should be constructed in the fifth grade classroom. Choice was limited to the theme that was currently being studied in social studies. The center was to be used as a supplemental activity to the class' social studies program, which consisted of a traditional social studies textbook and whole group discussion.

The classroom teacher, who had taught elementary grades for twelve years, had no previous knowledge about the concept of using a Literacy Play Center to foster engagement in literacy and/or social studies activities.

It was collaboratively decided to create a Time Machine, which focused on the study of explorers. The teacher, graduate students, and elementary students also discussed possible props and materials for the center. The graduate students were instructed to create an engaging, low-risk, self-contained, literacy/play enriched environment where the fifth graders could learn more about early explorers. It was also suggested to them to develop activities that focused on the following words: create (a drawing or map that traces the voyage of Columbus), imagine (you were lost in the ocean and had to develop a plan to stay alive), pretend (you are a doctor treating a sick seaman and need to decide what kinds of food and medicine should be used), design (an advertisement for selling a ship), or write (a news story about De Soto's voyage).

After the graduate students constructed the Literacy Play Center, they met with the teacher and students to introduce the center and explain the props, activities, and materials. The fifth grade students named the center CZ's Time Warp.

Props included a computer with internet access, goggles, a compass, a protractor kit, a globe, games, books, journals, maps, puzzles, and travel brochures. It also contained lapboards, pillows, writing tools, a bulletin board that had a timeline, stickers, and individual folders. The exterior side walls were bookshelves and the front entrance was made of thin plywood. Netting was placed from the ceiling to enhance the image of a time machine.

The Literacy Play Center was utilized in the classroom for seven weeks. The teacher provided forty minutes, five times per week for groups of four or five students to interact in the center. Generally, every student was able to work in the Literacy Play Center twenty minutes, twice per week. The methods employed in the study were surveys, interviews, and analysis of artifacts from the center.

The researchers and a graduate student observed the classroom weekly and took detailed field notes during each visit. Each observation lasted approximately one-half hour. The field notes were transcribed after each visitation. We looked at the students' mannerisms and verbal interactions. We wrote down conversations and described what each student or small groups of students did while they participated in the Literacy Play Center. In addition, we video taped the students while interacting in the play center three times during the seven week period. Photographs were also taken of the students. When the researchers viewed the video tapes, notes were taken. We were looking for evidence of engagement or non-engagement as well as interaction with others and choice of materials. These notes were compared to the field notes from the observations. Field notes were then expanded to include all new information.

In addition, we collected and analyzed artifacts from the center to further determine what kinds of literacy activities the students were engaged in during the time spent in the Literacy Play Center. The artifacts included journals, timelines, trip worksheets, and artwork. We compared this information with the patterns that emerged from the observations and video taping.

At the end of the study, the students were asked to write about their experiences in the Literacy Play Center. We utilized this information to design a questionnaire that was administered to the students at the conclusion of the study (Table 1). The questionnaire contained a five-point picture rating scale as well as several open-ended questions about the strengths and weaknesses of the experience. The students were asked to rate how they felt about the types of activities and their overall feelings regarding having the Literacy Play Center in the classroom. The mean and range of scores for each of the questions were analyzed. The open-ended questions were coded and compared with the information gleaned from the observational data.

Table 1. Student Literacy Play Center Questionnaire (n=19)

Name: _____ Date: _____ Teacher: _____

For each sentence, circle the picture that best matches how you feel about the time you spent in the Literacy Play Center that was built in your classroom by the Monmouth University graduate students.

1. How do you feel about the Literacy Play Center that was built in your classroom by the Monmouth University students?
   first dog (happiest), 18; second happiest dog, 1 (mean, 4.94)

2. How do you feel about the kinds of reading materials that are in the Literacy Play Center? **first dog (happiest), 11; second happiest dog, 7; middle dog, 1 (mean, 4.53)**

3. How do you feel about the kinds of writing materials that are in the Literacy Play Center? **first dog (happiest), 11; second happiest dog, 8; (mean, 4.60)**

4. How did you feel when you read the information that is in the Literacy Play Center? **first dog (happiest), 9; second happiest dog, 8; middle dog, 2 (mean, 4.36)**

5. How did you feel when you wrote about the information that you found in the Literacy Play Center? **first dog (happiest), 9; second happiest dog, 9; middle dog, 1(mean, 4.42)**

6. How would you feel about having another Literacy Play Center built in your classroom? **first dog (happiest), 17; least happiest dog, 2; (mean, 4.57)**

7. How do you feel about reading and writing? **first dog (happiest), 9; second happiest dog, 7; middle dog, 3 (mean, 4.31)**

8. What do you like best about the Literacy Play Center?
Trip Box; Journals; other activities

9. Is there anything that you would like changed in your Literacy Play Center?
nothing; fine the way it is
What changes would you like? **more time in center**

10. What other kinds of Literacy Play Centers would you like to have built in your classroom? **science, space, weather, oceans; health; sports**

11. Did you ever have a Literacy Play Center built in another class? **No**
What kind of center was it? What grade were you in?

Other Comments:
It is very cool.
I like it; I love it.
The Literacy Play Center is great.

Semi-structured interviews were also conducted (Appendix). Each student was individually presented with the information from his/her questionnaire. The students were asked to elaborate on the survey results to confirm or negate the information gleaned from the questionnaire. In addition, several questions were posed about their experience, what they completed while in the center, and how the experience compared with other social studies instruction.

The classroom teacher completed a questionnaire about her perceptions regarding the Literacy Play Center. She was interviewed regarding her thoughts on why she volunteered to have a Literacy Play Center constructed in her classroom and how she felt about the students' experience.

We used the constant comparative method (Glazer & Strauss, 1967) to analyze the observational data. Using our initial research question, we searched all of the data sources for emerging patterns and recurrent events. We continued this analysis throughout the study, comparing and contrasting new data with the existing categories. Both researchers read and reread the transcripts and viewed the video tapes. We wrote about the emerging categories and continued to search for new incidents. For data triangulation, the interview and questionnaire data was compared and contrasted with the observational data. The researchers discussed the emerging categories until agreement on the categories was reached. A graduate student, trained in coding procedures, served as an independent rater.

Results

The mean scores on the five point rating scales ranged from 4.31 to 4.94 (See Table 1). The lowest mean involved feelings regarding general reading and writing activities and the second lowest mean, (4.3) centered on feelings about the information that required reading during the time spent in the Literacy Play Center. The highest mean, (4.94) involved a question about their feelings regarding working in the Literacy Play Center.

Analysis of the interview transcripts, video tapes, student artifacts, and observational data revealed three categories: the physical environment, social interaction, and student motivation.

Physical Environment

The students frequently indicated that the environment was comfortable and cozy. They spoke a lot about feeling good while they were in the Literacy Play Center. They liked the physical boundaries (walls and net ceiling) of the center, the lapboards, and the freedom to sit on pillows while they worked. Some students indicated that it was very relaxing and felt like being at home. This was clearly evident during all of the observations and video tapes. The students anxiously waited for an opportunity to use the center.

They immediately sat on the floor, leaned on the pillows, and began to work on activities.

"It feels comfortable because it's enclosed."

"You just grab your assignment and sit back and relax."

"It is comfortable because we have pillows. It feels protective."

"It's nicer in there. It looks nicer, more comfortable, because of the pillows."

Social interaction

The students spoke about how much fun it was to participate in the center and to get the opportunity to be with other students. The students indicated that they liked being able to see their friends while participating and interacting in the center. They talked about how happy and excited they were when they working in the Literacy Play Center. During the observations, they assisted each other with the location and completion of activities, discussed information about various explorers, and shared the props. The students were very quiet during all of the social collaboration that took place. They spoke in low voices and there was no evidence of any dissension or disagreements.

"I feel happy and glad and happy to work with the other kids. I feel sad to leave the center."

"All the stuff in the center makes it fun."

"Good, because it's not only comfortable. I have friends in there."

Student Motivation

The students were actively engaged and motivated while in the center. This was apparent during all observations and analysis of the video tapes. They worked independently, in pairs, and in small groups. There was a high level of on-task behavior noted. In fact, in all the observations, every student in the Literacy Play Center was working on various activities or discussing information with other classmates. Students made the transition from one activity to another in an organized, thoughtful manner. In addition, as noted previously, the students were very quiet, even when they worked cooperatively in small groups. There was no evidence that the teacher had to exercise any behavior management techniques or facilitate any of the activities.

The students were even very motivated to complete activities in the Trip Box. This was surprising to the observers because The Trip Box was comprised of many paper and pencil tasks, some of which were commercially prepared worksheets that students might typically be assigned for seatwork or homework. At the beginning of the data collection, the classroom teacher assigned two of the trips. Initially it appeared that students completed the trips because of the assignment given by the teacher, but they continued to be motivated to work on them after they were given more freedom to choose their own activities. They did seem, however, to especially focus on "trips" that involved some aspect of art such as creating their own coat of arms and using reference books to label parts of a ship.

"They're (trips) fun. I loved to make my own underwater monster."

"The trips are fun to do and interesting."

"They're fun and there's competition. If there's a problem, you can look around the center and use the books."

Students also mentioned the availability of the computer and the reference books. They enjoyed the opportunity to choose the activities that they would be completing while in the center.

"I feel happy because I'm learning more things like where Christopher Columbus sailed to and ended."

" Great, I have time to do what I want like using the computer, reading the books, and using the gadgets."

Students also spoke about the social studies materials placed in the center. They indicated that the activities were more fun and interesting than reading and discussing material in traditional social studies texts. Work in the Literacy Play Center didn't seem like typical classroom learning to this group of students.

"I like working in here. It's better than doing regular social studies."

"It doesn't feel like I'm really doing social studies in there."

"It's better because it's much more fun than reading in the boring text-book. You can write in journals and look up a website on the computer."

"The teacher just talks and gives worksheets. In the center, you can take a book, go at your own pace, and instead of raising your hand, you can think things through in your head."

Conclusions

This pilot study investigated fifth grade students' perceptions and impressions about their experiences and peer interactions while working in the "Time Machine" Literacy Play Center. The center was constructed to provide content material to supplement their study of explorers which was a component of the social studies curriculum.

This study was limited to one fifth grade classroom in a suburban area and one type of Literacy Play Center. Lack of student diversity and lack of sustained time in the center were constraints. For example, since groups of students were only able to be in the Literacy Play Center for approximately fifteen to twenty minutes at one time, this greatly limited the opportunities for any sustained reading or writing as well as dramatic play activities (Christie, Johnsen, & Peckover, 1988). Specifically, one activity in the center was to construct an explorer journal and students frequently mentioned that they liked this activity. Careful inspection of the journals, however, revealed that most of the students did not write in them very often. Only a few pretended to be explorers writing about their adventures. Therefore, although the students liked the journals, they did not have the sustained time to use them for their reflections and creative expression.

Another constraint was that the classroom teacher did not receive any prior training regarding the concept of a Literacy Play Center. This lack of training lead to limited student choice when the center was first introduced and lack of adequate sustained time for the students to work in it.

The physical environment of the center, with its external boundaries, clearly defined space, and comfortable design seemed to have a favorable impact on the students. It was clearly evident from the observation and questionnaire/interview data that students preferred the cozy, relaxing place to work. This finding is consistent with previous investigations regarding space organization in early childhood classrooms (Roskos, 1995) and has implications for the design of intermediate grade rooms which often tend to be large open spaces with desks that are not comfortable.

In addition, the students reported feeling very happy and excited while in the Literacy Play Center. This was evident when analyzing observational data and the questionnaires. The positive feelings appeared to be a result of the social interaction that took place and the freedom to choose their activities. Interview and questionnaire data were rich with comments about how much they enjoyed working with their peers. As Gambrell (1996) has indicated, students who are engaged tend to be socially interactive as well as motivated, knowledgeable and strategic. The comfortable, inviting physical environment also appeared to positively affect the students' feelings.

The students were highly engaged and motivated the entire time they spent in the Literacy Play Center and during all activities. A high level of on-task behavior was noted during the observations and video taping. Further, the students liked the various activities, even the paper and pencil worksheet type tasks, that the researchers thought might be boring and tedious. It should be noted that their interest might be related to the opportunity to choose the activities that most appealed to them.

The students perceived the social studies activities and their involvement in the Literacy Play Center as much more interesting than when the content area subject was delivered via the traditional text and lecture method. In addition to the perceived interest level, students may have found the hands-on and varied, authentic activities as well as the multi-leveled materials to be more conducive to learning. Generally, the reading level of a content textbook is too difficult for many students to read and loaded with condensed factual information (Holmes & Ammon, 1985; Stewart, 1994). It appears that the addition of a Literacy Play Center in upper grade classrooms can support and enhance the understanding of content area material that is integrated with reading and writing. Future research should focus on evaluating the content area of study as well as investigating the students' interactions in the centers.

It appears that Literacy Play Centers can be employed in classrooms well beyond the early childhood years. In addition to fostering interest in literacy activities, they can enrich an intermediate classroom's social studies program and drive the content via reading, writing, and play. They have the potential to assist teachers in meeting the increasing content demands of today's schools and provide multiple opportunities for schema building. Students can link the significance of literacy tasks with the importance of having a knowledge base. Finally, a Literacy Play Center can engage and motivate students to construct knowledge in a social context and provide them with a voice regarding their thinking and learning.

References

Almasi, J.F., McKeown, M.G., & Beck, I.L. (1996). The nature of engaged reading in classroom discussions of literature. *Journal of Literacy Research, 28*, 1, 107-146.

Beck, I.L., & McKeown, M. (1988). Toward meaningful accounts in history texts for young learners. *Educational Researcher, 17*, 31-39.

Campbell, E.N., & Foster, J.E. (1993). Play centers that encourage literacy development. *Day Care and Early Education, 21*, 22-26.

Christie, J.F., Johnsen, E.P., & Peckover, R.B. (1988). The effects of play period duration on children's play patterns. *Journal of Research in Childhood Education, 3*, 123-131.

Dillon, D.R., O'Brien, D.G., Hopkins, C.J., Baumann, J.F., Humphrey, J.W., Pickle, J.M., Ridgeway, V.R., Wyatt, M., Wilkinson, C., Murray, B., & Pauler, S.M. (1992). Article content and authorship trends in *The Reading Teacher* 1948-1991. *The Reading Teacher, 45*, 362-65.

Dillon, D.R., O'Brien, D.G., Wellinski, S.A., Springs, R., & Stith, D. (1996). Engaging "At-risk" high school students: The creation of an innovative program. In D.J. Leu, C.K. Kinzer & K.A. Hinchman (Eds.), *Literacies for the 21st century: Research and Practice.* (pp. 232-244). Chicago, IL: National Reading Conference.

Dixon-Krauss, L. (1996). *Vygotsky in the classroom: Mediated literacy instruction and assessment.* NY: Longman.

Eccles, J.S., Wigfield, A., & Midgley, C. (1993). Negative effects of traditional middle schools on students' motivation. *The Elementary School Journal, 93*, 553-574.

Gambrell, L.B., Palmer, B.M., Codling, R.M., & Mazzoni, S.A. (1996). Assessing motivation to read. *The Reading Teacher, 49*, 518-533.

Gambrell, L., Codling, R.M., & Palmer, B.M. (1996). Elementary students' motivation to read. (Research Report No. 52). Athens, GA, & College Park, MD: National Reading Research Center

Gambrell, L.B. & Morrow, L.M. (1996). Creating motivating contexts for literacy learning. In L.Baker, P. Afflerbach, & D. Reinking (Eds.), *Developing engaged readers in school and home communities.* (pp. 115-136). Mahwah, NJ: Lawrence Erlbaum Associates.

Gambrell, L.B. (1996). Creating classroom cultures that foster reading motivation. *The Reading Teacher,* 50, 14-25.

Glaser, B.G., & Strauss, A.L. (1967). The discovery of grounded theory: Strategies for qualitative research. New York: Aldine.

Guthrie, J.T., Schafer, W., Wang, Y., & Afflerbach, P. (1993). Influences of instruction on reading engagement: An empirical investigation of a social-cognitive framework of reading activity (Research Report No. 3). Athens, GA, & College Park, MD: National Reading Research Center.

Guthrie, J.T. (1996). Educational contexts for engagement in literacy. *The Reading Teacher,* 49, 432-445.

Guthrie, J. T. & McCann, A.D. (1997). Characteristics of classrooms that promote motivations and strategies for learning. In J. T. Guthrie, & A. Wigfield (Eds.), *Reading engagement: Motivating readers through integrated instruction.* (pp. 128-148). Newark, DE: International Reading Association.

Holmes, B.C., & Ammon, R.I. (1985). Teaching content with trade books. *Childhood Education,* 366-70.

Jarrett, Olga. (1997). Science and math through role-play centers in the elementary classroom. *Science Activities,* 13-19.

Labbo, L. (1998). Social studies "play" in kindergarten. *Social Studies and the Young Learner,* 10, 4, 18-20.

McGuire, M. (1996). *Storypath: A strategy for meaningful learning in social studies.* Chicago: Everyday Learning Corporation.

McKenna, M.C., Kear, D.J., & Ellsworth, R.A. (1995). Children's attitudes toward reading: A national survey. *Reading Research Quarterly,* 30, 934-56.

Morrow, L.M. (1989). Designing the classroom to promote literacy development. In D.S. Strickland & L.M. Morrow (Eds.), *Emerging literacy: Young children learn to read and write.* (pp. 121-134). Newark, DE: International Reading Association.

Morrow, L., & Rand, M. (1991). Preparing the classroom environment to promote literacy during play. In J. Christie (Ed.), *Play and early literacy development.* (pp. 141-163). Albany: SUNY Press.

Morrow, L. (1997). *The literacy center: Contexts for reading and writing.* York, ME: Stenhouse.

Murden, T., & Gillespie, C.S. (1997). The role of textbooks and reading in content area classrooms: What are teachers and students saying? In W. Linek, & E.G. Sturtevant (Eds.), *Exploring Literacy.* (pp. 85-96). TX: College Reading Association.

Neuman, S., & Roskos, K.A. (1991). The influence of literacy enriched play centers on preschoolers' conceptions of the functions of print. In J. Christie (Ed.), *Play and early literacy development.* (pp.167-88). Albany: SUNY Press.

Neuman, S., & Roskos, K.A. (1992). Literacy objects as cultural tools: Effects on children's literacy behaviors in play. *Reading Research Quarterly,* 27, 203-225.

Neuman, S., & Roskos, K.A. (1993). Access to print for children of poverty: Differential effects of adult mediation and literacy-enriched play settings on environmental and functional print tasks. *American Educational Research Journal,* 30, 95-122.

Neuman, S., & Roskos, K.A. (1997). Literacy knowledge in practice: Contexts of participation for young writers and readers. *Reading Research Quarterly,* 32, 10-33.

Okolo, C.M., & Ferretti, R.P. (1996). Knowledge acquisition and technology-supported projects in the social studies for students with learning disabilities. *Journal of Special Education Technology*, 13, 91-103.

Oldfather, P. (1993). *Students' perspectives on motivating experiences in literacy learning.* (Perspectives in Reading Research, No. 2). Athens, GA, & College Park, MD: National Reading Research Center.

Oldfather, P. (1993). What students say about motivating experiences in a whole language classroom. *The Reading Teacher*, 46, 672-681.

Pellegrini, A.D., & Galda, L. (1993). Ten years after: A reexamination of symbolic play and literacy research. *Reading Research Quarterly*, 28, 163-175.

Preisser, G., Anders, P.L., & Glider, P. (1990). Understanding middle school students. In G.G. Duffy, (Ed.), *Reading in the middle school.* Newark, DE: International Reading Association.

Pressley, Michael. (1998). Reading instruction that works: The case for balanced teaching. New York: Guilford Press.

Roskos, K.A. (1995). Creating places for play and print. In J.F. Christie, K.A. Roskos, B.J. Enz, C. Vukelich, & S.B. Neuman (Ed.), *Readings for linking literacy and play.* (pp.8-17). Newark, DE: International Reading Association.

Stahl, S.A., Hynd, C.R., Glynn, S.M., & Carr, M. (1996). Beyond reading to learn: Developing content and disciplinary knowledge through texts. In Baker, L, Afflerbach, P. & D. Reinking (Eds.), *Developing engaged readers in school and home communities.* (pp. 139-164). Mahwah, NJ: Lawrence Erlbaum Associates.

Sternberg, R.J., B. Torff, & Grigorenko, E.L. (1998). Teaching triarchically improves school achievement. *Journal of Educational Psychology*, 90, 3, 374-384.

Stewart, R.A. (1994). A causal connective look at the future of secondary content area literacy. *Contemporary Education*, 65, 90-94

Stone, S.J., & Christie, J.F. (1996). Collaborative literacy learning during sociodramatic play in a multiage (K-2) primary classroom. *Journal of Research in Childhood Education*, 10, 2, 123-133.

Strickland, D.S., & Morrow, L.M. (1989). Environments rich in print promote literacy behavior during play. *The Reading Teacher*, 178-9.

Turner, J.C. (1995). The influence of classroom contexts on young children's motivation for literacy. *Reading Research Quarterly*, 30, 410-441.

Turner, J.C. (1997). Starting right: Strategies for engaging young literacy learners. In J.T. Guthrie, & A. Wigfield, (Eds.), *Reading engagement: Motivating readers through integrated instruction.* (pp. 183-204). Newark, DE: International Reading Association.

Vukelich, C. (1991). Materials and modeling: Promoting literacy during play. In J. Christie (Ed.), *Play and early literacy development.* (pp. 215-246). Albany: SUNY Press.

Walker, C.A., Allen, D., & Glines, D. (1997). Should we travel by plane, car, train, or bus? Teacher/child collaboration in developing a thematic literacy center. *The Reading Teacher*, 50, 524-527.

Weiner, B. (1990). History of motivational research in education. *Journal of Educational Psychology*, 82, 616-622.

Weinstein, C. (1977). Modifying student behavior in an open classroom through changes in the physical design. *American Educational Research Journal*, 14, 3, 249-262.

Wigfield, A. (1997). Children's motivations for reading and reading engagement. In. J.T. Guthrie & A. Wigfield (Eds.), *Reading engagement: Motivating readers through integrated instruction.* (pp. 14-33). Newark, DE: International Reading Association.

Young, S. A., & Romeo, L. (1998). Promoting literacy in play centers: The importance of adult facilitation. (Paper presented at the annual meeting of the Association for the Study of Play, St. Petersburg, Florida.)

Appendix. Literacy Play Center Interview

1. What activities have you done in the Literacy Play Center?
2. How do you feel when you're reading in the Literacy Play Center?
3. How do you feel when you're writing in the Literacy Play Center? Explain.
4. How does the Literacy Play Center compare to other things that you have done in social studies?
5. What have you worked on the most in the Literacy Play Center?
6. How do you feel when you're in the Literacy Play Center?

'No Somali! Only English!' A Case Study of an Adult Refugee's Use of Appropriate Materials When Learning English and Reading Skills

Judy S. Richardson

Virginia Commonwealth University

Abstract

This study is a participant-observer case study, using qualitative analysis. A representative "slice" of journal entries (Glaser & Strauss, 1980, p. 65) describing the instructional environment for an ESL learner is analyzed. Slicing enabled the author to see changes and consistencies over time in a more dramatic way than the day-by-day entries could reveal. The study focuses on types of materials that contributed to growth in oral communication and written literacy over time. Changes in proficient use of oral communication and reading progress are documented. Issues which surfaced consistently are described as well as how they influenced instructional approaches and use of materials. Because there is little research on the best approaches to helping women with literacy (Bowen, 1998), special attention was given to which materials were most suited to this woman's literacy development. Findings indicate that teachers ought to consider their students' cultural backgrounds and daily experiences, and then tailor lessons to them. This is especially true of women from cultures where they are expected to place a high value on their role as stay-at-home family caretaker of many children. One size does not fit all.

Background Information

I met Sadiya in the fall of 1996 when I volunteered through the Refugee and Immigration Office in Richmond, Virginia to tutor an adult in English conversation and reading skills. Sadiya and her family had arrived in Richmond, Virginia in July as refugees from Somalia. They fled Somalia after their home was invaded by bandits, who killed Sadiya's father-in-law and maimed her husband. Next, they had spent three years in a refugee camp in Kenya, awaiting entry into the United States and a sponsor. By the time I arrived on the scene, the church sponsoring this family had arranged for housing, settled the children in school, and helped the father enroll in an English Proficiency program as well as find work.

I have been tutoring Sadiya steadily from October 1996. I meet with her for one to two hours weekly—with some interruptions due to her schedule and mine. So far, we have logged over 150 hours. After each session, I write a journal entry in which I describe my feelings related to the instructional experience, events that occurred, questions about those events which might provide me with clues for teaching Sadiya effectively, Sadiya's accomplishments during the visit, the climate of the visit, and the instructional progress made. I have written more than 90 entries. My research goal is to provide insights about the process of learning to speak and read English through an in-depth analysis of one adult learner's journey over several years. This article is part of the story of the progress Sadiya and I have made over a 27-month period.

A Theoretical Framework

Because the subject of this study is an adult refugee who possessed no reading skills prior to my work with her, she represents the merging of three professional disciplines: adult education, reading, and English as a second language (ESL).

Adult Education

While teaching her, I relied on two adult theorists. Knowles (1980; 1987) advocates an andrological model of instruction, which is differentiated from a pedagogical, or child-oriented model, by the following characteristics. The adult learner: is a mutual partner in the learning process; has accumulated a reservoir of experience useful in instructional settings; is mature and problem-centered; is ready to learn and is internally motivated. In the most successful educational environment, the teacher is a facilitator and equal partner who expects to learn as much as the adult student. Knowles believes that the adult learner is self-directed. To explain how self-direction can be achieved, Grow (1991) proposes a model entitled Staged Self-Directed Learning (SSDL). Teachers guide adult learners from a stage of low to high self-direction by carefully matching the roles of learner and facilitator; individualizing the teaching to match learner needs; and being ever sensitive to the situations in which the learning occurs. This model prompts a learning climate that is rich with expectation, choice, and intention to learn.

Beginning Reading

Sadiya's lack of reading skills led me to draw on studies of early reading behaviors. Snow, Burns, and Griffin (1998), after reviewing several studies of early reading, list a number of literacy skills that kindergarten through third grade children can be expected to demonstrate. For the kindergarten—or most basic level—these include basic literacy tasks and concepts about print, such as knowing parts of a book and its functions; making appropriate switches from oral to written language; and writing one's own name. Bear, Invernizzi, Templeton, and Johnston (1996) call the first stage of orthography the "Preliterate Stage" and the second the " Letter Name Stage." The preliterate learner often represents phonemes through pictures rather than graphemes. At the Early and Middle Letter Name Stage, students correctly use several letters of the alphabet, directionality, and letter-sound correspondences.

English as a Second Language

I relied on three theorists of second language acquisition to help me identify appropriate methods and materials for teaching English as a second language (ESL). Schumann (1978) identifies conditions for successful acculturation and language acquisition in his now-classic model. The best learning environment would include: social variables such as an even balance between the target and native culture (so that the learner does not rely more heavily on the native culture), an expectation that the two cultures will "intermingle;" a balance of the two cultures so that one does not dominate; an expectation that acculturation will occur; and positive attitudes towards both cultures.

In his Monitor Model, Krashen (1982; 1989) argues for a balance between determinism and environmental factors as contributors to second language acquisition. He bases his model on a critical age factor, which states that second language learning becomes more difficult due to lateralization of the brain hemispheres. Krashen argues that this neurological "shut down" occurs at about age five. Five hypotheses comprise his model. The first hypothesis is that any language is acquired unconsciously more than through direct learning. The power of acquisition ought to be used more effectively in teaching ESL. For instance, less reliance on organized learning through workbooks and more reliance on learner environment are necessary components of effective ESL instruction. The next hypotheses are interrelated. Learners monitor their learning but they need sufficient time to focus on form and specific knowledge of when to apply rules. Since these conditions are very difficult to meet during most communication—which demands quick responses—explicit rule teaching or error correction will slow down or impede progress. The natural order hypothesis suggests that language learners acquire language "rules" in a natural, predictable sequence rather than by direct instruction. Studies of English orthographic development (Bear and Templeton, 1996) seem to support this hypothesis. Fourth, as a logical extension, natural communication seems to provide a relaxed setting for language learning. Learners do best when language input is comprehensible and just beyond their current level of knowledge. Krashen calls this comprehensible input "i + 1" where i is input and 1 is the challenge level. Fifth, socio-emotional factors strongly influence language learning and may well account for those older learners who do master a second language in spite of that critical age factor. Krashen calls this the affective filter hypothesis; he writes that it is the single most important variable in language learning. When the filter is high, it represents a tense, highly anxious socio-emotional climate and learning is greatly impeded.

Cummins (1979; 1994) argues that a distinction must be made between conversational language proficiency, which he calls Basic Interpersonal Communication (BICs), and Cognitive Academic Language Proficiency (CALP), which is more formal academic instruction. Learning English for conversational and functional purposes is less cognitively stressful and more immediately practical. This notion supports Krashen's fourth hypothesis, that of natural communication in a relaxed setting as the best vehicle for learning English.

The Variable of Time

Several second language experts discuss the variable of time in language acquisition. Cummins (1994) suggests that achieving conversational proficiency might take approximately two years, while achieving academic proficiency might take as much as five to seven years. Leki (1992) writes that time is the single most important factor in ESL learning, as do Peregoy and Boyle (1997). A study by Lee and Shallert (1997) suggests that solid second language proficiency is a better facilitator of literacy acquisition in a second language than is literacy proficiency in the first language. This second language proficiency takes time, as Snow, Burns, and Griffin (1998) indicate when they recommend that ESL children develop oral proficiency before beginning reading instruction; they indicate that this oral proficiency may take as much as a year.

Implications of the Theoretical Framework

Based on the theories and literature in these three disciplines, I expected that Sadiya would be an eager, motivated learner with purpose and goals. I expected that she would have a repertoire of experiences far beyond those of a child. I anticipated that she would need guidance in basic literacy skills. Although I understood that Sadiya's age might interfere somewhat with her learning progress, I also expected that her adult status would be an asset. Phonemic analysis would be an essential link between her first and second languages. I hoped to find a positive support base in her home. I was resolved that our journey to literacy might take several months.

I expected to work on oral language for some time before witnessing a break-through in reading. I wanted to take advantage of a natural environment for learning and show rules only in context of the language use. Cummins' BICs approach seemed to me the most logical, as it merged the richness of an adult's experience with language experience. I expected from the start to use materials and print in the home.

The Study Design

This study is a participant-observer case study, in which I employ qualitative analysis. In order to reflect on the entries over time, I wrote a set of questions to guide my consideration of each entry. The questions were:

What was the learning climate like?

What approaches and techniques seem apparent?

What materials seem most applicable?

Why, in light of knowledge about adult learning, reading, and English as a second language, are these approaches, techniques and materials employed?

For this study, I selected a representative "slice" of the entries (Glaser & Strauss, 1980, p. 65) as a manageable subset of the entries. This enabled me to take an ecological perspective (Lier, 1997) and retroactively focus on differences over time. Slicing enabled me to see changes and consistencies over time in a more dramatic way than the day-by-day entries could reveal.

The eleven entries I selected included: a beginning point, my first tutoring session in October 1996; four consecutive entries from November to December 1996; an entry in October 1997 to roughly parallel the first entry; four consecutive entries from November to December 1997 to roughly parallel the four in 1996; and as an ending point, an entry in April 1998.

As I reflected on the entries, I looked for changes in proficient use of oral communication and reading progress. I wanted to determine how much growth had occurred, and in which areas. I also wanted to determine what issues surfaced consistently, and how they influenced my approaches and use of materials. Because there is little research on the best approaches to helping women with literacy (Bowen, 1998), I wanted to pay attention to how materials were most suited to Sadiya's literacy development. In family literacy, often the adult's literacy needs are second to the child's (Auerbach, 1989).

The Family

All of our interactions occurred against a family backdrop. In Somali culture, the mother is expected to take care of the daily needs of her family—usually including several children—waiting on them and putting their interests above her own. Sadiya's husband is about ten years older than she is. He is typical of many Suni Muslims in Somalia: he is literate in the Somali language, he is well educated (having the equivalent of a high school diploma), and he speaks five languages—some better than others. He speaks fairly good English, well enough to communicate basic needs but not well enough to do the same job he did in Somalia. Currently he is working as a dishwasher. He is a practicing Muslim and often attends prayer meetings. Sadiya is his second wife; he divorced his first wife.

In his culture, as the oldest son he is expected to care for his mother and any of her unmarried children. Therefore, his mother and her youngest son lived with the family for the first several months after they arrived in Richmond. In February of 1997, the mother-in-law moved to live with a married daughter in another state and the youngest son went another direction to seek his fortune.

Sadiya and her husband had four children when they arrived in Richmond, a son and three girls. The son is now in middle school; his sisters are in second, first, and pre-school grades. In March of 1997 Sadiya gave birth to another son, who is a United States citizen. All of the family—even the baby—who is now almost two, are speaking English with greater facility every day. For Sadiya, the struggle is the greatest.

Sadiya

Sadiya is in her mid-thirties. She is nearly always cheerful and optimistic. Her smile and eagerness to learn lights my day, even when I arrive harried and tired. She is devoted to her husband and children, although at times shows impatience with her older three (what mother doesn't!). When we met Sadiya spoke only Somali, and read in no language, in contrast to her husband's and brother-in-law's skills. Why did Sadiya want to learn English? For her sponsors, a long-term goal is employment, but Sadiya has not expressed such an interest. Because Somali is spoken at home, she does not need English to communicate there, and—for the past three years—she has been outside of her home very little. Her children are learning faster then she is, so it is not to teach or coach them (Puchner & Hardman, 1996). Sadiya wants to learn because she wants to be part of the United States. She has no plans to return to Somalia. She wants to accomplish the everyday tasks that require reading and writing. She enjoys learning and our time together.

The Setting

I tutored in the midst of this family, in their home. Most often, at least four people were nearby while I taught Sadiya. Sometimes her husband was at home on his day off. Sometimes his friends were visiting. If I could not arrange my schedule to arrive before the school bus, the two school-aged daughters and oldest son were at home and they "helped" with our lesson. Always, during the segment of time this study encompasses, the youngest two children were home. Noise and distraction were part of our instructional environment. The home is small by American standards, and often messy with the imprint of five children and two adults.

The Journey
Our First Meeting

Learning Climate. Our first meeting was chaotic. I was greeted by the mother-in-law who then disappeared upstairs. Looking flustered, Sadiya peered from the kitchen but returned to cooking an omelet. The two-year old girl eyed me suspiciously as she sat in her toy car. I sat on the couch by myself for about ten minutes before the mother-in-law reappeared with her youngest son, who was to be the translator. However, he left again as Sadiya finally came to sit on the couch with her mother-in-law and me.

Method/Technique/Materials. I tried a language routine. "Hello, my name is Judy." I gestured for them to repeat this to me, which is exactly what I got: "Hello, my name is Judy." I tried again, pointing to Sadiya and saying, "My name is Sadiya" and then to the mother-in-law with "Hello, my name is _____." After practicing this routine for a few minutes, I showed pictures of my family. I focused on the words, "grandmother, husband, wife, daughter, son" as I showed the pictures. When the son returned, I pulled out an atlas to show where Richmond, Virginia was in comparison with Mogadishu, Somalia. He was quite interested but his mother and Sadiya ignored me. She spoke sharply to Sadiya, who immediately got up and went to the kitchen to complete a chore. I had to wait some time for her return. The tension in the air was palpable. I put away the atlas and moved to some active learning. I made a map of the living room and kitchen in their notebooks and walked to locations while naming objects: "This is a chair. This is a rug. This is a kitchen." Then I wrote the words "chair, rug, and kitchen" in their notebooks.

Observations. The dominant technique in this lesson was language-based routines. I used no rules, but did present the syntax of the language in a conversational setting and used real-life, functional materials, as both Krashen and Cummins would advocate. Cultural differences were outstanding in this session. The females deferred to the male, waiting for him to start the lesson. However, they also ignored him and me when the conversation was not relevant to them. Sadiya deferred to her mother-in-law. Household duties took precedence over the lesson. Time and appointments were valued differently. Schumann's acculturation model seemed to fit this situation. Learning a second language requires validation of one's own culture and a balance between the native and second culture. It was apparent that a balance did not yet exist.

Sadiya seemed very uneasy with her mother-in-law during the lesson. Something was going on which caused friction. The mother-in-law gave enthusiastic responses, ignoring her daughter-in-law or frowning at her. While Sadiya seemed to want to learn, she also seemed to be highly anxious and notself-confident. Her affective filter was so high that learning was being blocked.

Sadiya had no reading skills at this point. While she did know that words represent objects and can be written down, she did not know how to read or write any letters, in Somali or English. Sadiya had very few of the skills that Snow, Burns, and Griffin (1998) list for kindergarten learners. Her performance of those few she did possess was profoundly influenced by her ESL status. Of the 29 kindergarten tasks, she could do only three. For instance, "begins to trace print when listening to familiar text being read" (p. 80) was impossible for her because she was not familiar with any English text, nor was she familiar with any Somali text. She did know directionality and the purpose of books. She did not use pictures to represent graphemes, but from the beginning attempted to write letters to match phonemes; most likely her experiences over time had informed her about the grapheme-phoneme relationship. Here was an older learner, who brought a rich life experience but limited knowledge of American culture to the lessons. She was interested but distracted. At this point, I could not tell if she was introverted or overwhelmed by her mother-in-law and household responsibilities.

After this first lesson, it was apparent that we would have a long way to go, and needed much time to get there. Sadiya was not literate in her home language. She spoke no English, only Somali. When we used language routines, her pronunciation of English words showed that she would have great difficulty with several English phonemes, perhaps never achieving the pronunciation level of a native speaker. Her culture expected very different roles of her than my culture expected of me. I would need to use materials that were concrete and interesting. Labeling objects might be a good start. Experiential and language-based learning would work well. Structure in language use, such as language routines, would be necessary. I relied on Birch (1998), who describes her program for developing phonemic awareness in ESL learners. The first goal is to teach how to segment spoken English words; the second is to help students recognize letter shapes and names and associated sounds. Birch advises that "the best way to teach the patterns of English is within the context of a whole language reading program." (p. 21).

One Month Later: Four Slices

Learning Climate, 11/25/96. On November 25, 1996, Sadiya greeted me at the door with a hug, kiss and an English sentence: "Hello, Judy, how are you?" Her mother-in-law was visiting friends. The two-year-old was asleep.

Methods/Technique/Materials, 11/25/96. The focus on learning was blissful! Using Jean Craighead George's *The First Thanksgiving* (1993), I explained what Thanksgiving means to Americans. We cut, pasted, and labeled pictures of turkey, salad, and sweet potatoes from newspaper ads. Sadiya knew "salat" from Somali. She recognized the sweet potato. The picture helped her know "turkey." The lesson ended with my writing this piece in her notebook:

"I learn much in October and September.

This month is November.

Thanksgiving is Thursday.

We will eat turkey and sweet potato and salad."

As I packed up, we practiced our standard phrases: "My name is Sadiya. How are you? I am fine. It is a nice day. Have a nice day."

Observations, 11/25/96. With no distractions from other members of the household, Sadiya's affective filter was low and learning was high. I was able to rely on her experiences as a refugee to introduce a new concept, Thanksgiving. This introduction reminded me of Krashen's i + 1. Using the similar food words, I was able to make a transfer from Somali to English. Phonemic practice could be rooted in those words.

Learning Climate, 12/8/96. "Judy, Nadifa's bus not come." Thus Sadiya greeted me on December 8, 1996. Instead of a lesson, I drove Nadifa to her school, only to discover that this was an early dismissal day so the bus driver had come earlier. School was almost finished when we arrived. So I drove her back home. Although her eldest son had told Sadiya of this schedule change, Sadiya had not understood.

As I entered for the second time, Halimo (Sadiya's mother-in-law) hugged me but then went immediately upstairs and never returned. The rest of the children arrived from school. The husband came in. Now there were eight in the home.

Methods/Techniques/Materials, 12/8/96. I spent some time talking to Sadiya's husband. I had not realized that he had no use of the left side of his body, due to a severe beating by bandits in Somalia. For the remaining time, I made words cards for *one* through *five*, and made matching cards on which the numerals were written. Sadiya repeated the numbers after me, and tried to match the word to the numeral. However, the girls were fascinated by this activity and interjected themselves into the lesson. Sadiya spoke sharply to them. Her husband seemed oblivious and did not intervene. I also made word cards for the names of each family member, and showed Sadiya the first letter of each name. Then we practiced saying each name, emphasizing the sound of the first letter in each name. I copied some sentences into Sadiya's notebook after she put her notebook and a pencil in front of me and said, "Judy, homework?" I wrote some of our language routines: "This is a chair; this is a table; this is a couch; this is a door."

Observations, 12/8/96. As often happens with adult learners, other agenda intrude on a lesson. The oldest son had already made great strides in acculturation and expected that his mother would understand easily what he understood. The critical age factor was evident in the oldest son's rapid acquisition of information and in the girls' interaction in the lesson. Sadiya had little time to concentrate, and many distractions, even though I was attempting a very functional, BICs-type lesson. Her affective filter was simply too high to promote a good learning climate. Yet, she tried to salvage the lesson herself, as many adults would, by asking for homework. I was the minority culture on this day; Somalia was the dominant language of all others in the house. I learned about Somali culture.

Learning Climate, 12/16/96. I accompanied Sadiya to an ESL night school. She was the only Somali in a class with five more advanced Chinese adults, and the only non-literate in the class. She was seven months pregnant and very uncomfortable in child-sized chairs. The teacher was very animated.

Method/Technique/Materials, 12/16/96: The teacher shared an explanation of Christmastime. She encouraged the students to name body parts as she pointed to them. They sang "Dem Bones" to reinforce the words. Next, they reviewed colors. Last, the teacher handed out play money and held up items "for purchase." She gave a price, and asked if the students had enough money to buy the item. From my journal:

> "The older Chinese couple caught on, but the three girls were somewhat confused, and Sadiya was totally lost. I sat beside her and helped form numerals and say number words because she could do the activity. She was making 2, 3, 4, and 5 backwards. I tried to guide her hand. The classroom was too distracting for her to attend to me. During break, she led me straight to the restroom, indicating that she was very capable of learning survival skills!"

Observations, 12/16/96. The teacher called me aside after the lesson to tell me that Sadiya was probably learning disabled. I was not ready to accept this diagnosis. Sadiya's behaviors seemed more like those of a preliterate child. I felt that she needed a lot more time before any diagnosis was to be made. While the lesson was appropriate for the Chinese students, it was i + 15 for Sadiya! The lesson was far beyond her. It seemed to me that this evening was an example of "one size does not fit all," where the teacher's goals and plan dominated at the expense of the learner (Bowen, 1998). As a result of the class, I could see that writing numbers and letters was very difficult for her. I decided to next use a salt tray as a means of kinesthetic practice.

Learning Climate, 12/23/96. From my journal:

"Today was the last day of tutoring before a three-week break, and I was reluctant to go because I really just wanted to rest. But, of course, I did go because I knew how much Sadiya depends on me for English, especially since night school will not work out for her at this point."

The children were all home for Winter Break, plus the nephew and Sadiya's husband. Halimo greeted me but then retreated. Both men wanted to talk to me about Somalia. I enjoyed learning about Mogadishu and some Somali history, although this meant less time for Sadiya. The noise level was high. For our lesson, I suggested the kitchen table, but Sadiya wanted to be in the living room at the coffee table. The girls wedged between us.

Methods/Technique/Materials, 12/23/96. We counted play money. We traced numerals in the salt tray. I noted the beginning letters of *one, two, three, four, five* and *ten.* We practiced naming body parts and colors. I shared some Christmas books to develop a concept for Christmastime in the United States. Then I thought I was done, but Sadiya wanted to practice the sentences I had written in her book. She could now say these sentences pretty clearly, so I altered the language routine to "What is this?" and guided her to respond, "This is a couch."

Observations, 12/23/96. Repetition with language routines was helping Sadiya to practice and use grammar. I had not introduced any rules, but the patterns and context provided her with enough information to use English more effectively. Some phonemic awareness was evident as she now could recognize some first letters of words, and write them in the salt tray. I was using children's literature to help her learn about our culture. The self-direction of the adult learner was evident in her request to review sentences when I had thought the lesson was done. Even amidst the many distractions, Sadiya remained more focussed than I could have been. She had disregarded what could have been a very high affective filter.

Overall Observations for This Set of Lessons

The four lessons in this segment showed active learning using language to connect the abstract to everyday examples. Modified language experience stories and language routines dominated the instruction. Interactive discussion was implemented as often as possible. Because the mother-in-law became ill and stopped attending lessons, and the brother-in-law was not at home during some of the lessons, Sadiya was more focussed and less pulled to do chores. The girls were part of some lessons, listening and pointing when Sadiya and I practiced counting or naming body parts. As I had originally anticipated, Sadiya was a motivated and self-directed learner. Her English speaking and reading skills were very limited but slowly getting better. Second language theories seemed to be validated at every turn. Time was definitely a factor, with progress being slowed by the limited exposure to English, the dominant Somali culture in the home, the age of the learner, and the many distractions to learning.

Ten Months Later: Another Slice

Sadiya gave birth to a baby boy in April 1997. This child became an integral part of the instructional setting. Often I rocked him, amused him and cajoled him while Sadiya worked hard on her language practice. Even as I was rocking him, she would call to me, "Judy, please. This OK?" I had to ignore her baby for a minute, as she demanded my attention. Her youngest daughter became very withdrawn when the baby arrived; now she hardly spoke and hid her head. The setting had now become consistently noisy and distracting. Two youngsters demanded someone's attention—Sadiya's or mine. Yet what could have been a high anxiety environment was instead a relatively low affective filter because of Sadiya's intense motivation to learn.

Learning Climate, 10/10/97. We had a good lesson. Sadiya's youngest daughter hugged me shyly; her baby loves to receive a hug and kisses on both cheeks. They both "helped" with the lesson, pointing to body parts and putting magnetic letters in the ice trays. The baby made sounds as he heard Sadiya and I making them.

Method/Technique/Materials, 10/10/97. Sadiya and I sorted words by first letters. At this time, she sorted words beginning with H, M, N, D, J, and S because these are the first letters of family members' names. For instance, *Sadiya* was sorted with *S* and *Judy* was sorted with *J*.

Observations, 10/10/97. A year after our first lesson, Sadiya could count and recognize numbers from one to ten, and stumbled through 11-20. She recognized the entire upper case alphabet and many of the lower case letters. As she sorted "H" words, she commented in her own words, "Halimo (mother-in-law) wrist, ankle hurt. In bathtub. Water." When I showed her a word card for "much," and read the word to her, she said, "I like you very much." She watched my mouth and tongue placement to understand how to make the sounds of English phonemes. She printed her own name to receive food stamps, and could print all of the upper case letters with guidance.

1996-1997

My materials during the year of 1996-97 included: magnetic letters and numbers and ice trays in which to sort them; words from her environment, such as family names, body parts, and household objects; children's books when I could find some with consistent, linguistic patterns to show rimes; newspaper ads; labels from products; pictures of her family and mine; Longman's *ESL Literacy* workbook; and a salt tray to practice formation of troublesome letters and numbers.

Four More Slices

Learning Climate, 11/21/97. For the first 30 minutes, it was Sadiya, the two youngest children, and I. We had learned to pace instruction and study around and with them. However, the two older girls descended upon us and chaos erupted! They were so energetic and noisy. They demanded attention. They teased and frustrated the youngest girl, who started to scream and cry. This upset Sadiya, who became angry. I closed the lesson.

Method/Technique/Materials, 11/21/97. I had clipped several articles about the Somali floods. People were fleeing to the highest ground, competing for space with bandits and wild animals. I thought that the pictures of Mogadishu and the starvation of her people would create a conversational lesson.

From my journal entry:

"But when I started to show her, she looked a bit puzzled, then frowned, and said,"No Somali. Only English." I tried to explain that this was about where she had lived, but she was adamant. I had to agree that talking about this subject would be fruitless, so I put it away as quickly as I could!! This goes back to the adult learning principle that the learner will learn what she is interested in, and not necessarily what the teacher intends."

We went back to a lesson on money. I had purchased some disposable diapers and showed her the receipt. We made this amount from the play money.

Observations, 11/21/97. Sadiya's affective filter continued to affect the lesson success. When the children were all home, chaos and distractions impeded learning. The children were correcting her, which caused her to feel shy and anxious. Even her high motivation and sense of purpose could not overcome this climate. My materials from the newspaper were not relevant to her, even though I had selected them based on her experiences. However, progress with recognizing money and realizing how much an amount will buy was apparent: The lesson was short because I was there only thirty minutes before the older girls came home. The baby was fussy.

He would not sit still, so I held him while Sadiya completed some work in a workbook. For the first page, he was amused by me. By the second page, he was restless. By the third page, he was fussy and unhappy. Sadiya kept right on, ignoring her son and me and her daughter. She was so determined that she shut them out. After the older children arrived, we spent some time looking at the alphabet and having her say each letter. We also looked at pictures and I talked to her about each one, to practice English. The girls participated also.

Learning Climate, 12/5/97. This was a great lesson but short because I arrived at 1:30 and all of the children were home from school by 2:00. After that, the house was too noisy and full of distractions for us to concentrate. Until 2:00, Sadiya worked intensively in the Longman workbook. I amused the baby but even when he became fussy, she ignored us both and kept right on to the finish! When the other children arrived, I asked if she wanted to stop, but she hardly heard me. She was determined to continue and tried to shut them out. Unfortunately, neither of us could ignore them for long. One of the girls started "helping" her mother form letters; all of the children came crowding around us wanting attention. I stopped the lesson; everyone sang and talked before I left.

Method/Technique/Materials, 12/5/97. We used a workbook because Sadiya could concentrate on it while I attended to her children. When I had to explain and help her manipulate materials such as letters for a sorting activity, I could not also watch the children. She was able to recognize and say the alphabet, but relied on the letters being in order. The girls "helped" her understand my dialogue about the pictures by translating into Somali.

Observations, 12/5/97. I would have preferred that the children not speak Somali; Sadiya relied too much on the native language and it became dominant. Sadiya controlled the affective filter as long as only the younger children were home. The workbook helped her remain focused, although it was not my first choice of an effective material. I preferred the alphabet practice and dialogue, but with four children present, even these BICs-based materials were not effective. Although she had an intense sense of purpose, the climate simply became too confusing.

Learning Climate, 12/12/97. When I arrived early in the morning, a man was outside digging up her yard. Sadiya was very nervous about who he was. The youngest girl was asleep and the baby was eating. Sadiya said, "So sorry, baby. Mommy English. Half a minute, Judy." I assured her that we could speak English under any circumstance. I talked about the rice cereal. I showed her apples on the jar and said he was eating applesauce. I pointed to the word pears and said he was drinking pear juice.

Method/Technique/Materials. 12/12/97. We used the materials of the moment, those for feeding the baby. Next, she completed some workbook pages as I held the baby. When he fell asleep, she copied sentences from the workbook into her notebook. She spaced between words, an improvement over past occasions. I asked her to match the upper and lower case letters of the alphabet. Last, she showed me a cold blister on her youngest daughter's lip and brought me a bag with Blistex in it. I explained by showing and talking how to use it on the sore. I had planned to review money and numbers, but no time remained.

Observations, 12/12/97. Adults assume that other adults will speak and understand their language. The workman did not know what to do when Sadiya spoke Somali, so he ignored her. Someone gave Sadiya the medicine but did not take the time to explain its use in clear, simple English with gestures. Sadiya was frustrated and thus less able to learn during our lesson. I capitalized on the familiar, using the foods and the medicine to salvage the lesson.

Learning Climate, 12/19/97. The youngest girl was asleep and Sadiya was feeding the baby. But the little one awoke and the older girls arrived very shortly afterwards. One of them had left her coat at school; since school would be closed for the Winter Break after this afternoon, I took her back to the school to retrieve it. This left very little quiet time for a lesson.

Method/Technique/Materials, 12/19/97. We began by practicing upper and lower case letters. I wrote them, and she copied, saying them as she wrote. I guided her as needed. This was short-lived. I gave them a picture of my family members and we talked about who they were. Then I gave them the Christmas presents I had purchased. As they opened them, Sadiya pointed to a picture of Santa Claus and asked, "Judy, what is this?"

Observations, 12/19/97. By mid-December, 1997, Sadiya could read the names of her family members on the Christmas presents I brought. We were becoming accustomed to distractions. Her learning was no longer so influenced by the disruptions. She either tuned them out, or we improvised. However, the learning was slow, due to the many distractions.

Overall Observations for this Slice of Lessons

The progress was evident. Clear evidence of early conceptualization was surfacing. She had developed a schema for English language and was refining it. She was taking such control of her own learning that I had to alter my behavior from that of only 'teacher' to also 'babysitter'. Her motivation was so high that even "tedious" workbook tasks absorbed her while I rocked her baby and amused her youngest daughter. Her affective filter was lower more of the time and the learning curve continued to climb. Phonemic awareness was strong and she was beginning to read.

One and a Half Years Later, the Last Slice

Although three men were visiting her husband and all of the children were home, Sadiya and I had a very productive lesson on April 10, 1998. She simply shut them all out and continued to work. She was now adeptly balancing her native and new cultures. When the men arrived, she donned her gubashir—a drape that covers a Muslim woman to indicate modesty—and greeted them respectfully, watched as I shook their hands, and then went right back to the table to practice her writing.

Sadiya studied and sorted alphabet letters. I had collected different fonts for each letter, both upper case and lower case, and presented her with three groups of letters at a time. She sorted first by putting all versions of one letter in a pile. Next, she sorted the upper from the lower case. Then she initiated a count of the number of letters in each sorted pile. She asked to copy each letter and variation into her notebook. From my journal:

> "I thought the lesson was over, when she got up and pulled a package of Reynolds Wrap from the counter, asking was this an 'R'? I pointed to each letter and spelled the words for her. She proceeded to copy 'Reynolds Wrap' into her notebook! WOW!"

Her baby began to point at letters and numbers as I asked Sadiya to recognize and say them. He tried to say them too. Her daughter was beginning to open up again, hugging me when I arrived and smiling often.

Theoretical Applications to our Lessons

I have exposed Sadiya to materials which she is likely to see and use daily in her home, materials which are suitable to her needs as a female and mother who is expected to run a household. The materials were specifically chosen for a nonliterate woman (Bowen, 1998). When the affective filter was too high during a lesson, I could see that learning would be minimal. I often adjusted by simply putting away materials she could not concentrate on and asking her to name and point to parts of the body, or to recite letters and numbers while identifying them. The anxiety would then ease up and she would become more confident. I found that some lessons, for instance my lesson on Somalia, were not appropriate. Part of the reason is that understanding maps was too difficult for Sadiya, beyond i + 1; another part was that happenings in her homeland were experiences she wished to ignore.

At times, Sadiya's frustration with the slow pace of her learning was evident, as she watched her school-aged children come home daily with more and more fluency in English speech and literacy. However, we continued to meet weekly and practice. Because her exposure to English is so limited, and Somali is so dominant in the home, I have realized that learning English will take more time than I had anticipated.

When Sadiya and I started working together, I was not sure what her aptitude was. The affective filter was so high that her learning was blocked. Yet, when the affective filter lowered, I understood that she does have a good aptitude and high motivation to learn. Sadiya tends to learn best from that which surrounds her, which is why I have approached lessons from a language experience base and used materials in her environment. As the lessons progressed, I could see that Sadiya does have a strong sense of purpose and now demands opportunities, shutting out even her children so that she may practice.

A language is closely tied to a culture. Puchner and Hardman (1996) explain that different cultures view the role of familial influence on learning differently. Older family members from a Southeast Asian culture might not wish to learn English, fearing that this new language will erode their own customs. They may resist their children learning English. Sadiya lives her culture in her role at home, but she is fierce about her children's opportunities, relishing her youngest son's use of English. The title for this article, taken from the lesson on 11/21/97, shows that Sadiya wants to embrace this new culture; at that time, she seemed to want to erase Somali from her life. Now, however, she seems to want to acculturate but maintain the balance Schumann says is necessary. Of course, she is conflicted when her children correct and interrupt her, but she perseveres.

Observations about Approaches and Materials

Sadiya continues to learn English. She has shifted from me as the authority to me as the consultant. She, the learner, generates the instruction. The learning climate has become more relaxed. Schumann's acculturation theory is evident when Sadiya moves easily from her Somali acquaintances to me.

I have been using a balanced approach to reading instruction, as Birch (1998) advocates. Materials which best suit the circumstances are used, but the predominant approach is functional language, language experience, and letter and word practice based in contextual knowledge (Cummins, 1994). Sadiya has moved to a Late Letter Name Stage of orthographic development. She can now complete all but seven of the 29 kindergarten tasks listed by Snow, Burns, and Griffin (1998).

I believe that my use of basic communication for learning oral and written communication was consistent with her needs, and—indeed—often overruled my plans altogether. I used functional materials: experiences about which we wrote and talked, a workbook as a structured aid, children's books for thematic learning (Christmas, Easter, Thanksgiving) and artifacts (photographs, newspaper ads, play and real money, word and letter cards related to family names, manipulative letters). These materials were specifically selected for Sadiya's needs as a mother and homemaker.

Table I provides a comparison of oral communication and reading progress over the eleven lessons. During this period, roughly eighteen months, Sadiya has achieved a high level of oral communication fluency, moving from none to self-generated sentences. She has achieved less progress in reading skills, but has moved through perhaps two and a half stages, from no lit-

Table 1. Summary of Approaches & Materials

Lesson Date	Approaches/Strategies	Materials
10/7/96	BICS; Direct Method; Language routines; labeling; experiential learning;	Photographs; maps; furniture; notebooks & pencils; our own bodies
11/25/96	BICS; Language routines; modified language experience phonemic awareness practice	Newspaper ads; children's books
12/9/96	Functional & thematic approach	Word cards of family names
12/16/96	Language routines; singing; role playing; experiential learning	Music; labels; worksheets; monopoly money
12/23/96	Language routines;VAKT/guided practice; experiential learning; functional & thematic approach	Salt tray; play money; pictures; children's books at Christmas
10/10/97	Language routines; Direct approach; phonemic awareness practice	Word sorts by first letters; magnetic letters & board; children's alphabet book; workbook; notebook
11/21/97	Thematic & functional; Language routines	Newspaper article; workbook; money & receipts & purchases
12/5/97	Language routines; Direct approach; LEA	Alphabet guide; workbook; pictures
12/12/97	BICS; Guided learning; Communicative approach; Experience	Medicines; workbook; notebook; baby food jars
12/19/97	Experiential; Communicative	Workbook; family photographs; gift labels
4/10/98	Thematic; Communicative; Direct; Functional & Experiential; LEA; decoding	Word sorting by first letters; Letter sorting by caps, lower case, different styles; household items; coins; notebook

eracy to beginning reading (Bear, Invernizzi, Templeton, and Johnston, 1996).

In our lessons, some issues were hurdles to overcome or compensate for. Sadiya's age was a handicap to rapid acquisition of phonemes (Krashen, 1982). Her lack of any literacy hindered her conceptual development of words in print. The high affective filter when her older family members were present meant a low learning climate (Krashen, 1989). At that point, I wondered—as her night school teacher had—if Sadiya had a learning disability. But she is overcoming the hurdles because she is so motivated (Grow, 1991); she is cheerful and tries again and again. Her self-direction and purpose are so high (Knowles, 1980; 1987)that she overcomes my hesitations and fatigue.

Implications of This Study

This is a longitudinal case study, so application to a larger group should be made with caution. However, Sadiya's case does seem to validate many notable reading and ESL theories which have been based on observations of children. These theories appear to be true for Sadiya, an adult, as well. Furthermore, Sadiya's case validates adult education theories. Most likely, these theories would apply to other adult refugees with little or no native literacy skills. The best approaches would seem to be BICs, modified language experience, and work with phonemic awareness. Indicated materials are manipulative, household items, and objects which are familiar to the learner. For the first several months, concentration should be on oral communication. Teachers ought to consider what their students will know about and experience daily and tailor lessons to them. This is especially true of women from cultures where they are expected to place a high value on their role as stay-at-home family caretaker. One size does not fit all.

References

Auerbach, E. R. (1989). Toward a contextual approach to family literacy. *Harvard Educational Review, 59,* 165-181.

Bear, D. R. & Templeton, S. (1996). Explorations in developmental spelling: Foundations for learning and teaching phonics, spelling, and vocabulary. *The Reading Teacher, 52,,* 222-242.

Bear, D. R.; Invernizzi, Templeton, S.; & Johnston, (1996). *Words their way: Word study for phonics, vocabulary and spelling.* Upper Saddle River, New Jersey: Merrill.

Birch, B. (1998). Nurturing bottom-up reading strategies, too. *TESOL Journal, 7,* 18-23.

Bowen, B.A. (1998). Four puzzles in adult literacy: Reflections on the National Adult Literacy Survey. *Journal of Adolescent and Adult Literacy, 42,* 314-323.

Cummins, J. (1979), Linguistic interdependence and the educational development of bilingual children. *Review of Educational Research, 49,* 222-251.

Cummins, J. (1994). The acquisition of English as a second language. In Spangenberg-Urbschadt, Karen and Pritchard, Robert (Eds.) *Kids come in all languages.* Newark, Delaware: International Reading Association.

George, J.C. (1993). *The First Thanksgiving.* New York: Philomel Book.

Glaser, B.G. & Strauss, A. L. (1980). The Discovery of grounded theory: Strategies for qualitative research. Hawthorne, New York: Aldine Publishing Company.

Grow, G. (1991). Teaching learners to be self-directed: A stage approach. *Adult Education Quarterly,* 41, 125-149.

Knowles, M.S. (1980). *The modern practice of adult education: From pedagogy to andragogy.* New York: Cambridge Books.

Knowles, M.S. (1987). Adult Learning. In R. L. Craig (Ed.), *Training and Development Handbook.* New York: McGraw-Hill.

Krahsen, S. (1982*). Principles and practices in second language acquisition.* New York: Pergamon Press.

Krashen, S. (1989*). Language acquisition and language education.* Englewood Cliffs, New Jersey: Prentice-Hall.

Kreuger, E. & Townshend, N. (1997). Reading clubs boost second-language first graders' reading achievement. *The Reading Teacher, 51,* 122-127.

Lee, J & Schallert, D. (1997). The relative contribution of L2 language proficiency and L1 reading ability to L2 reading performance: A test of the threshold hypothesis. *TESOL Quarterly,* 31, 713-739.

Leki, I. (1992). *Understanding ESL Writers, A Guide for Teachers.* Portsmouth, New Hampshire: Boynton/Cook Publishers.

Lier, L. V. (1997). Observation from an ecological perspective. *TESOL Quarterly,* 31, 783-787.

Nishio, Y. W. (1991) ESL Literacy Student Book. New York: Longman Publishing Group.

Peregoy, S. & Boyle, O. (1997). *Reading, Writing, & Learning in ESL, A Resource Book for K-12 Teachers.* White Plains, NY: Longman.

Puchner, L. D. & Hardman, J. (1996). Family literacy in a cultural context. *NCAL Connections,* Fall. University of Pennsylvania: National Center on Adult Literacy.

Schumann, J. (1978). Second language acquisition: The pidginization hypothesis. In E. Hatch (Ed.), *Second Language Acquisition.* Rowley, MA: Newbury House.

Snow, C. E.; Burns, M. S.; & Griffin, P. (Eds.) (1998). *Preventing Reading Difficulties in Young Children.* Washington, D.C.: National Academy Press.

Teaching Effective Research Strategies to Elementary School Students

Julie K. Kidd, Ed.D.

George Mason University

Abstract

This program description describes a schoolwide effort to develop a program designed to build students' research strategies and skills. It was implemented in grades 2 through 6 in a Northern Virginia elementary school. The program was developed by a reading specialist and a library media specialist in collaboration with the classroom, talented-and-gifted, learning disabilities, Chapter 1 reading, and English-as-a-second-language teachers. Emphasis was placed on (a) establishing a collaborative environment; (b) designing a program that built on previously learned reading, writing, and research strategies; (c) integrating reading, writing, and research with the content areas; (d) providing appropriate instruction; and (e) encouraging students to move toward greater independence in their inquiries. Specific strategies for selecting topics, activating prior knowledge, generating questions, locating information, thinking critically about what was read, recording relevant data, and synthesizing information were taught to the students. Modeling of the strategies and feedback sessions were critical to the success of the program. As a result of the program, students learned how to conduct successful inquiries and approached research with confidence and enthusiasm.

Learning is a process in which learners interact with the world around them to construct and reflect upon their understanding of the world. Student-centered schools and teachers recognize that "schooling must be a time of curiosity, exploration, and inquiry . . ." (Brooks & Brooks, 1993, p. 9). At the same time, students need effective tools to help them make sense of their surroundings and their experiences. Therefore, it becomes the task of teachers to teach effective learning strategies as they "invite students to experience the world's richness, empower them to ask their own questions and seek their own answers, and challenge them to understand the world's complexities" (Brooks & Brooks, 1993, p. 5). As students investigate their world, research, defined as "focused, systematic inquiry" (Duthie, 1996, p. 162), becomes a powerful tool that enables students to acquire, interpret, evaluate, and apply information about a variety of topics, concepts, and issues.

An emphasis on inquiry as a means of encouraging students to learn about their world is prevalent throughout the curriculum. Professional organizations and associations have worked toward developing standards for the various content areas that include a focus on inquiry and, more specifically, on research as a means of carrying out successful inquiries. In *National Science Education Standards,* the National Academy of Sciences (1996) describes inquiry as being "the central strategy for teaching science" (p. 31). It explains that "teachers can take an inquiry approach as they guide students in acquiring and interpreting information from sources such as libraries, government documents, and computer databases—or as they gather information from experts in industry, the community, and government" (National Academy of Sciences, 1996, p. 31). Likewise, the International Reading Association and National Council of Teachers of English (1996) include the following statement in *Standards for the English Language Arts:* "The ability to identify good topics, to gather information, and to evaluate, assemble, and interpret findings from among the many general and specialized information sources now available to them is one of the most vital skills that students can acquire" (p. 39). Therefore, it is essential that teachers model "a thoughtful approach to inquiry" (National Council for the Social Studies, 1994, p. 12) and provide students with effective strategies for conducting research.

To support successful student inquiries, teachers in a Northern Virginia school planned and implemented a schoolwide program designed to begin teaching students effective research strategies in the primary grades and to continue to build on the strategies throughout the middle grades. The goal was to provide students with a firm foundation in research strategies early in their school experience in an effort to encourage students to become increasingly more sophisticated in their approaches to research and more independent in their inquiries. In addition, they hoped to make the complex research process an exciting endeavor for all students regardless of their academic abilities. To accomplish these goals, the teachers examined strategies that are designed to enhance comprehension of informational texts and determined ways in which the strategies could be employed to help students engage in effective research. The following is a description of the research program that evolved over years of experimenting, modifying, reflecting, and refining.

Background Information

The idea to design and implement a schoolwide program for developing students' research strategies began when Lillie Newman (a library media specialist) and I (a reading specialist) examined the research students were conducting at our school. From an initial investigation of the students' work, it was evident that few students approached research as a complex process in which planning, investigating, synthesizing, creating, evaluating, and sharing occur. Instead it appeared that many students approached research as a task that involved locating a source and copying the information verbatim with some minor paraphrasing or as an activity that required the researcher to paraphrase each sentence or paragraph read (Newman & Kidd, 1994). They seemed to view research as the process of "accumulating information" or "transferring information" rather than one of "transforming information." (Many, Fyfe, Lewis, & Mitchell, 1996, p. 18).

Dahl and Farnan (1998) explain that the first group of students in the Many et al. Study (1996) accumulated information. They "gathered interesting material, often turning to random discoveries without an overriding plan, and adjusted their planning webs after the fact to include each additional find" (p. 75). Thus, as they made decisions about the information, selecting interesting pieces of information seemed to be more important than seeking out relevant information.

Students in the study who viewed research as transferring information typically recognized the need to use several sources and to select relevant information, but did not synthesize the information. Instead, they tended to paraphrase the sources using a sentence-by-sentence method of translating each sentence into their own words or by reading and then writing down what they remembered from a particular source (Many et al., 1996).

A third group of students in the study approached research as transforming information. Planning, reviewing the information covered, and considering the audience were prevalent in their work. They were able to synthesize the information gathered by selecting relevant information, organizing the data, and connecting the information among the sources (Many et al., 1996). Thus, to encourage students in our program to become transformers of information rather than merely accumulators and translators of information, we determined that students would need to be taught various effective research strategies. We wanted students to have the tools to implement effective research as they engaged in a variety of inquiries (Newman & Kidd, 1994).

To help students develop the strategies necessary for effective research, it is important that teachers view research as a complex process that requires students to employ a variety of problem-solving strategies (Rankin, 1992). In successful programs, teachers and library media specialists teach students how to organize their task and apply effective strategies as they (a) define the task and set goals; (b) seek and locate reference materials, (c) extract and record data, and (d) use, synthesize, and evaluate information (Eisenberg & Brown, 1992; Guthrie et al., 1996; Rankin, 1992). To become effective researchers, students should be taught to view research as a recursive process in which they utilize a variety of effective strategies as they plan, search, investigate, create, share, and assess (Newman & Kidd, 1994).

The type of program we envisioned was one that begins in kindergarten and continues to build upon previously learned skills and strategies throughout the elementary school years. We saw the role of the teachers as facilitators who would create an atmosphere conducive to research, implement developmentally appropriate instruction, and provide support while at the same time leading the students to greater independence. Our task was to identify effective strategies and determine ways to share them successfully with the students.

Participants

Initially, the research program was designed and implemented in grades two to six in a Northern Virginia elementary school in the suburbs of Washington, D. C. Approximately 240 students attended the school located in a middle-class townhouse community bordered by upper-middle class houses and low-income housing. Students from all three of these communities attended the school resulting in a wide socio-economic range. Approximately 30% of the students were classified as African American, 30% as Caucasian, 30% as Hispanic, and 10% as Asian and other. The students represented a wide range of academic abilities, as well. In addition to the typical classroom students, students participating in the Talented and Gifted (TAG) program, the Learning Disabilities (LD) program, the English-as-a-Second-Language (ESL) program, the Chapter 1 Reading (Chapter 1) program, and the Remedial Reading program were included in the research program. Three years later, the research program was implemented in grades three to five at a multi-cultural school of approximately 750 students and then four years later at a school of approximately 300 diverse students.

Background Preparation

Because research should connect with learning that takes place throughout the school day and in the content areas (Eisenberg & Brown, 1992), we initiated the research program by enlisting the assistance of all teachers in the school. This included the library media specialist, reading specialists, LD teachers, ESL teachers, and classroom teachers. In a previous study in which teachers implemented a process approach to teaching research strategies and skills, Kuhlthau (1993) concluded that one element of a successful research program "was a strong team approach, with administrators playing an integral role" (p. 16). Therefore, participation of a variety of teachers was encouraged not only in the planning phase but throughout the entire process. As a team of teachers, we developed, planned, and prepared the schoolwide research program. We also reviewed the curriculum and determined what topics and issues to emphasize, what concepts to develop, and what objectives to address. Our goal was to engage students in "problem-directed research, rather than artificially imposed research assignments that only peripherally relate to the context, content, and objectives of the course of study" (Kuhlthau, 1993, p. 12). Using the information gathered, we designed a plan for incorporating research into the curriculum that built upon previously learned strategies not only from September to June, but also from year to year. After developing a framework that served as a guide for inte-

Figure 1. Letter to Parents

Dear Parents and Guardians:

During the third quarter, the fourth-grade students successfully completed their animal research. Not only did the students learn new and interesting facts, but they also familiarized themselves with new resources and research techniques. Their posters and oral presentations were very informative. Their classmates enjoyed listening to the facts that were shared.

It is now time to build on these skills and strategies through a more formal research project. Each fourth grader will research a person who has contributed to American freedom and will write a research paper. Throughout the project, the students will be expected to

1. select a topic;
2. brainstorm what they know and want to know;
3. identify the types of reference materials available;
4. record bibliographic information;
5. record notes on data charts;
6. organize their notes using a mapping strategy;
7. compose, revise, and edit their drafts; and
8. publish a final report.

Time will be allotted in class for students to work on each aspect of the research project. However, students will need additional time set aside at home to continue and complete each phase of the project. You can assist your child further by taking time to visit the public library.

We hope to see the excitement continue as we lead the students through the process of writing a research paper. If you have any questions, please call us. We appreciate your support.

Sincerely,

grating research with the goals and objectives for the content areas, our efforts focused on designing instruction, scheduling lessons and work sessions, locating materials, assessing students' needs, and determining specific requirements, due dates, and expectations.

Once these elements were in place, we communicated with parents and students to ensure that all people involved knew what was expected. A letter was sent home to parents explaining the research project, describing how it related to the curriculum, outlining the procedures for accomplishing the project, stating the specific requirements and due dates, and requesting appropriate assistance (see figure 1). To assist students with planning, scheduling, and self-evaluating, we provided students with calendars, checklists, charts, and rubrics with information on due dates, requirements, and criteria that would be used when evaluating students' work. The goal of the communication with parents and students was to help students take responsibility for their own learning while providing the support and structure needed for them to move forward with confidence and ease.

Teaching strategies

According to Vacca and Vacca (1999), "The process of inquiry . . . works best when it occurs in steps and stages" (p. 191). "The teacher must carefully plan inquiry-centered projects, giving just the right amount of direction to allow students to explore and discover ideas on their own. The research process isn't a do-your-own-thing proposition, for budding researchers need structure" (Vacca & Vacca, 1999, p. 193). For this reason, the instructional support provided by teachers throughout the research process is crucial. To ensure that students received adequate instruction, modeling, and feedback, it was important to schedule ample time for students to work under the guidance of the team of teachers (Kuhlthau, 1993). During the preparation period, we developed a tentative calendar outlining specific times for lessons, use of the library, work sessions, feedback sessions, and after-school opportunities. Also, we determined what strategy lessons needed to be developed (see figure 2), who would take responsibility for teaching the lessons, and what types of modifications must be made for specific students. Although we sketched out a detailed plan, we recognized that our plan needed to remain flexible to meet the needs that arose throughout the project.

As we developed the plan, we discussed what types of teaching strategies should be employed as we introduced and reinforced various research strategies. Because we believed "learners need to receive many demonstrations of how texts are constructed and used" (Cambourne, 1988, p. 33), we decided that modeling or demonstrating was essential to the students' success. Our reasoning was that when teachers demonstrate how to apply spe-

Figure 2. Research Strategies

- Identify audience, purpose, topic, and form using a planning sheet
- Generate topic ideas by brainstorming, examining written materials, taking field trips, making observations, etc.
- Select a topic with audience and purpose in mind
- Brainstorm what is known about the topic using the K part of the KWL
- Generate questions using the W part of the KWL
- Identify types of reference materials available
- Locate and retrieve reference materials
- Record bibliographic information
- Locate information within texts
- Read passages related to topic
- Identify relevant information
- Categorize information gathered
- Record notes on data charts in appropriate category
- Organize and synthesize notes using a mapping strategy
- Compose, revise, and edit written drafts or sketch and revise visual displays
- Create and share a final product

cific learning strategies to the research process, students have a clearer understanding of what to do and how to do it. They hear and see what effective researchers do and have an opportunity to implement the strategies themselves. Therefore, when beginning new projects, we selected a topic which the class, as a whole, researched. Each time a new strategy was introduced or a previous strategy was reviewed, we modeled how to implement it.

We determined that guided practice that would allow students to apply what they learned under the guidance of a teacher was important, as well. Therefore, following the demonstration, we provided time in class to apply the strategies modeled. This enabled the students to ask questions and receive immediate feedback from teachers and peers. Likewise, we knew we wanted to encourage students to employ the strategies independently, which meant we needed to establish time for students to work during class and at home to work on their own. To do this, we established conference days in which students worked independently while teachers met individually with students to provide feedback. In addition, we assigned parts of the project for homework.

Occasionally, students required additional support and attention. During work sessions and feedback sessions, all teachers on the team, including the library media specialist, conferenced with students and provided individual or small-group instruction as needed. This time gave us the opportunity to assess the students' progress and determine how to meet their needs. Strategies were adapted or modified to provide for students who needed greater support and for those who needed greater challenges. In addition, we found that this was a perfect time to invite parents and community volunteers to share in the learning process. The more attention each student received, the greater the chance of success.

Research Strategies

Strategy instruction was an essential element in designing and implementing the research program. The goal, over time, was for the students to internalize the strategies; however, we recognized the need to provide appropriate structure throughout the learning process (Vacca & Vacca, 1999). Therefore, instruction was designed to provide a well-organized and systematic approach to pursuing inquiries.

Students began the research project with instruction on how to employ planning strategies to keep their research progressing. Planning is an element of research that occurs throughout the entire process but requires a concentrated effort at the beginning. Students began by identifying the audience, determining the purpose for the research, selecting a topic, and identifying the form in which the information would be shared. The students recorded this information on a planning sheet (see figure 3). From their writing instruction, students knew that the audience, purpose, topic, and form have an impact on the direction of their writing. Therefore, when selecting their topics, they reflected upon who would be their audience, why they were sharing the information, and how the information would be shared.

Early in the process, students learned that there are a variety of strategies to assist them in selecting a specific topic. Brainstorming is a simple

Figure 3. Planning Sheet

Audience:	fourth grade students, teachers, and parents
Purpose:	to inform
Topic:	Americans who contributed to freedom
Form:	written report
Possible Topics:	George Washington
	Rosa Parks
	Thomas Jefferson
	Martin Luther King, Jr.
	Susan B. Anthony
	Harriet Tubman

strategy which enables students to generate a list of possible topics. However, this strategy can be limiting because it narrows the choices to familiar topics. Therefore, other strategies were also employed. For example, a class beginning reports on animals took a trip to the zoo, made lists of animals as they visited the exhibits, and then chose research topics from that list. Students undertaking biographical research examined myriad biographies and then chose one of the people to research. Another teacher provided an overview of the various Native American tribes before students selected one to research. In all of these cases, teachers created an environment which encouraged students to explore possible topics before making a final choice.

Because research involves finding answers to questions, students explored their selected topics by accessing what they knew and developing questions to guide their research. To facilitate this process, students employed Ogle's (1989) KWL chart to record their prior knowledge and questions. They began by brainstorming a list of words and phrases relating to what they knew about their topic. Then they listed questions that could be answered through research.

Once questions were generated, students grouped the questions to develop focus categories for the research. They did this by chunking similar questions together and creating labels. This required the students to analyze the questions to determine which questions were related and how they were related. For example, students researching Americans who contributed to freedom generated several questions relating to their person's childhood. Others were about that person's adult personal life. Another group of questions pertained to the person's accomplishments. These categories become the basis for the data chart (see figure 4), which is a graphic organizer designed for recording notes (Hoffman, 1992; McKenzie, 1979).

In the primary grades, students generally created two to three categories, and middle grade students generated three to six main ideas or headings. Because of its format, the data chart helps students maintain a focus and organize the information they collect. Students began by gathering sources, examining the table of contents and index, locating relevant passages, and skimming the text for content. If students decided to use a source, the bibliographic information was recorded at the top of a data chart. It is important for students to understand that when they use someone else's work, they must give them credit for it. Therefore, the students recorded notes only from one source on a particular data chart. When referring to a new source, they used a new data chart and began by recording the bibliographic information.

To take notes, students read the information carefully. If information was relevant, it was recorded using words and phrases in the appropriate category on the data chart. Students continued in this manner as they read. Any

Figure 4. Data Chart

Name: _____ Date: _____ Topic: _____

Author: _____ Source: _____

City of Publication: _____ Publisher: _____ Copyright Date: _____

Childhood	Adult Personal Life	Accomplishments

information that did not relate to the identified categories but was considered interesting and unique was recorded either on the back of the data chart or in a category labeled, "other." The intent was to allow for the possibility that some interesting information could be discovered that wasn't initially anticipated, but that was too important to ignore. After the information from the first source was recorded, students began the process again with additional sources. Each time they referred to a new source, they began a new data chart.

After taking notes, students combined and organized them by drawing upon the mapping strategy (see figure 5) used when writing (Heimlich & Pittelman, 1986). The students placed the topic in the middle of the map. The categories were written in the circles as the main ideas, and the details were recorded for each main idea. The students began with one of the data charts and recorded the information around the appropriate ideas. This continued until all of the information was recorded on the map. They followed the same process for the second and third data charts. However, if a piece of information was already recorded, it was not recorded again. This enabled the students to synthesize information from multiple sources.

As students became more proficient, the mapping became more sophisticated. Instead of creating one map for all of the information, older students were able to develop a map for each category. This required students to analyze the information in each category and create subheadings. Therefore,

Figure 5. Mapping

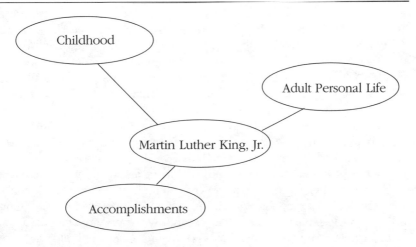

Students write details from data charts around each main idea.

for a report on a famous person, map I focused on the person's childhood and was divided into (a) family, (b) education, and (c) events. Map II emphasized the person's adult personal life, and map III stressed the person's accomplishments. This strategy helped students organize their information and prepared them for using linear outlines in the future.

After students completed the map(s), they used the synthesized information to create a final product. Although students assessed their progress throughout the process, evaluation at this time was critical. Students analyzed the information they collected, determined what was to be shared and how it was to be shared, and evaluated the final product as it was created. Through the process of drafting the product, revising it to make it better, and editing it to make it error free, students examined their work critically. The result was a visual display, a model, a dramatization, a written report, and/or an oral presentation. Students concluded the project with a sense of accomplishment and a desire to delve into research again.

Implications

By the time I left the initial school four years after the program's inception, a schoolwide program for developing effective research strategies was in place in grades two through six, and teachers had begun to experiment with how to engage kindergartners and first graders in the research process. The program included a framework that outlined how each grade level would develop research strategies throughout the year and how each year would build on the previous year.

Being aware of what students had learned in previous years gave teachers a sense of where to begin instruction in subsequent years. The teachers felt confident knowing that they were aligning new instruction with previous instruction because it meant the students could move forward more efficiently. With this type of coordination among and within grade levels, the students entered each grade with a more consistent repertoire of strategies. This was not the case prior to implementing a schoolwide program. In previous years, students from different classes might range from having no research background to having an extensive research background. In addition, teachers had approached research in a variety of ways making it more difficult for the current teacher to build on previous experiences. The effort to build a schoolwide program that promoted inquiry-based learning established some consistency throughout the school and ensured that teaching students how to implement effective research was a priority of all teachers.

In a similar manner, teachers realized the importance of building strategies throughout the academic year rather than assigning one big project. As a result of the program, teachers began introducing the strategies to promote comprehension of content area texts within a variety of contexts. One group of third-grade teachers had students apply reading and writing strategies while gathering information about rocks. They developed a data chart with appearance, properties, and uses as categories. They used this as an opportunity to teach and reinforce how to (a) gather information by reading a text, (b) determine the relevancy of information, (c) categorize the information, and (d) record the information on a data chart. By learning how to gather, classify, and record information, the students not only engaged in reading to learn, but also developed strategies that they were able to apply more independently when conducting a more formal research project.

Because this type of scaffolding was built into the program, students seemed to approach research in a positive manner. To these students, research appeared to be exciting and fun because they had the tools and resources to be successful. They were ready for new learning because it built upon previous learning. They knew what was expected of them and knew they would have support reaching those goals. It was evident that this systematic and well-planned research program promoted excitement in research that we had not noticed in the students prior to its implementation.

A clear example of this enthusiasm surfaced one day near the end of one school year. I entered a fourth-grade classroom ready to teach a mathematics lesson. One child, who was in the ESL and LD programs, became excited and started bouncing up and down in his chair. When his hand shot up, I called on him. He asked if we were going to do a new research project. I indicated that we were going to do math today, but next year we could conduct more research. He responded, "I want to do it today. I won't be here next year." His simple comment made me realize that if our program could create an interest in research and motivate a child who often struggled with learning, then we must have a plan worth continuing and sharing.

As I moved to two other schools over the course of the next few years and as Lillie Newman worked with new teachers in the initial school, we continued to build upon our initial program. In both of my schools, I worked with teachers to implement a plan for conducting research in grades three to five. As in the first school, teachers seemed to put more emphasis on inquiry-based learning after the program was implemented. An improvement in students' research strategies was noted, as well as, an increase in students' excitement and interest in conducting research.

As one who sees the importance of teaching students how to research, I am puzzled by the number of times my own son, now 16, has brought home a list of requirements for a research report, but has received little instruction in how to approach the tasks involved in researching and creating a product to share. I have heard other parents groan about the research papers they had to help their children write. As I have shared some of the strategies from our program with these parents, they have remarked on how much more pleasant the research process was with their children.

Overall, students need to be taught effective research strategies in a systematic way that begins when they enter school and continues to build throughout the grades. If this is to happen, school communities need to examine their own practices related to developing students' research strategies and design a plan that will fit the needs of their students. Students involved in the program described here seemed to be highly interested in conducting research, thus it would be interesting to survey students to determine if they are in fact more motivated to research when given support. It would also be interesting to find out what factors contributed to their interest in research and to their success in applying effective research strategies.

Conclusion

Over the years, it has been fascinating to watch students grow as researchers. We have sensed the excitement as they moved from selecting a topic, to developing questions, to reading to gather information, to taking notes, to organizing their information, and finally to creating and sharing a product. Because teachers worked together as a team to develop and implement the research projects, they provided students with the instruction and support they needed to engage successfully in research. This resulted in students who felt comfortable approaching research and were confident and excited about conducting their own.

References

Brooks, J. G. & Brooks, M. G. (1993). *In search of understanding: The case for constructivist classrooms.* Alexandria, VA: Association for Supervision and Curriculum Development.

Cambourne, B. (1988). *The whole story: Natural learning and the acquisition of literacy in the classroom.* Auckland, New Zealand: Ashton Scholastic Ltd.

Dahl, K. L. & Farnan, N. (1998). *Children's writing: Perspectives from research.* Newark, DE: International Reading Association and National Reading Conference.

Duthie, C. (1996). *True stories: Nonfiction literacy in the primary classroom.* York, ME: Stenhouse Publishers.

Eisenberg, M. B. (1992). Current themes regarding library and information skills instruction: Research supporting and research lacking. *School Library Media Quarterly, 20*(2), 103-109.

Guthrie, J. T., Van Meter, Peggy., McCann, A. D., Wigfield, A., Bennett, L., Poundstone, C. C., Rice, M. E., Faibisch, F. M., Hunt, B., Mitchell, A. M. (1996. Growth of literacy engagement: Changes in motivations and strategies during concept-oriented reading instruction. *Reading Research Quarterly, 31*(3), 306-332.

Heimlich, J. E. & Pittelman, S. D. (1986). *The semantic mapping. Classroom applications.* Newark, DE: International Reading Association.

Hoffman, J. V. (1992). Critical reading/thinking across the curriculum: Using I-charts to support learning. *Language Arts, 69*(2), 121-127.

International Reading Association and National Council of Teachers of English. (1996). *Standards for the English language arts.* Newark, DE: Authors.

Kuhlthau, C. C. (1993). Implementing a process approach to information skills: A study identifying indicators of success in library media programs. *School Library Media Quarterly, 22*(1), 11-18.

Many, J. E., Fyfe, R., Lewis, G., & Mitchell, E. (1996). Traversing the topical land scape: Exploring students' self-directed reading-writing-research processes. *Reading Research Quarterly, 31*(1), 12-35.

McKenzie, G. (1979). Data charts: A crutch for helping pupils organize reports. *Language Arts, 56*, 784-788.

National Academy of Sciences. (1996). *National science education standards.* Washington, DC: National Academy Press.

National Council for the Social Studies. (1994). *Expectations of excellence: Curriculum standards for social studies.* Washington, DC: Author.

Newman, L. and Kidd, J. K. (1994). *Research strategies and skills for elementary school students.* Unpublished manuscript.

Ogle, D. M. (1989). The know, want to know, learn strategy. In K. D. Muth (Ed.), *Children's comprehension of text* (pp. 205-223). Newark, DE: International Reading Association.

Rankin, V. (1992). Rx: Task analysis or, relief for the major discomforts of research assignments. *School Library Journal, 38*(11), 29-32.

Vacca, R. T. & Vacca, J. L. (1999). *Content area reading: Literacy and learning across the curriculum.* New York: Addison-Wesley Educational Publishers, Inc.

New Directions for Developmental Reading Programs: Meeting Diverse Student Needs

Jeanne L. Higbee

The University of Georgia

Abstract

While legislators are questioning the provision of instruction in reading at the college level, developmental educators and other reading education professionals are examining a variety of models for meeting the educational needs of college students with deficits in reading and other areas. At some institutions there is no longer a choice; required "remedial" reading courses will not be offered. Yet at every institution, regardless of size or type, there will be some students who are underprepared compared to the standard for that institution. The purpose of this paper is to discuss alternative models for learning support for all students.

In many states legislators are questioning the provision of developmental education programs at public expense, especially at four-year colleges and universities. Even those who might support developmental mathematics and writing courses, realizing that students have different strengths, find it difficult to support reading programs. Certainly anyone who is capable enough to be admitted to college is able to read. Unfortunately, what these legislators fail to understand is that many students *can read*, but do not know *how to read*. In one state after another, legislators are threatening to cut funding or to relegate all developmental education programs to two-year institutions. When viewed from this perspective, the future of developmental reading programs appears bleak. However, reading educators who approach this problem with creativity can find myriad solutions. At every institution, regardless of size or type, there will be some students who are underprepared compared to the standard for that institution, or who are better prepared in some academic areas than others. Many students, including high achievers from high school, are not adequately prepared for the rigors of college level academic work; they do not know how to read textbooks, annotate, review, and prepare for exams. Because they are bright, they were able to be successful in high school without learning how to study. There are numerous students who would benefit from assistance, whether they realize it or not (Hardin, 1988, 1998; Henry, 1995). Educators who embrace Astin's (1985) talent development model, who support the "paradigm shift from teaching to learning" (Arendale, 1997, p.1), will continue to provide learning support to assist these students. The purpose of this article is to discuss several models that work and may be adapted in a variety of settings to fit institutional needs. In many cases these programs can be more cost effective than providing required reading courses for high risk freshmen.

Serving Diverse Populations

Developmental education is defined as " a field of practice and research within higher education with a theoretical foundation in developmental psychology and learning theory. It promotes the cognitive and affective growth of all postsecondary learners, at all levels of the learning continuum" (National Association for Developmental Education, 1995). Developmental education no longer connotes required classes for high risk, provisionally admitted, or underprepared students. Instead, developmental educators provide courses and other forms of academic assistance and support for *all* students. The field is growing, not declining. It is critical to the future of the profession that developmental educators, regardless of academic discipline, reevaluate how their programs are defined and perceived on their own campuses, and then address the challenge of informing other faculty, administrators, alumni, legislators, the press, and the public about their mission and goals. These constituencies can also provide feedback that can be very helpful in planning for the future (Higbee & Dwinell, 1996, 1997; Higbee, Thomas, Hayes, Glauser, & Hynd, 1998).

Students know what developmental educators do, and they welcome the expansion of services. Programs often receive more publicity via word-of-mouth than through traditional modes like posters, ads, and announcements in the student newspaper. Although programs and courses with voluntary participation do not always attract some of the students who may need them the most, many students will take advantage of the opportunity to enhance their skills in order to earn higher grades. At the University of Georgia (UGA), despite an ultimatum by the Chancellor and Board of Regents regarding the admission of developmental studies students to research universities in the state of Georgia, the Division of Academic Assistance (ACA) is serving more students than ever before. The division provides a wide array of courses and programs for a diverse population that includes honors students, international students, graduate and professional school students, and other students who previously did not know where to turn when they needed help. The Division of Academic Assistance has demonstrated that it is possible to expand the breadth of developmental education services beyond those for high risk students without significant increases in budget. Meanwhile, by creating new courses and programs to meet diverse student needs, the division has escaped budget cuts or the elimination of the program, hardships experienced by other institutions in the University System of Georgia.

Investigating Joint Ventures

One means of expanding the target audience for programs and services to meet diverse student needs is collaborating with other units within both Academic and Student Affairs. Developmental education programs can establish liaisons to academic departments, especially those offering high risk core curriculum courses; to offices serving specific populations, such as students with disabilities; and to student services such as orientation programs, residence life, and Greek life. Then these services can work together to brainstorm student needs and ideas for meeting them.

Piloting New Programs

Different models fit different institutions, depending on size or location, type of college or university, organizational structure, budget, and other factors, and specific student needs. Fortunately, there is a wide array of models to choose from and each can be adapted to better meet the goals of the institution. Some programs, such as learning communities, can be implemented with little or no additional expense to the institution, depending upon the model chosen. Others, like elective courses, can replace required courses, serve a broader population, and assist in eliminating the stigma that may be associated with developmental education programs on some campuses. Reading educators can play an instrumental role in designing and implementing new programs such as integrated courses, Supplemental Instruction, freshman seminars and workshops. (Casazza & Silverman, 1996; Commander, Stratton, Callahan, & Smith, 1996; Farmer & Barham, 1996; Maxwell, 1997, 1998; Simpson, Hynd, Nist, & Burrell, 1997; Wilkie, 1993).

Integrated Reading and Writing Courses

One of the trends during the past decade has been the reintegration of reading and writing (McKusick, Holmberg, Marello, & Little, 1997; Quinn,

1995; Stern, 1995). The potential problem with these courses is that neither the reading nor the writing faculty have been adequately trained to teach them (Ecung & Fry, 1998). One solution, though often problematic from the standpoint of budget and courseload, is courses that are team-taught. Working collaboratively, reading and writing faculty can support one another, try out new approaches, and perhaps reduce teacher burn-out.

Freshman Seminars

There are many different models for freshman orientation courses, First-Year Experience programs (Fidler & Fidler, 1991), and content-based freshman seminars. These classes assist freshmen in adjusting to college while also providing an opportunity to become well acquainted with a small group of their peers in a supportive environment that promotes learning. Many of these courses include the integration of reading and study skills instruction. Some are taught by faculty hired specifically for this purpose, others are taught by volunteers from both academic departments and Student Affairs. Reading educators may be involved in administration, faculty training and development, and instruction for these courses.

Adjunct, Paired, and Linked Courses

Similarly, there are a variety of models for courses in reading and study strategies that are taught in conjunction with core curriculum courses (Blinn & Sisco, 1996; Bullock, Madden, & Harter, 1987; Byrd & Carter, 1997; Commander, Callahan, Stratton, & Smith, 1997; Commander & Smith, 1995; Dimon, 1981; Kerr, 1993; Resnick, 1993; Simon, Barrett, Noble, Sweeney, & Thom, 1993; Weinstein, 1995; Wilcox, del Mas, Stewart, Johnson & Ghere, 1997). Participation may be voluntary for any student taking the course or mandatory for specific sections. Some are taught for graduation credit, some for non-degree credit, and some may be considered laboratories that bear no additional credit. The advantage of adjunct, paired, or linked courses is that skills are taught for learning specific content. For example, a student would not use the same approach to read both a history text and a mathematics text (Bohr, 1996; Campbell, Schlumberger, & Pate, 1997; Waycaster, 1993).

Supplemental Instruction

Supplemental Instruction (SI) is another model that has proven effective in educating students about how to apply learning strategies to specific course content (Arendale, 1998; Martin & Arendale, 1993, 1994; Martin, Blanc, & DeBuhr, 1983; Peled & Kim, 1995). SI differs from adjunct, paired, and linked courses in that students may choose to attend as many or as few SI sessions as they wish, depending upon their perceived need. Students are not required to make a semester-long commitment to SI. Students may not know at the beginning of a term, when it would be necessary to enroll in an adjunct course, that they will need assistance in order to be successful. The flexibility inherent in SI is attractive to students. Another reason that Supplemental Instruction has gained acceptance from students, faculty, and administrators alike is that it targets high risk courses rather than student populations. Thus, the stigma that is often associated with developmental education courses does not apply to SI. A student striving to maintain a 4.0 may participate for different reasons than a student struggling to achieve a 2.0, but both can benefit.

Unlike faculty and graduate students who teach paired, linked, and adjunct courses, SI leaders are student peers who facilitate sessions to assist students in assessing their notetaking, mastering the textbook, reviewing lecture material, predicting exam questions, developing test-taking strategies, and other skills. Reading educators are the ideal personnel to train and supervise SI leaders. At some institutions reading faculty teach SI leader courses comparable to tutor training courses.

Learning Communities

The term "learning community" is currently being used in the literature to refer to a variety of different models that encourage collaborative learning. Some models are literally communities, housed in college and university residence halls (Dolan, 1998). Others are blocks of courses in which all participating students are simultaneously enrolled, much like how many professional schools operate. The students attend all their classes together and also study together outside of class. Another model resembles an advisor's group (Carter & Silker, 1997). Students meet as a group on a regular basis with an advisor or other facilitator to learn strategies, discuss common problems, and provide support. Regardless of the model, reading educators can play a key role in establishing and facilitating learning communities.

Learning Centers, Tutorial Services, and Workshops

There are many examples of institutions that have transformed their developmental education learning laboratories, which once served only high risk or provisionally-admitted students, into learning centers that serve the entire student body. Often a wide variety of services are offered on both an individual and small group basis. Tutorial services may be included, or there may be a separate tutoring center. Some institutions offer workshop series through their learning centers. Workshops for students may be presented on site, at campus residence halls or Greek houses, or in classes. Workshops for faculty may be conducted in departmental meetings or at brown bag lunch seminars. Reading educators may also provide workshops in the community.

Workplace Literacy Projects

The theme of the 42nd annual College Reading Association conference was "Advocating for Literacy." Reading educators have been instrumental in promoting literacy efforts both within and outside educational institutions (Wall, Longman, Atkinson, & Maxcy, 1993; Longman, Atkinson, Miholic, & Simpson, in press). During the 1990s workplace literacy projects have been established in prisons, factories, and major corporations, often piloted with the use of grant money from a variety of sources. Whether university-based or employed by industry or a government agency, faculty working with these programs reap numerous rewards in terms of personal satisfaction and the opportunity to gain an understanding of how people from diverse backgrounds learn best in different settings.

Institutional Fit

Developmental educators must examine how models can be adapted to fit their own institutions. Typical questions include whether programs should be centralized or decentralized, if services should be staffed by professionals or peers, if courses should be taught for degree or non-degree credit, and whether programs should be housed within Academic Affairs or Student Affairs. The answers to these questions should depend upon what will work at a particular institution, taking into consideration factors like availability of facilities, budget, and administrative structure. What is the most efficient and effective way to meet student needs?

One Institution's Response: Academic Assistance at UGA

The University System of Georgia's Chancellor and Board of Regents determined that it is not the mission of Georgia's public research universities to provide "remedial" education. Educators throughout the state and around the country interpreted this policy statement as the death knell of programs like the Division of Academic Assistance at The University of Georgia. Meanwhile, a building was remodeled for the division's use, and the program received a technology grant to equip its new learning center. The division conducted a national search and hired a new director, a reading educator from within the program. The division received a $10,000 semester conversion grant to conduct an assessment of how to best meet student needs during a period of transition (Higbee et al., 1998). The university's curriculum committee approved new courses to be taught by ACA faculty. The faculty created their own model, and while other developmental education programs in the state are threatened, the division is thriving.

The Division of Academic Assistance currently offers 19 different University (UNIV) courses. All courses earn institutional credit. Two of these courses, "Learning to Learn" (UNIV 1102), taught by reading faculty, and "Strategies for Academic Success" (UNIV 1103), taught by counseling faculty, were created almost ten years ago to provide academic support for non-developmental studies students. Following the semester conversion grant report, courses were piloted in the areas of problem solving and critical thinking (Chaffee, 1992). These courses have become very popular; waiting lists are generated each time they are offered.

New UNIV courses to be taught by ACA reading faculty members include "Text Comprehension and Vocabulary Improvement," "Improving Reading Rate," and "Study Strategies Adjunct," which can be offered in conjunction with other courses, most commonly high risk core curriculum requirements. UNIV 1101, "Topics in Academic Assistance," enables faculty to pilot new course ideas prior to seeking curriculum committee approval. Courses taught by other ACA faculty include "Improving Grammar, Usage, and Style," "Basic Report Writing for College and Beyond," "Introduction to Academic Writing," "Resources for Research," "Introduction to the Research Paper," "Basic Composition for Multilingual Writers," "Academic Writing for Multilingual Students," "Preparation for Statistics-Based Courses," "Preparation for Pre-Calculus," "University Success for Freshmen," and "Strategies for Success for Nontraditional Students." One reason these courses have been so popular, despite offering institutional (i.e., nondegree) credit only, is that they were designed to meet specific student needs. Several sections of some courses (e.g., UNIV 1102 and 1103) are taught each semester, while for others only one section may be taught per year. Students are often referred by faculty members and advisors from throughout the university.

Conclusion

Faculty members in the Division of Academic Assistance at the University of Georgia foresee that it is likely that required courses for high risk students will be phased out in the near future. Instead, the division will offer an even broader variety of elective courses to meet all students' academic needs. Part of the success of this curriculum must be attributed to the efforts of ACA faculty to seek input from both students and other university faculty in order to create a program appropriate to this institution, without requiring additional faculty and staff. The Learning Center and Tutorial Services are thriving, the division has established strong bonds with other academic units, and the faculty have developed various series of workshops to meet specific student needs (e.g., adjusting to semester conversion, workshops for international students). The future is bright.

Reading educators are now positioned to take their place in the leadership of programs that enhance access, retention, and diversity in higher education. If viewed through creative lenses, opportunities abound. Through assessment of institutional and student needs, it is possible to implement programs that serve more students without increases in funding.

References

Arendale, D. (1997). Leading the paradigm shift from teaching to learning. *National Association for Developmental Education Newsletter, 20*(2), 1.

Arendale, D. (1998). Increasing efficiency and effectiveness of learning for freshman college students through Supplemental Instruction. In J. L. Higbee & P. L. Dwinell (Eds.), *Developmental education: Preparing successful college students* (pp. 185-197). Columbia, SC: National Resource Center for The First-Year Experience & Students in Transition, University of South Carolina.

Astin, A. S. (1985). *Achieving educational excellence.* San Francisco: Jossey-Bass.

Blinn, J., & Sisco, O. (1996). "Linking" developmental reading and biology. *National Association for Developmental Education Selected Conference Papers, 2,* 8-9.

Bohr, L. (1996). College and precollege reading instruction: What are the real differences? *Learning Assistance Review, 1*(1), 14-28.

Bullock, T., Madden, D., & Harter, J. (1987). Paired developmental reading and psychology courses. *Research & Teaching in Developmental Education, 3*(2), 22-29.

Byrd, E. H., & Carter, E. C. (1997). Study-reading for paired courses. *National Association for Developmental Education Selected Conference Papers, 3,* 1-3.

Campbell, A. E., Schlumberger, A., & Pate, L. A. (1997). Promoting reading strategies for developmental mathematics textbooks. *National Association for Developmental Education Selected Conference Papers, 3,* 4-6

Carter, J. A., & Silker, G. L. (1997). Academic enhancement groups: Transformational process for academically deficient students. *National Association for Developmental Education Selected Conference Papers, 3,* 7-8.

Casazza, M. E., & Silverman, S. L. (1996). *Learning assistance and developmental education: A guide for effective practice.* San Francisco: Jossey-Bass.

Chaffee, J. (1992). Critical thinking skills: The cornerstone of developmental education. *Journal of Developmental Education, 15*(3), 2.

Commander, N. E., Callahan, C. A., Stratton, C. B., & Smith, B. D. (1997). Adjunct courses and Supplemental Instruction: A ten step workshop. *National Association for Developmental Education Selected Conference Papers,3,* 14-16.

Commander, N. E., Stratton, C. B., Callahan, C. A., & Smith, B. D. (1996). A learning assistance model for expanding academic support. *Journal of Developmental Education, 20*(2), 8-16.

Commander, N. E., & Smith, B. D. (1995). Developing adjunct reading and learning courses that work. *Journal of Reading, 38*(5), 352-360.

Dimon, M. (1981). Why adjunct courses work. *Journal of College Reading and Learning, 21,* 33-40. Reprinted in M. Maxwell (Ed.) (1994), *From access to success.* Clearwater, FL: H & H.

Dolan, A. (1998, November). Welcome to the neighborhood. *The Iowa Stater, 24*(3), 3.

Ecung, V., & Fry, A. (1998). Views and processes for integrating reading and writing for successful developmental practice. In P. L. Dwinell & J. L. Higbee (Eds.),

Developmental education: Meeting diverse student needs (pp. 35-44). Morrow, GA: National Association for Developmental Education.

Farmer, V. L., & Barham, W. A. (1996). Selected models of developmental education programs in postsecondary institutions. *National Association for Developmental Education Selected Conference Papers, 2,* 10-11.

Fidler, P. P., & Fidler, D. S. (1991). *First National Survey on Freshman Seminar Programs: Findings, Conclusions, and Recommendations.* Columbia, SC: National Resource Center for the Freshman Year Experience.

Hardin, C. J. (1988). Access to higher education: Who belongs? *Journal of Developmental Education, 12,* 2-6.

Hardin, C. J. (1998). Who belongs in college: A second look. In J. L. Higbee & P. L. Dwinell (Eds.), *Developmental education: Preparing successful college students* (Monograph No. 24) (pp.15-24). Columbia, SC: National Resource Center for The First-Year Experience and Students in transition, University of South Carolina.

Henry, J. (1995). *If not now: Developmental readers in the college classroom.* Portsmouth, NH: Boynton/Cook Heinemann.

Higbee, J. L., & Dwinell, P. L. (1996). Seeking feedback to enhance developmental education counseling programs. *Research and Teaching in Developmental Education, 13*(2) 85-88.

Higbee, J. L., & Dwinell, P. L. (1997). Do developmental education programs really enhance retention? A commentary. In P. L. Dwinell & J. L. Higbee (Eds.), *Developmental education: Enhancing student retention.* Carol Stream, IL: National Association for Developmental Education.

Higbee, J. L., Thomas, P. V., Hayes, C. G., Glauser, A. S., & Hynd, C. R. (1998). Expanding developmental education services: Seeking faculty input. *Learning Assistance Review, 3*(1), 20-31.

Kerr, L. (1993). Content specific study strategies: A repertoire of approaches. *Journal of College Reading and Learning, 26*(1), 36-43.

Longman, D., Atkinson, R., Miholic, V., & Simpson, P. (in press). Building long-range workplace literacy projects: The ABC reading apprenticeship and task analysis. In J. Higbee & P. Dwinell (Eds.), *Developmental Education: An Expanding Role.* Morrow, GA: National Association for Developmental Education.

Martin, D. C., & Arendale, D. (Eds.). (1993). *Supplemental Instruction: Improving first-year student success in high risk courses*(Monograph N0.7). Columbia, SC: National Resource Center for The Freshman Year Experience.

Martin, D. C., & Arendale, D. R. (Eds.). (1994). *Increasing achievement and retention.* San Francisco: Jossey-Bass.

Martin, D. C., Blanc, R. A., & DeBuhr, L. (1983). Breaking the attrition cycle: The effects of Supplemental Instruction on undergraduate performance and attrition. *Journal of Higher Education, 54*(1), 80-89.

Maxwell, M. (1997). *Improving student learning skills* (Revised ed.). Clearwater, FL: H & H.

Maxwell, M. (1998). A commentary on the current state of developmental reading programs. In J. L. Higbee & P. L. Dwinell (Eds.), *Developmental education: Preparing successful college students* (Monograph No.24) (pp. 153-167). Columbia, SC: National Resource Center for The First-Year Experience and Students in Transition, University of South Carolina.

McKusick, D., Holmberg, B., Marello, C., & Little, E. (1997). Integrating reading and writing: Theory to research to practice. *National Association for Developmental Education Selected Conference Papers, 3,* 30-32.

National Association for Developmental Education (1995). Definition and goals statement. Carol Stream, IL: Author.

Peled, O. N., & Kim, A. C. (1995). Supplemental instruction in biology at the college level. *National Association for Developmental Education Selected Conference Papers, 1,* 23-24.

Quinn, K. B. (1995). Teaching reading and writing as modes of learning in college: A glance at the past, a view to the future. *Reading Research and Instruction, 34,* 285-314.

Resnick, J. (1993). A paired reading and sociology course. In P. Malinowski (Ed.), *Perspectives in Practice in Developmental Education* (pp. 62-64). Canandaigua, NY: New York College Learning Association.

Simon, J., Barrett, L., Noble, L., Sweeney, S., & Thom, H. (1993). Interdisciplinary models of pairing at three institutions. *Proceedings for the 17th Annual Conference of the National Association for Developmental Education,* 17-18.

Simpson, M. L., Hynd, C. R., Nist, S. L., & Burrell, K. I. (1997). College academic assistance programs and practices. *Educational Psychology Review, 9*(1), 39-87.

Stern, C. (1995). Integration of basic composition and reading. *National Association for Developmental Education Selected Conference Papers, 1,* 29-31

Wall, P., Longman, D., Atkinson, R., & Maxcy. D. (1993). Capitalizing on workplace literacy instruction for industrial construction workers. The ABC's of ABC. *Proceedings of the 17th Annual Conference of the National Association for Developmental Education,* 19-20.

Waycaster. P. (1993). Teaching mathematics study skills. *Proceedings for the 17th Annual Conference of the National Association for Developmental Education,* 15-16.

Weinstein, G. L. (1995). Mathematics survival: A linked course. *National Association for Developmental Education Selected Conference Papers, 1,* 38-40.

Wilcox, K., del Mas, R., Stewart, B., Johnson, A., & Ghere, D. (1997). The package course experience and developmental education. *Journal of Developmental Education, 20*(3), 18-20, 22, 24, 26.

Wilkie, C. (1993). Types and structures of developmental education programming in Pennsylvania. *Proceedings for the 17th Annual Conference of the National Association for Developmental Education,* 10-12.

Perceptual Understanding and Preservice Teachers' Literacy Learning

LEARNING FROM EXPERIENCE: PRESERVICE TEACHERS' PERCEPTIONS OF LITERATURE DISCUSSIONS

JoAnn Rubino Dugan

Clarion University of Pennsylvania

Abstract

This study explored the development of preservice teachers' perceptual knowledge of literary response. Forty elementary preservice teachers read books and conducted eight discussions with children in primary and elementary classrooms. The preservice teachers kept journals in which they reflected about what they learned from the experience. The overarching research question was: What do preservice teachers learn about literary response from literature discussions? Journal reflections and written responses to two questionnaires were analyzed qualitatively using grounded theory methods (Bogdan & Biklen, 1992; Glaser & Strauss, 1967). Major themes of understanding that emerged included a focus on instructional practice, student response, grouping practices, intertextual connections, collaboration, reading and writing connections, cultural awareness, and factors of engagement. An overwhelming majority of preservice teachers' perceptions focused on the children's interactions and meaning constructions. Reflections revealed that they perceived reading and response to literature as a transactional experience of exploration and of personal involvement in the story world. One of the challenges mentioned by several was managing the abundance of talk. Nonetheless, the majority of preservice teachers felt that children benefited from the free and open discussion forum because it allowed for multiple responses that encouraged active meaning-making. All of the preservice teachers indicated that they would definitely hold literature discussions in the future.

Experience is an essential element in learning. In educating teachers, the field teaching experiences are learning situations for developing practical knowledge about teaching. As Kessels and Korthagen (1996) assert, teaching experiences are "concrete situations to be perceived" wherein future teachers develop perceptual knowledge about their practice. Hence, what preservice teachers come to know about teaching may be determined to a great extent by their participation in actual teaching experiences and their own perceptions of what they understand about these experiences. Therefore, preservice teachers' perceptions of their teaching experiences offer a lens through which educators can view the development of practical knowledge about teaching and learning.

This study was concerned with preservice teachers' knowledge about reading instruction and literary response in the course of literature discussions. According to literary response theory (Rosenblatt, 1938, 1978) reading is a transaction between the reader and text in which the reader experiences the text emotionally as well as intellectually. Readers play an active role in this creative process of making sense by responding to a text based on the knowledge and experiences they bring to the reading. Because of the individual nature of a reader's background, responses may vary and texts may have more than one meaning as readers respond and interpret them based on their own backgrounds.

Literature discussions provide opportunities for children to express their personal responses to literature in an open forum to develop an aesthetic appreciation of children's books and to enhance understanding through the sharing of multiple perspectives. Discussions are consistent with the notion that meaning is not singular and predetermined, but is constructed and negotiated through social interactions and dialogue with others (Bakhtin, 1986; Vygotsky, 1978). Literature discussions have been found to foster engagement with reading and increase understanding of literature (Gambrell & Almasi, 1996). Book discussions are also a medium in which teachers may use scaffolded instruction to model meaning-making strategies and build on children's ideas to help them more fully develop their initial responses (Dugan, 1997; Vogt, 1996).

Teachers' ability to facilitate literature discussions may depend on the teachers' perception of literary response as well as an ability to apply it in real teaching situations. Wolf, Carey, and Mieras (1996) found that preservice teachers who perceived meaning as text-based limited children's exploration of meaning; however, preservice teachers who perceived meaning as a construct of the reader encouraged children's exploration of multiple meanings. Wolf and colleagues suggested that preservice teachers should learn about literary response by actually reading and responding to books with children because feedback from the children and from teacher educators serves to guide and develop preservice teachers' practical understanding of literary response. Building on this premise, this study explored preservice teachers' perceptions of literature discussions to determine what they learned from the practice of facilitating discussions, encouraging children's responses, and enhancing an appreciation of literature. The overarching research question was *What do preservice teachers learn about literary response from literature discussions?*

Methods

Participants

Forty elementary preservice teachers participated in this study. All were enrolled in a reading specialization course taught by the author. During this final semester of their senior year, the preservice teachers also were completing a yearlong, field teaching experience. They were placed with mentor teachers in four rural school districts located in southwestern United States. Under the guidance of mentor teachers, they taught school on a daily basis and attended six university-based classes that met in the evening about every two weeks. One of the goals in the reading specialization course was to develop a deeper understanding of instructional methods in the teaching of reading with children's literature. Reading specialization assignments were designed to be integrated with the field teaching experiences so that preservice teachers could apply concepts and principles of reading instruction in real classroom teaching situations.

Procedures

To familiarize the preservice teachers with a framework for facilitating literature discussions, small group literature discussions were conducted "in the round" during the first two class meetings. Small groups of preservice teachers participated as discussants and responded to children's books read aloud by their instructor while the rest of the class recorded their observations and perceptions of the interaction. The framework used for facilitating discussions and scaffolding response consisted of a cycle of activities for previewing and selecting a book, developing prior knowledge, and helping children think aloud and reflect in writing during the read alouds both spontaneously and at specified intervals (Dugan, 1997). The instructor emphasized that the framework was to be used as a flexible guide for instruction rather than a rigid, lock-step procedure. Following the demonstrations, the preservice teachers discussed their observations and perceptions of the interaction and dialogue, identified the roles of teacher and students and explored the implications for classroom instruction. Reader response theory and concepts such as active meaning-making, appreciation of literature, and free exchange of ideas were also a focus of these debriefing sessions.

Preservice teachers were then asked to hold eight literature discussions while reading trade books with children in their classrooms. According to the preservice teachers, reading trade books aloud was a routine daily activity, but book discussions were not. Nevertheless, with the approval of mentor teachers, preservice teachers were able to conduct a total of eight discussions during the fifteen-week semester. Following each discussion, they reflected in journals. The author provided the following questions to guide their reflections:

1. How did the children respond to the story?
2. How did they interact with each other? Why?
3. What kind of questions did I ask? Why?
4. What did I learn?

Preservice teachers were asked not to limit their reflections to these questions, but to write freely about their perceptions of the discussions.

In addition, two questionnaires were used to gather the preservice teachers' perceptions. Questionnaire #1, given about the seventh week into the semester, asked the preservice teachers to respond in writing to questions that tapped their perceptions of practices they were employing to encourage response and changes they had noticed thus far in the children's interactions. At the end of the semester, Questionnaire #2 was used to gather the preservice teachers' final overall impressions of the literature discussions. (Specific questions on the questionnaires are provided in the Findings section of this report)

The three data sources—journal reflections, Questionnaires #1 and #2—enabled the author to triangulate the data analyses and confirm findings from each source.

Data Collection and Analyses

After each discussion, the preservice teachers kept journals and submitted these reflections as they were completed throughout the semester. The author read and responded with comments and questions to encourage preservice teachers to think deeply about their experiences and make connections to concepts being discussed in class. Reflections were returned to students the following week so they could read and benefit from the feedback. At the completion of the semester, journal reflections were collected and copied with preservice teacher's permission.

Qualitative analyses were conducted using grounded theory (Bogdan & Biklen, 1992; Glaser & Strauss, 1967). A first reading of the journal reflections involved highlighting descriptive passages in which preservice teachers had focused on what they perceived and learned from the experience. A major portion of their journal reflections consisted of comments related to the discussions; however, brief summaries of the books were also included but not analyzed. In a second reading, specific insights about what worked and what they had learned were identified. For example, "small groups work better than large groups," "the teacher plays a vital role in determining student participation," and "children like reading stories about things they enjoy doing." These insights were compiled as a running list. Similar insights were then clustered to form categories which were assigned headings reflecting major themes.

Responses on the questionnaires were analyzed qualitatively by listing all responses for each question on a chart, reading them to determine the main focus of each and highlighting the key ideas, and then identifying the common ideas across the group of responses for each item.

Findings

Generally, these preservice teachers viewed the literature discussions as a positive and valuable learning experience for themselves and for the children. Many commented that they learned a "vast amount" not only about facilitating discussions, but also about the children and their insightful responses to books, and the value of literature for developing interest in books and a love of reading.

Journal Reflections

Analyses of the journal reflections revealed that preservice teachers developed understandings about the following areas: instructional practice, student response, grouping, intertextual connections, collaboration, reading and writing connections, cultural awareness, and factors of engagement.

Comments related to *instructional practice* dealt with the need for modeling meaning-making strategies, building prior knowledge, selecting books, and managing the talk (particularly in the first few discussions). Preservice teachers reported that they helped children become engaged from the beginning by encouraging them to make predictions about the stories based on the book covers, titles, and illustrations. They stated that prior knowledge was important and they were helping children make connections between the text and their own lives by encouraging them to relate to the characters, share their own personal stories, and discuss unfamiliar words. They managed the talk by encouraging children to use common courtesy by responding and listening to each other and "respecting different opinions."

In terms of *student response*, preservice teachers acknowledged multiple personal responses rather than expecting one correct interpretation. They noted that discussions provided opportunities for both disagreement and problem solving among children, and realized the critical need for student control or "ownership" of the process of generating hypotheses and forming interpretations. Many preservice teachers described their role as a "facilitator," "monitor," and "listener" while the children were described as the "leaders" of the discussions.

A few preservice teachers noted *gender differences* in children's interaction and response. When reading different versions of Cinderella stories, one preservice teacher stated, "The boys did not seem to be interested in the story and remained quiet throughout the reading except when they were asked to read aloud. This experience taught me that I must be aware of gender differences and interests for reading." In another discussion about the story of astronaut Jim Lovell, the same preservice teacher again noted, "Boys dominated the discussion. They were especially interested when they learned that one time Lovell landed in the dark without any lights at all." "Next time," she wrote, "I would involve girls...by addressing the fact that if they think females are able to accomplish this training and asking them to provide names of the first female pilot and astronaut."

In terms of *grouping*, preservice teachers held most of the discussions with the whole class, but several indicated that they preferred small groups because it was "much easier to manage the talk" and "gave more students a chance" to participate. They pointed out, nevertheless, that both small groups and large groups "required teacher direction" to encourage children to work cooperatively and to "focus their attention" on one common goal or objective.

Variations of *intertextual connections* were frequently noted by many of the preservice teachers with respect to reading different genres, multicultural literature, and comparing and contrasting texts. There emerged from the reflections a desire on the part of preservice teachers to expose children to a wide variety of texts. They followed through with this by reading books of different genres, fiction and informational, on a wide range of subjects. All felt that by exploring books with the children they were "encouraging them to read more texts on their own" and were developing a "love of reading." Several preservice teachers indicated that books presented many possibilities for learning, but some books were better for "stimulating writing," while others were better for "stimulating thinking and discussion."

The preservice teachers described the interaction among the children as "learning to get along," "respecting other ideas," " learning to agree and disagree," "to share," "to work toward common goals," to engage in "shared thinking" and "to come to a decision." Hence, this category was labeled *collaboration* for the purpose of socially constructing meaning.

A few preservice teachers identified *reading and writing connections.* These were noted in lessons in which preservice teachers encouraged students to respond in writing or to write their own stories using literature as a model.

The participation in literature discussions seemed to raise a *cultural awareness* and respect for diversity in teachers and students. As one preservice teacher stated, "Reading opens many avenues of thinking and exploring diversity issues." Another noticed that reading of multicultural literature helped children understand that "we are all special."

Factors that affected children's *engagement* with books were a concern for many preservice teachers. They identified the book as a positive influential factor related to children's engagement in the discussions. The book had to be one the children could relate to. Also, teachers themselves needed to prepare for discussions by reading the book in advance, by anticipating how children might respond, and by sharing their enthusiasm for the book with the children. Several said that the book had to be selected with the children's interests in mind for it to hold their attention.

Timing was also another factor that influenced engagement. Preservice teachers felt that teachers have to choose the right time of day when children are able to relax and focus. Also, in terms of timing, some preservice teachers said that they could not stop too often or too long during a reading to discuss the story or they would "lose the children," and they needed to "pay attention to the children's response" to determine when to move on. Along with this, space was important. Many preservice teachers said they preferred to have the children "gathered together and seated around on the floor rather than at their desks."

Responses to the Questionnaire #1

1. *What changes have you noticed in children's interactions during discussions?* In terms of the changes in children's interactions, preservice teachers noticed that the children became more open and responsive as they became accustomed to discussing the books. At first, responses were directed toward the teacher, but with time, the children began to talk more to each other.
    - They are realizing they are allowed to talk freely about the story. They have also had to learn to be respectful of others' opinions about the books.
    - They feel more free to discuss the story with me and with each other.
    - They seem more verbal as days go by. Some of the shy children are talking more. They try to predict what the story is about and discuss it with each other.
    - There are more interactions. At first only a few kids would participate in the discussion. Now almost all the kids participate.

2. *What kind of responses have you noticed?* Preservice teachers said that children's responses were based on their personal experiences as well as the text, included their feelings, likes, and dislikes, and usually involved thoughtful and creative responses.
    - The students love to tell about their past experiences.
    - I have been pleasantly surprised at the thoughtful responses I have been

getting. Sometimes they get off the subject, but most of the time they are right on track.

- I've noticed that they haven't always noticed what I thought they would.
- Thoughtful responses, free responses, wrong responses, unusual predictions.

3. *How are you encouraging students to appreciate the story?* To help children appreciate the story, preservice teachers said they tried to tie it to something personal and familiar in the children's own lives and every day experiences. They also indicated that discussion was a way of encouraging students to enjoy the story.

- By asking questions about the author's motive for writing the story and by questioning which parts or events they really liked or disliked and having them explain why!
- Reading with feelings and enjoyment.
- By involving them and giving them the control to get out of it what they can from each other instead of telling them what they need to notice and why.
- I always share with them the author and make a note if I know a book by the same author that they might be familiar with. After reading I ask them what they liked or didn't like about the book.

4. *How are you helping students understand the story?* Most of the preservice teachers said they were helping students understand the story through discussions. Many indicated the importance of relating the story to students' lives. More specifically, during discussions they asked a few key questions, built on students' responses, explained unknown words, clarified confusing sections, emphasized important points, and encouraged students to help each other by answering their questions and sharing ideas.

- I am helping students understand the story by relating it to their lives and experiences. I am discussing new vocabulary, new phrases, and new ideas.
- If they do not understand, they know they can ask questions. I also try to ask questions to help them understand.
- I like to ask them to place themselves in the character's position and see how they would feel and what they would do. I think this helps them get more out of the story.
- I am using prediction charts, cause/effect charts, and difference/similarity examples.

5. *What have you done differently since the first discussion?* Many of the preservice teachers said that they were allowing the children to initiate more, ask more questions, and talk to each other.

- I have really talked less. I allow the kids to lead the discussion and interact more freely.
- I pause more and let the students discuss anything they are thinking. I am more perceptive about when to pause and when to encourage questions for discussion.
- I am letting students make more predictions and ask more questions rather than me.
- I have tried to ask open-ended questions. I tried to wait for the students to answer the questions and to think—to allow think time.

Responses to Questionnaire #2

At the completion of all discussions, preservice teachers were asked to respond in writing to several questions to gain a sense of their overall impressions about literature discussions and have them evaluate what they had learned.

1. *What have you learned about student response to literature?* Preservice teachers' understandings reflected the following themes of engagement in meaningful reading and respecting children's idiosyncratic responses.
   - Sharing books help them build on their prior knowledge and engaged them in the story.
   - Children enjoy voicing their opinions about a topic and like to discuss stories after they've been read.
   - The more chances you give the children to interact with the text the more meaningful it becomes to them.
   - Children love to be participants in the story reading process. They learn more when they verbalize their thoughts rather than when they sit quietly and only listen.

2. *What have you learned about facilitating book discussions?* Preservice teachers reported that they learned a great deal about encouraging children to respond and interact appropriately, managing the discussions, and creating a risk-taking environment that would invite free expression.
   - It's important for you (teacher) to provide opportunities for the children to respond and interact.
   - The teacher doesn't always have to be the one to initiate the discussion or to constantly ask the questions. The teacher needs to provide an environment in which the children feel free and safe to share ideas.
   - If I am excited about the book and find it enjoyable, then the children usually are too.
   - It is important to ask students what they think the story is about and to stop at parts in the story to allow the children the opportunity to make predictions.

- It is best to back off and allow students to lead the discussion, but be there for them as a facilitator.

One preservice teacher found it difficult to integrate literature discussions into the regular classroom schedule and had some difficulty working with the students.

- I have learned that the children have to be willing to read with you and to be willing to participate. I am in an intermediate school and it has been hard for me to get the 5th and 6th graders to cooperate. It has also been hard to take time out of my teacher's schedule to do this.

However she said she would hold discussions in her future classroom.

- I hope to do this in my future classroom so I can get to know my students and I can check their levels of comprehension.

3. *What do children learn when they discuss books?* Active and meaningful reading, comprehension strategies, and participation strategies were general themes reflected by preservice teachers' responses to this question.

- Discussing books helps get the children actively involved in the reading with active participation rather than passive listening. And the children learn to pay attention to the details of the story.
- When children discuss books they learn that the written word has meaning. Print makes sense. Children learn that their opinion has merit— what they have to say is important. This raises their self-esteem.
- They learn how to comprehend (make predictions), comprehension strategies that will help them when they read other texts.
- They are learning to think and say how they see things. They find out that not everyone sees things the same way.
- They learn how to predict, recognize detail, sequence events, which are all useful in independent projects.
- They learn a good life lesson on how to conduct themselves in a group discussion.

4. *Will you continue to hold book discussions in the future?* All of the preservice teachers answered "Yes" to this question. Their reasons varied but reflected common themes of positive benefits of discussion for enhancing understanding, actively involving students in reading, and engagement with books and other creative activities.

- Book discussions are great springboards that open doors to numerous activities and lessons. They are a creative way of teaching.
- Students definitely benefit from this. They learn that reading can be enjoyable.
- Discussions help students comprehend. They hold their interest and keep them actively involved in the reading.
- Book discussions get them interested in the book, and allow them the

opportunity to become involved in the story. I feel involvement will enhance their comprehension of the reading material.

Discussion

This study explored preservice teachers' literature discussions with children in an attempt to discover what practical knowledge they might learn about literary response and active meaning-making. According to Kessels and Korthagen (1996), perceptual knowledge, or phronesis, is practical knowledge that is context specific. Phronesis involves an understanding of complex and ambiguous situations by studying the concrete details of each case. With respect to the relationship between theory and practice, the educator's job is to "help the student become aware of salient features of the experience . . . ," and "not to teach a number of concepts" (Kessels & Korthagen, 1996, p. 21).

One of the major benefits of this study was that the preservice teachers were in the position to study the concrete details of their own literature discussions. Through reflection about their discussions, preservice teachers were able to study children's idiosyncratic responses and interactions that were unique to the situation. They experienced for themselves the liveliness of children enthusiastically sharing their personal understandings and socially constructing meaning (Bakhtin, 1981; Vygotsky, 1986). As a result, these preservice teachers saw and heard the transactional theory in action (Rosenblatt, 1978). Reader response was no longer merely an abstraction, a theory that they read about in their textbooks or talked about in their courses. Now preservice teachers had first-hand knowledge and convincing evidence that children's responses to books were a springboard to lively discussions and active meaning-making. They saw the fabric of discussion as it was richly woven with children's responses, colored with personal knowledge and experiences, and focused on understanding the story. They heard thought-provoking questions and insightful comments as they came from the children. Moreover, the preservice teachers quickly learned that they did not have to "be the sage on the stage." They perceived that it was not necessary to quiz the children. Instead, the children initiated the talk and set the agenda for discussion based on their personal responses to the books (Dugan, 1997; McGee, 1996; Vogt, 1996).

As these preservice teachers interacted with the children, they learned how to be flexible and facilitate response-centered talk. According to McGee (1996) teachers need to plan for and manage this talk by establishing routines, encouraging the children to be active listeners, and to take turns sharing ideas. These preservice teachers perceived that student ownership of the discussion was crucial and discovered that this required them to ask fewer explicit questions, and allowed for more open questions. However, this resulted in highly energized discussions in which many children were talking at once. Several preservice teachers wrote about how uncomfortable and out of control they felt. Yet, they did not throw in the towel. Instead, they learned to manage the interaction by encouraging students to take turns, listen to one another, and respect what their classmates had to say.

A strong affective element was evident in the preservice teachers' perceptions of children's enjoyment and satisfaction derived from reading together and discussing books. This is important because children's attitudes toward reading and interest in reading can influence their engagement in reading (Wigfield, 1997). The discussions serve to stimulate interest in reading, scaffold the process of forming interpretations, and encourage children to take responsibility for making sense of the book by putting them in the center of the meaning-making experience (Gambrell & Almasi, 1996).

Affect is also evident in a reciprocal relationship between teacher perceptions and student perceptions of learning (Skinner, Wellborn, & Connell, 1990). That is, teachers positively influence students' sense of control over learning through shared activities and choice; and students' sense of control over their learning, in turn, positively influences their academic performance by increasing engagement (Sweet, 1997). Given this relationship, teachers need to realize that they can positively influence children's reading attitudes and should examine instructional methods that will promote interest and engagement in reading. As Kessels and Korthagen (1996) assert, ". . . the task of the teacher educator is to help the student teacher explore and refine his or her perceptions" (p. 21).

One preservice teacher discovered "a moment of truth and revelation" when she realized that "the safe environment and social reinforcement allowed students to come out of themselves." Underlying this comment was a hint of skepticism. Some preservice teachers admitted that they had doubts at first about the potential benefits of literature discussions, but in the end were proven wrong. The discussions were a time and place where students could take risks with their thinking, but it was not until preservice teachers experienced this that they were convinced. These preservice teachers found discussions to be enlightening, satisfying, and enjoyable not only for the children but also for themselves. As one preservice teacher reported, they realized how much "fun" they themselves could have along with the children "when they all take part in the storytime event."

In terms of literary response theory (Rosenblatt, 1938, 1978), the reflections of preservice teachers indicated that they perceived meaningful reading to be more a matter of responding to the story with feelings and personal stories than a matter of getting the right message. In a practical sense, these preservice teachers realized that they needed to approach the reading with an open mind to invite various responses from students. An overwhelming majority of preservice teachers' perceptions focused on the children and their meaning constructions, as well as their own efforts to help the children participate in this process. Similar to findings of Wolf, et al (1996), viewing reading as a constructive process, these preservice teachers encouraged and accepted multiple responses from the children. They also recognized the importance of actively involving students in reading as a meaning-making experience by sharing ideas and reported that the children "loved being involved in the text" as a result of "predicting" and "responding." They perceived that "children were learning from one another" as well as "from the story," and acknowledged the importance of bringing children's prior knowledge to the reading. As one preservice teacher put it, "I saw those little prior knowledge wheels fast at work."

Reflection proves to be a powerful medium for the development of perceptual knowledge about teaching (Schon, 1983). Reflection can help preservice teachers self-evaluate and self-monitor their teaching. According to Shulman (1987), reflection is valuable because it can make implicit meanings explicit. Within the context of preservice teachers' reflections, teacher educators can engage in dialogues with prospective teachers to call attention to the key elements of the process of instruction and learning to help them see how and why specific interactions are effective. Reflection can also promote meaningful inquiry about teaching by bringing questions out in the open. As with the preservice teachers in this study, reflection can help prospective teachers take a problem–solving approach toward their own instruction to address the challenges of teaching and explore alternative solutions through dialogues with more experienced teachers.

Implications for Teacher Education

These findings have significant implications for educators who want to shift instruction from transmission, teacher-directed to transactional, student-centered formats. Do we want teachers who teach strictly by the script without thought or consideration for the children? Or do we want teachers who are responsive and sensitive to the children? Teachers need to involve children in active and meaningful reading. Response-centered discussions allow children to participate in the process of making sense. However, teachers, especially novice teachers, need actual teaching experiences with discussions so they know what to expect in terms of children's talk and interactions. And they need frameworks that support their efforts so they will be successful. To invite children to share responses, then follow their lead and build discussions around their responses requires teachers to be perceptive and responsive. They must tune in to the children, or be "kid listeners" (Walker,

1996). Listening to children's talk about books, preservice teachers "learned what the children knew and were thinking" so that they could "build on their responses." Scripted lessons cannot accomplish this. A teacher can.

Teachers must be willing to explore and teacher educators must be supportive of inquiry and reflection. Responsive teaching "is thoroughly subjective" (Kessels & Korthagen, 1996, p.21) and concrete situations are essential so that knowledge can be reconstructed. Teacher educators cannot expect to transmit perceptual knowledge, or phronesis, to their students. Likewise, students should not be expected to become perceptive automatically in a few short weeks of student teaching. Perceptual knowledge develops out of teaching experiences that can be perceived.

Finally, teacher educators need to take advantage of opportunities in which scaffolding and reflection can be used to raise preservice teachers' awareness of the elements of responsive instruction in connection with real teaching experiences. Teacher education programs should be closely linked with children, teachers, and schools so prospective teachers *see* and *feel* the complexity and diversity of teaching.

Future Research

Ashton (1996) calls for an expansion of programs that offer prospective teachers "time to develop the complex understandings of self and students . . . , and . . . research to help identify important content and ways to enable prospective teachers to incorporate that knowledge into their practice in meaningful ways" (p. 22). We must look for ways to involve preservice teachers in ongoing teaching experiences and provide the guidance of experienced teachers who can scaffold reflection and encourage exploration of the complex details of real teaching situations. Professional development schools offer a wide range of integrated and collaborative teaching experiences (Darling-Hammond, 1994). These programs should be explored to provide a clearer description of the experiences offered, to determine how the experiences are perceived by preservice teachers, and to investigate how reflection about teaching impacts novice teachers' ability to shift into learner-centered, responsive teaching modes.

References

Ashton, P. T. (1996). Improving the preparation of teachers. *Educational Researcher, 25*(9), 21-22, 35.

Bakhtin, M. M. (1981). *The dialogic imagination.* Austin: University of Texas Press.

Bogdan, R. C., & Biklen, S.K. (1992). *Qualitative research for education: An introduction to theory and methods* (2nd ed.) Boston, MA: Allyn & Bacon.

Darling-Hammond, L. (1994). *Professional development schools.* New York, NY: Teachers College Press.

Dugan, J. (1997). Transactional Literature Discussions: Engaging students in the appreciation and understanding of literature. *The Reading Teacher, 51*(2), 86-96.

Glaser, B., & Strauss, A. (1967). *The discovery of grounded theory.* New York: Aldine.

Gambrell, L. B., & Almasi, J.F. (1996). *Lively discussions! Fostering engaged reading.* Newark, DE: International Reading Association.

Kessels, J.P.A.M., & Korthagen, F.A.J. (1996). The relationship between theory and practice: Back to the classics. *Educational Researcher, 25*(3), 17-22.

McGee, L. M. (1996). Response-centered talk: Windows on children's thinking. In L. B. Gambrell & J. F. Almasi (Eds.) *Lively discussions! Fostering engaged reading* (pp. 194-207).

Rosenblatt, L. M. (1938). *Literature as exploration.* (4th ed.) New York: Modern language Association.

Rosenblatt, L. M. (1978). *The reader, the text, the poem: The transactional theory of the literary work.* Carbondale, IL: Southern Illinois University Press.

Schon, D. A. (1983). *The reflective practitioner: How professionals think in action.* New York: Basic Books.

Shulman, L. S. (1987). Knowledge and teaching: Foundation of the new reform. *Harvard Educational Review, 57*(1), 1-22.

Skinner, E. A., Wellborn, J. G., & Connell, J. P. (1990). What it takes to do well in school and whether I've got it: A process model of perceived control and children's engagement and achievement in school. *Journal of Educational Psychology, 82*, 22-32.

Sweet, A. P. (1997). Teacher perceptions of student motivation and their relation to literacy learning. In J.T. Guthrie & A. Wigfield (Eds.) *Reading engagement: Motivating readers through integrated instruction* (pp. 86-101). Newark, DE: International Reading Association.

Vogt, M. (1996). Creating a response-centered curriculum with literature discussion groups. In L. B. Gambrell, & J. F. Almasi. (Eds.) *Lively discussions! Fostering engaged reading.* (pp. 181-193). Newark, DE: International Reading Association.

Vygotsky, L. S. (1986). *Thought and language.* Cambridge, MA: MIT Press.

Walker, B. J. (1996). Discussions that focus on strategies and self-assessment. In L. B. Gambrell, & J. F. Almasi (Eds.) *Lively discussions! Fostering engaged reading.* (pp. 286-296). Newark, DE: International Reading Association.

Wigfield, A. Children's motivations for reading and reading engagement. In J. T. Guthrie & A. Wigfield (Eds.) *Reading engagement: Motivating readers through integrated instruction* (pp. 14-33). Newark, DE: International Reading Association.

Wolf, S. A., Carey, A. A., & Mieras, E. L. (1996). "What is this literachurch stuff anyway?": Preservice teachers' growth in understanding children's literary response. *Reading Research Quarterly, 31*(2), 130-157.

Appendix. Themes of Preservice Teachers' Reflections on Literature Discussions

Instructional Practice
Teacher needs to model strategies for mapping, organizing, and brainstorming ideas.

Teacher needs to build prior knowledge before reading.

Teacher needs to arouse students' interest.

Teacher needs to manage the talk.

Teacher needs to highlight and discuss literary techniques.

Sometimes teacher needs to discuss vocabulary that *students* call attention to or question; meaning may differ because of context.

Teachers need to manage discussion.

Teachers didn't have to ask questions, but merely asked students to share thoughts wonderings, this worked well!

Teachers must make decisions about book selection; group arrangement, activities, focus, interaction.

Student Response
Responses vary from student to student; unexpected responses; creative responses.

Gender differences in response depending on interests and knowledge.

Students disagree, but come to a conclusion students need to learn from mistakes.

Students respond by relating personal stories.

Students respond by relating to the characters.

Students respond with feelings and emotions.

Student theories are important to the meaning-making.

Individual theories are important understanding the story.

Students need to solve problems themselves.

Increased involvement enhances their enjoyment and comprehension.

Teachers should read students more books so they have more experience responding, making mistakes and learning from them.

Making animal sounds in response to the reading.

Teachers can learn about the children through discussions: they are people with emotions; they can understand, empathize, and are considerate and kind.

Grouping
Students need more participation in small groups.

Some teachers prefer small group, but still they must monitor interaction.

Teacher should assign roles and encourage groups to work on one goal or
objective.

Teacher groups students to encourage problem solving and more participation.

Students form groups and teacher places anyone who has not chosen a group.

Children gather in a group and sit on the floor.

Intertextual Connections

Reading across texts for compare/contrast variations of genres, multiculturalism.

Using other resources for text, i.e. internet.

Genres-fairy tales, mysteries, expository and narrative texts are not just for
gifted children.

Books present many possibilities for learning.

Teachers explore different ways of encouraging students to interact with texts.

Some books are better for prewriting, thinking and discussion.

Repetitive patterns of text encourage students to read along.

Collaboration

Students generate several theories, all come to decision through collaboration, shared thinking.

Students respect other ideas, learn to get along, learn to agree; all because of
collaborative atmosphere.

The atmosphere needs to be *collaborative* so students will share and respect
each other.

Students need common goals so they will work together.

Reading and Writing Connections

Reading leads to writing that students want to do.

Reading and writing go hand-in-hand.

Reading a discussion helps develop an awareness of text language.

Literature provides springboards for writing their (students) own books.

Both are creative processes.

Children use their imaginations to read and write.

Cultural Awareness

Reading opens many avenues of thinking and exploring diversity issues.

Celebrating differences.

Helping children understand that we are all special.

Children need to learn to respect other's opinions.

Children learn about each other, who they are and where they come from,
in discussions.

Factors that Affect Engagement

Sometimes students don't want to listen to the story; timing and the book are important; choose the right book and the right time to read it.

Learn to hold students' attention, especially younger children; not stopping too often or too long to discuss the story; discuss before and after; but not as much during.

Depends on the group when discussion works best. But when students read along they are more attentive and can discuss during as well.

Children who have been read to appear to be more involved and entertained.

Encouraging Metacognitive Awareness in Preservice Literacy Courses

Jane Brady Matanzo
Deborah L. Harris

Florida Atlantic University

Abstract

Metacognition means knowing about knowing or one's self knowledge as a learner, knowledge of given tasks, and the ability to monitor oneself during learning experiences. The authors hypothesized that the more preservice reading methodology students become metacognitively aware, the more importance and value they will give to building like metacognitive awareness in their students. It initially was found that the preservice students had limited knowledge of what metacognition involved, its relationship to reading and learning effectiveness, and what they did themselves metacognitively as readers. Course instruction was planned to enhance and develop more metacognitive awareness in the preservice students and to observe metacognitive behaviors as they worked with elementary students in the schools. The findings are that the more metacognitive preservice students became, the more they encouraged students with whom they interacted to be metacognitive in terms of self-appraisal, task understanding, and self-monitoring.

You know, I finally *understand* how and why to do such things as comparing two characters in depth or to monitor my reading and thinking when it doesn't seem to make sense. I'm thinking about thinking more! I know you said a goal was for us to be strategic in our teaching so we could help our students be strategic in their reading. I have a large store of strategies to use and am now doing them more automatically. It's making a difference in how I'm interacting with my students and getting them to think more about thinking and why they do what they do.

This comment was part of a journal reflection made by a former methodology course student during her internship. It was as if the discovery light bulb suddenly clicked and the input she had during her literacy methodology courses about metacognition and strategy instruction now made sense and became a more activated presence in her teaching. In considering the implications of this remark, it occurred to us that perhaps the more metacognitively aware our students could become during their university preparatory courses, the more importance and value they might give to instilling metacognitive awareness in their future students and in students with whom they interacted during preservice clinical experiences. We found ourselves contemplating ways to increase meta-awareness about metacognition!

To ascertain just what our students did know and practice in terms of their own metacognitive awareness, we devised both individual and small group consensus questionnaires. Our findings encouraged us to modify and extend our emphasis on metacognitive development as we instructed our courses. This article presents a pre- and post analysis of our students' metacognitive awareness, strategies used during our courses to increase metacognitive awareness, and the effect such modifications had on both the preservice students and their professors.

Theoretical and Definitional Support

Prior to beginning our project, we felt we needed to base what we would do in our classes theoretically. In addition, we needed to agree on a definition of metacognition and the scope of it that we would emphasize. This led us to seek answers to three questions:

1. What is metacognition and how is it defined?
2. Can university students become more metacognitive?
3. Does a teacher's own metacognitive knowledge facilitate the transfer and/or the importance of that knowledge?

What is Metacognition and How is it Defined?

The term, metacognition, coined by cognitive psychologists, was initially defined by Flavell (1978) who claimed it was "knowledge that takes as its object or regulates any aspect of any cognitive endeavor" (p. 187). Stewart and Tei (1983) have defined it as thinking about thinking which they elaborated as one having an awareness of his or her knowledge. They felt that age and one's reading experiences were related to the extent of one's awareness. Brown (1985) felt metacognition had two specific aspects which were knowing what one knows and being able to regulate that knowledge. However, the latter aspect, regulation, is not constant and may be dependent on the strategies they know and use, their awareness of their knowledge, and any prior knowledge of what is being learned. The skills associated with regulation are planning, evaluation, and monitoring with the consciousness of monitoring increasing gradually (Baker & Brown, 1984; Paris, Lipson, and Wixson, 1984). Palincsar and Brown (1984) did a series of studies and found that four cognitive activities, summarization, questioning, clarifying, and predicting, helped to improve reading comprehension and control of the reading act by students. These four categories are encompassed in the Reciprocal Teaching Strategy (Palincsar & Brown, 1984).

Paris, Lipson and Wixson (1983) categorized metacognition as declarative, conditional, and procedural knowledge. In terms of reading, they noted that the three areas referred to readers knowing what strategies worked and being able to verbalize what was used and why, knowing when they needed to employ a strategy and why, and knowing how to use given strategies effectively. Vacca, Vacca, & Gove (1991) also divided metacognition into three categories: self-knowledge, task knowledge, and self-monitoring. They felt that metacognition encompassed one's self-concept or knowledge of oneself as a learner or reader, knowledge of what strategies are appropriate to a task, and the ability to self monitor. Wixson and Peters purported that the skills needed for these three areas are critical for efficient reading. (1987). In general, the literature supports the notion that metacognition is knowing about knowing. Regardless of what definition or sub-categories are implemented, the value of relating metacognition to reading is that increased focus is put upon the knowledge, responsibility, and decisions made by the reader (Babbs and Moe, 1983).

Can University Students Become More Metacognitive?

It has been shown that the older and more proficient the reader, the more metacognitive that reader should be (Stewart and Tei, 1983). Metacognitive processing, for the most part, appears to be late in development, is not constant, and is related to more formal thought (Brown, 1985; Brown and Smiley, 1977; Costa, 1991; Tunmer, Herriman, and Nesdale, 1988).

Learning log assignments in university courses can contribute to making more conscious one's own awareness and processing by having students reflect on specific cognitive behaviors and having them explore and evaluate their own thinking and learning (Commander, N. E. and Smith, B. D., 1996).

Several university programs have developed processes to attempt to strengthen the metacognitive awareness of their students. An interdisciplinary science and mathematics course was established to increase students' metacognitive awareness of the learning processes involved in their use of core skills, critical thinking, and relating content learned to real life experiences. Faculty-student interviews, student portfolios, and focus group interviews were used to ascertain growth at the end of the semester. Those who seemed more metacognitive in their thinking and understanding of the subject matter appeared strongest in procedural and subjective ways of knowing. Negative attitudes toward the subject areas at the beginning of the study seemed the most resistant to change (Freeman, C. C. & Smith, D. L., 1997). Professors of a general chemistry course integrated cooperative learning, class discussions, concept mapping, and lecturing into their course and observed student levels of participation. They found that by incorporating multiple modes of learning that the metacognitive skills necessary for mastering the content of the course increased. They felt that the different modes of information delivery were reinforcing and helped the students transfer their knowledge to other learning situations (Francisco, J. S., Nicoll, G, and Trautmann, M., 1998). Concept mapping also was used as an instructional technique in a graduate psychology course. This technique guided and facilitated students to construct knowledge as a metacognitive strategy. It also helped students monitor the expansion of their knowledge and to discard misconceptions (Gravett, S. J. & Swart, E. (1997). One university department designed the Strategic Content Learning (SCL) Approach to help students with learning disabilities become more self-regulated in their completion of academic tasks. Students were tutored individually and in small groups to gain an awareness of strategies that would help them learn and retain content more effectively. Findings indicated a significant increase in what students believed, knew, and expressed metacognitively about tasks, strategies, and ways they now monitored themselves while learning content. Before the study, the 19 students did minimal to no self-regulation (Butler, D., 1997).

Mack and Tama (1997) explored ways preservice teachers could expand their own metacognitive knowledge by doing a series of case studies which also showed the application of what the students learned to practicum experiences with secondary students. They developed two assessment forms, Metacognitive Check on Teaching and Diagnostic Awareness of Students' Abilities. Comments which emerged from these two forms indicated that preservice teachers were able to examine what they did in classrooms and were developing strategies to modify what might be needed to improve their teaching experiences. The latter checklist helped them to see that students with whom they worked seemed to exceed at tasks when they were given opportunities to reflect upon what they had done and to make decisions about what might work the next time they did such an activitiy. The greater degree to which these preservice teachers were able to verbalize awareness of their own metacognition, the more insight and skill they appeared to have to increase the metacognitive abilities of their students. Risko (1995) developed video disc classroom case studies focusing on remedial reading instruction for both graduate students who were classroom teachers and students in her preservice classes to view and analyze. By the end of the semester, the preservice teachers were more aligned with the experienced teachers in perceiving what remediation was needed to help a struggling reader in multi-dimensional terms. They also appeared more aware, verbal, and confident as to what elements constituted appropriate strategies and what they themselves could do as readers, thinkers, and implementers. The use of the videodiscs and opportunities for reflection and discussion influenced preservice students' beliefs and actions concerning literacy and its classroom applications.

A University of New England study (Hollingworth, R., 1998) suggests, in terms of outcomes with university chemistry students, that professors could be more effective in developing metacognitive skills in students they teach. They discovered that many students entering the university had not been taught strategies for examining or improving their metacognitive or self-knowledge abilities. They learned through interactions with students that the most lacking element of knowing what one knows was to link that knowledge to the real world. Immediate feedback and increased control by students for their own learning helped them succeed to a higher degree.

An important finding gleaned from most of the studies was that students reported that the university classroom environment was supportive in helping them understand what they were doing themselves in terms of literacy and it gave them opportunities to simulate ways to transfer their understandings to students they would work with in classrooms. The studies cited reinforced our belief that we could stimulate metacognitive awareness among our preservice education students and encourage them to transfer the 'what, why, how, and when they know' to students they will impact.

Does a Teacher's Own Metacognitive Knowledge Facilitate the Transfer and/or the Importance of that Knowledge?

Since we are preparing teachers to teach reading and the degree of metacognitive development appears to be pivotal to reading comprehension, we were curious if the extent of a teacher's metacognitive knowledge might affect his or her modes of instruction. Pressley implies this relationship when he states that "the most compelling comprehension strategies instruction probably is being designed in schools by people who have both knowledge of the research and theoretical literature and the realities of classrooms" (Pressley, M., et. al., 1995, p. 211).

Weir (1998) returned to teaching middle school students after a 12 year absence and found her students to be passive readers and poor comprehenders. She took the initiative to read and study current professional literature and literacy research and found that developing the metacognitive abilities of students was a common theme that had come to the forefront of literacy instruction during her non-teaching years. She developed two inquiry questions for her students to ask themselves as they read: 1)How can we know if we understand what we read? and 2) What can we do to make sure we understand what we read? (p.459) She next made a list of possible strategies and analyzed the tasks involved that students would need to be successful in meeting the demands of these questions. She instructed her students in the given strategies and the result was that her students became more active readers as well as metacognitive thinkers and practicioners. However, the underlying accomplishment of this action research is best stated in the author's words: "I see now that my students were not the only ones who received a metacognitive jump-start. . . . reading professional research has prompted me to examine my teaching and seek innovation" (p.467). This teacher found that by becoming more aware of her own metacognition and seeing how her knowledge and skills might relate to her students, her students gained in their own metacognitive development.

Many researchers imply metacognitive awareness is gained through teacher modeling of practices such as think-alouds, and a teacher understanding, sharing, and explaining strategies that will help one be more knowing about what one knows as well as knowing and monitoring what one needs to do under various literacy related situations (Forget, M. A. & Morgan, R. F., 1997; Beeth, M. E., 1998; Bourner, T., 1998; Baumann, J. F., Jones, L. A., & Seifert-Kessell, 1993; Ratekin, N., Simpson, M., Alvermann, D. E., & Dishner, E. K., 1985; Barton, M. L., 1997; Gijselaers, W. H., 1996; Seng, S. 1997; Underwood, 1997). Teachers must guide students and, as a prerequisite, they must understand the processes and be able to know and express clearly what they know and understand themselves (Murphy, 1997). The literature indicates that teachers must be metacognitive in terms of what they do to be literate and be able to articulate their knowledge and skills to the students they teach.

Method
Setting and Participants
This study was conducted with 62 preservice students enrolled in one of two courses, with 30 students in two sections of Reading: Elementary School 1 , and 32 students in two sections of Reading: Elementary School 2. They will hereafter be referred to as Reading I and Reading II students. A section of each of the courses was taught by two different professors from two separate regional campuses of a southeastern state university. The students participating were in their junior and senior years of a teacher preparation program respectively. The first course was a comprehensive Foundations of Reading course. The second course was a Diagnostic Reading course where students administered at least two informal reading inventories and remediated

given students a minimum of three times. The first course was a prerequisite and provided the base for the second reading course.

Definition Selection

Since two professors and four classes were involved, it was felt we needed to select a similar delineation and scope of metacognition that we would present to all four classes and that would be represented in our surveys. We selected the Vacca, Vacca, & Gove (1991) three stated categories of metacognition as they provided a simplistic and easy to understand format for our students. Therefore, for this study, metacognition is defined as knowing about knowing in terms of 1) f self-knowledge, 2) task knowledge, and 3) self-monitoring.

Procedure

The procedure included an individual metacognitive pre-assessment, a group metacognitive pre assessment, modifications in instructional delivery, observation of preservice students teaching and interacting with elementary students, and post-course metacognitive reflection and response. Students in all four classes completed the same assessments so comparisons between students who had not yet had a reading course and those who were beginning a second reading course could be made.

Individual Pre-Assessment. An open-ended individual response form was administered preservice students during the first meeting of each of the four classes. The two professors developed items they felt would give them insight as to how metacognitive the preservice students were prior to beginning formal instruction. The Individual Metacognitive Pre-assessment is in Appendix A.

Group Pre-Assessment. An open-ended response form was administered preservice student discussion groups of four to six students, depending upon enrollment, during the first meeting of each of the four classes. Students were instructed to take their individual pre-assessment for reference to the group setting to which they were assigned randomly from a precourse roster. This group reflection opportunity after reflecting personally was planned because researchers have found that social exchanges and contextual factors such as group sharing and reflection affect metacognitive knowledge and behaviors (Gijselaers, W. H., 1996; Beeth, M.,1998; Alexander, J. M. & Manion, V., 1997; Hansen, J. & Hubbard, R., 1984; Masataka, K., 1997; Chiu, C. W. T., 1998). We were interested to observe if students were reinforced or swayed through peer interaction with some of the metacognitive related items they had responded to individually and what they would do and negotiate in a group setting as the group needed to present one response for group interaction. The Group Metacognitive Pre-Assessment is in Appendix B.

Modifications in Instructional Delivery. We brainstormed possible instructional strategies that might apply to encourage metacognitive development. The research (Langer, J., 1984; Graves, Penn & Cooke, 1985; Herber, 1978; Nagy, 1988, Johnson & Pearson, 1978; Raphael, 1986; Hansen and Pearson, 1983; Ogle, 1986; Wong and Au, 1984; Bean, Singer, and Cowen, 1985; Kintsch & Van Dijk, 1978; Lapp and Flood, 1986; Stow, W., 1997; Palincsar & Brown, 1986; McNeil, 1984; Flood, 1984; Sanacore, 1984; White & Frederiksen, 1998; Barton, M. E., 1997; Weir, 1998; Hollingworth, 1998; Commander, N. E. & Smith, B. D., 1996; Butler, D. L., 1997; Geimer, T, Krzystofczyk, Luczak, S, & Talach, S., 1998; Kirby & Pedwell, 1991; Cunningham, 1990, Heller, 1986; Schallert & Kleiman, 1979; Costa, 1991; Shore & Dover, 1987; Pearson & Gallagher, 1983; Garner, 1987; Seng, 1997) recommends many instructional means to encourage metacognitive development including activating prior knowledge, making inferences, identifying the most important content, summarizing, using fix-its like looking back in the text or reading on to make sense, retelling, doing teacher and student think-alouds, employing concept maps and other graphic organizers, utilizing peer or larger cooperative groups, holding focused discussion groups, doing self and reciprocal questioning, and using anticipation and study guides.

The two professors involved decided to consider the before, during, and after aspects of reading as well as ways for students to reflect. They did not try to replicate each other but agreed to teach strategies that would focus on prior learning and purpose setting, monitoring while reading, retelling, and providing a time at the end of each class period for the preservice students to reflect upon themselves as readers and learners individually and in cooperative groups throughout the course.

Among the strategies emphasized by the professors were 1) KWLSH (What do you *know?*, What do you *want* to know?, What have you *learned?*, What do you *still* want to know?, and *How* will you find that information?) (Matanzo, 1997); 2) doing professor, small group, and individual think alouds; 3) using fix-it strategies such as asking does it make sense, reading a passage again, reading ahead, or practicing given word attack strategies; 4) retelling parts of chapters from their texts; and 5) journaling or reflecting orally individually and in small groups at the end of each class session on what was learned that day, what was not understood, what needed further explanation, and why they thought so.

Observations of Preservice Students' Teaching and Interacting with Elementary Students. Each of the courses had a clinical component where the students were observed teaching small groups of elementary students approximately four times each semester. During this time, the professors kept anecdotal records and noted any metacognitive development encouraged by the preservice teachers. Primarily, they were observing to see if they were modeling any of the metacognitive behaviors previously modeled or experienced by them during the regular course sessions.

Post-Course Metacognitive Reflection and Response. At the conclusion of the course, the individual pre-assessment and the group pre-assessment were returned. Students were asked to reflect on their initial responses and compare that knowledge to what they knew and practiced now metacognitively. They did this orally with their original group on the Group Metacognitive Pre- assessment. Reactions were shared with the other groups in the class. The students in Reading II were asked to reflect on their metacognitive growth in terms of what they had learned and experienced in both Reading I and Reading II as they found it difficult to separate the continuity and knowledge gained from one course to the other. Hence, for their prompt, course was plural. Each student was then asked to respond in writing to the following prompt:

> An aspect stressed in this course(s) was the development of metacognitive knowledge: 1) knowledge of oneself as a reader/learner; 2) knowledge of given literacy tasks and how to approach them; and 3) the ability to monitor and adjust one's reading to achieve greater understanding and enjoyment.

> Reflect on what you have gained in this course(s) in terms of your own literacy and if and how the content and experiences have or have not affected YOUR OWN metacognition as a learner in the above three areas, particularly as they relate to your own reading and writing.

> In other words, do you feel you have grown in your own reading/ writing/thinking abilities and processes as a result of this course(s)? Has what you learned affected how you read and write and feel about being a reader or writer yourself? How? Do you use any of the strategies taught in your own learning and/or for university assignments? If so, which ones do you use and how have your found them helpful to you? If you don't use any of the strategies learned in this course(s) in your own learning/assignments, support why you haven't. Do you think a teacher's own self-knowledge in these three metacognitive areas will make him or her a more effective teacher of reading? Support why you do or don't think so.

Data Collection

The data was collected in five ways: 1) Written responses on the Individual Metacognitive Pre-assessment; 2) Written responses on the Group Metacognitive Pre-assessment; 3) Anecdotal records by the professors during the in school teaching experiences of the preservice students; 4) Post-course oral group reflection and sharing; and 5) Post-course individual written reflection for the given prompt.

Limitations

Several limitations were considered as the data were analyzed. Although the two professors taught from syllabi with common objectives, personalities and the preciseness and emphases of their delivery varied. The time frame for collecting data was similar but varied slightly at times during the semester due to holidays and other variations in class schedules. Many of the students involved in the Reading II classes had different professors at various of the university's four campuses including adjunct professors which may have affected the degree of some of the metacognitive knowledge and attitudes expressed.

Since two of the data analysts were professors of the given courses for this study, their attempt to be fair in their interpretations of the data gathered were subject to natural bias. Having an additional, non-involved party analyze the data and work significantly with them to establish a common consensus of agreement, hopefully balanced any bias that might have affected the findings.

The emphasis of the metacognitive instruction and its subsequent analysis focused upon the three aspects of metacognition delineated by Vacca, Vacca, and Gove (1991). Although students' reading assignments and the extension the professors provided during their teaching went beyond these three designated aspects, they were the focus of this study as they were easily defined, understood, and categorized.

Data Analysis

Since qualitative data were collected, the professors and one independent reviewer analyzed the five sets of data seeking patterns of response and categorizing those findings using an agreed upon interpretive stance to guide their analysis (Atkinson, Delamont, & Hammersley, 1988). A random sample of data was collected and analyzed on the three metacognitive criteria and ideas conveyed through the written expression of Reading I and Reading II preservice students by each of the three analysts. Interpretations were compared and showed relative concurrence at a minimum of 90% on all items analyzed. A grid was developed to correlate findings. Two stances were used: the professorial point of view in terms of strategy appropriateness and effectiveness and the university students' point of view in terms of self-awareness and her/his implementation of metacognitive instruction. The analyses compared responses made on the individual and group pre-assessment data items with post-course group data and post-course individual reflections to ascertain if any behaviors, beliefs, or knowledge were expressed differently. The data were analyzed for patterns of growth in terms of the three categories given our definition of metacognition. In addition, the anecdotal records were analyzed and categorized for patterns of behavior expressed while the preservice students worked with elementary school students.

Findings
Individual Metacognitive Pre-Assessment
The findings were analyzed and discussed under five categories: 1) Individual metacognitive pre-assessment; 2) Group metacognitive pre-assessment; 3) Anecdotal records; 4) Post- course oral group reflection; and 5) Post-course individual written reflection for the given prompt. This latter category is divided into four segments: 1) Knowledge of self; 2) Knowledge of task; 3) Knowledge of ways to self-monitor; and 4) Preservice teachers' perceptions about whether a teacher needs to be metacognitive to encourage one's students to be metacognitive.

Students were asked to respond to 12 items (See Appendix A) ranging from defining metacognition, describing what they do before, during, and after reading, to describing themselves as readers. When asked to define metacognition, 66 percent of the Reading I students and 43 percent of the Reading II students gave no answer.

The 33 percent of the Reading I students who responded appeared to be guessing with 18 percent knowing it had something to do with knowing or thinking. Fifty percent of the Reading II students knew it had to do with knowledge of oneself and knowing how to learn. The most frequent response was knowing what you know, knowing when you don't know, and knowing what to do about it which related to the three dimensions of our definition.

Items 2, 3, 4, 5, 6 and 12 dealt with what they would do to help students be more metacognitive and what they would do before, during, and after reading with students. When asked ways they would help a student be more metacognitive, 80 percent of the Reading I students left the item blank and those who responded suggested that students be shown examples and that one should take time to answer questions and explain. Reading II students were slightly more astute with 56 percent responding and offering answers such as to help them understand the mistakes they are making on a regular basis and to know why they may be making them, have them read and think aloud to see how thinking about thinking helps get more of their own meaning out of the selection, make use of KWL charts, encourage them to read more, ask questions and reflect on what they read, and know the best ways in which each student learns.

When asked what they would do with students before, during, and after reading, 83 percent of the Reading I students and 100 percent of the Reading II students responded. Although the Reading II answers were more sophisticated and often reflected what was taught and experienced by them in Reading I, the Reading I students' answers were serious in nature and, generally, appropriate. Responses for before reading for both groups included looking at the title and pictures to making predictions, scanning the book, giving an overview and involving the students, making sure they were familiar first with the words and ideas in the story, and introducing vocabulary. During reading responses included circulating among the students and helping them, encouraging them to think about what will happen next and what the final outcome will be and why, checking to see if predictions were correct and then making additional predictions; asking them questions , jotting down unknown words or looking them up, pausing to check for understanding, and having them reread a paragraph if it wasn't clear.

When asked what they would do if students encountered a problem during reading, the Reading I students made three categories of responses: sound out the words, skip that part, or reread. The Reading II students made those responses and, in addition, offered to help the students connect what they already knew about to what they were reading, had them read with a partner, and asked questions to probe their thinking.

Response differences were apparent between the Reading I and Reading II students when they were asked what they would do with students after they finished reading. Seventy five percent of the Reading I students responded they would ask questions. Nine percent made miscellaneous comments such as go over difficult words, review and reinforce concepts learned, and encourage students to reflect on the book and relate it to personal experiences. Sixteen percent gave no response. All of the Reading II students responded with the most frequent answer categories being to have students reflect and discuss with others what was read, review the main ideas, retell the story in their own words, think about how they felt about the story and how it connected to their lives, have them ask themselves what questions they were able to answer; and go through the story again to prove and disprove their predictions.

Item 12 required the students to describe briefly a lesson they would teach second graders based on Frog and Toad are Friends (Lobel, 1971). Twenty six percent of the Reading I students described a cohesive lesson that included finding out what students knew about toads and frogs, making and checking predictions, having them ask questions if they didn't understand, and asking them questions for understanding. Five percent would integrate the book with other subject areas. Forty seven percent did not indicate what they would do. Sixty six percent of the Reading II students responded and also gave cohesive lesson descriptions. Most included before reading and after reading steps. During reading strategies were not noted except to prove predictions which was primarily indicted at the end of the lesson. Strategies they included were discussing and comparing frogs and toads, previewing the story and making predictions, defining unknown vocabulary, setting a purpose for reading, using graphic organizers, asking critical thinking questions, having students retell the story, and planning a closure activity.

Items 7, 8, 9, 10, and 11 dealt with each preservice student's perception of his or her reading and what they did before, during, and after reading. When asked what they did before reading, the majority of Reading I students were concerned with finding a comfortable place with few distractions and getting a drink. Thirty three percent noted they looked at the text, illustrations, sentence structure, and length of the book, and then skimmed the text and read the summary. Only one student in the Reading II class mentioned comfort and it was mainly in finding a quiet reading place. Most of their responses related to interactions with the book, mainly by skimming and finding out about the author. They mentioned the importance of looking at the illustrations, the bold headings, and the questions at the end of the reading first. Their answers related to textbook or expository reading rather than narrative. Interest in the topic and having the opportunity to discuss what was to be read with others was noted.

When asked what they did during reading, eighty six percent of the Reading I students responded to claim they reread parts they didn't understand, looked up words, thought about what would happen next, skipped ahead and then came back if they didn't understand, and took breaks. Ninety one percent of the Reading II students said they stopped periodically to check understanding, used a highlighter, tried to visualize what was being read, gathered notes, organized facts, predicted, tried to relate to the characters, and attended closely to important details. One student also indicated writing down questions about parts of the text that were unclear.

Item 9 asked if, during reading, they had ever read something that seemed unclear to them and, if so, what did they do? Eighty six percent of the Reading I students said yes and 10 percent said something had been partially unclear. All of the Reading II students answered yes. The predominant answer that students from both groups gave was to reread the text until they could understand it. One student commented that if the book was not a subject of interest, s/he would put it aside. If it were interesting, s/he would continue reading it even if it was difficult.

When asked what they did after reading, 63 percent of the Reading I students responded and said they liked to talk about what they read with friends, reflect on what was read, go back over things not understood, relax, or go to sleep. Eighty one percent of the Reading II students responded and claimed they asked themselves questions, looked up vocabulary words, understood how the character changed, reviewed main ideas and the summary at the end of the chapter, reflected on what was read, proved predictions, and retold what they read in their own words.

The last item to be discussed from the Individual Metacognitive Pre-assessment urged students to describe themselves as readers. There was a 100 percent response from both Reading I and Reading II students. No categories of readers were given but students assigned themselves a designation of excellent (41%), good (52%), mediocre (6%), or inconsistent (1%). Students who claimed to be excellent readers said that several of them were early readers and were read to considerably when they were children, they liked a variety of reading materials, and remembered what they read. One excellent self-designated reader claimed that s/he especially liked science and technology books but read entertaining books as well. Students who claimed to be good readers said they do read but are particular about what they choose, read different types of materials, do best when the subject is of interest, read for the gist of the story, do better silently than orally, and reread sometimes to make sure they understood the authors' messages. One student said s/he was an ESOL student who likes to read but often has to read and reread selections a number of times in English to make sure that the information makes sense. Many students favored autobiographies, novels, and entertaining books. Those who designated themselves as mediocre (their choice of term) noted that silent reading was very hard and things had to be reread many times, that reading had always been difficult, and they were told they weren't good readers. One person designated him/herself as an inconsistent reader. S/he wrote that the level of interest often dictates how well s/he reads and the level of retention is not always what is desired.

Group Metacognitive Pre-Assessment. The group pre-assessment findings mirrored the individual findings for both groups since the students tallied their items on the group list. The unexpected finding from this collaborative experience was that as students shared ideas from their individual pre-assessment, they began exchanging ideas about what worked for them and how they would do given things. One Reading II student told how tabbing sections of her text with sticky notes helped her and explained and showed others how she did it. At the following class session, 43 percent of the students were using brightly colored post-its! As the students shared, they used reading terms, and appeared to consider and reconsider some of their own literacy practices. Both Reading I and Reading II students seemed more confident and secure when deciding how they would teach narrative text as compared to teaching expository text. Their exchanges reinforced research findings that there is value in having students reflect and brainstorm collectively (Gijselaers, 1996); Beeth, 1998). The Group Metacognitive Pre-assessment is in Appendix B.

Anecdotal Records. The Reading I students taught two lessons to primary aged students and two lessons to intermediate students. There were four to eight students in the various groups. The Reading II students conducted IRI's and did a minimum of three follow-up lessons based on their findings with at least three students. Similar anecdotes were recorded for both sets of preservice teachers. A majority of those teaching did think-alouds, encouraged the students subsequently to do think-alouds, used graphic organizers, led the students to revise and extend their thinking, modeled strategies such as fix-its, used reciprocal questioning, and included retelling at the conclusion of most lessons. The students were not required to do these things as they planned, taught, and evaluated their lessons. However, they were using what had been modeled, taught, and practiced in class. When comparing what the preservice teachers had planned on paper and were doing with students, it was found that approximately 53 percent of the students incorporated various metacognitive related strategies when they were appropriate to what their elementary students were or were not doing rather than adhering strictly to their preconceived plans. The observers found that an increasing number of metacognitive strategies were being incorporated in these lessons in more overt ways than had been done in previous semesters when the metacognitive strand had not been as stressed during university instruction.

Post-course Oral Group Reflection and Sharing. At the last class session, the collaborative groups that worked together during the first class session were reformed and the group was presented its original input on the Group Metacognitive Pre-assessment. The students reviewed their input and then shared informally with the whole class what they would keep, modify, add, or delete from their original responses. They expanded significantly on their original input and were interacting knowingly with each other using appropriate literacy terms and reflecting on all three aspects of the metacognitive definition chosen for this study.

Post-Course Individual Written Reflection for the Given Prompt. After responding and reflecting upon the Group Metacognitive Pre-assessment, students then were asked to respond to the prompt given earlier in this article. Their reflections were analyzed in terms of what they now knew about themselves as readers, what they knew about the task of reading, and how they self monitored themselves. A critical additional part of the prompt was their perception as to whether a teacher needed to be metacognitive before effectively encouraging elementary students to be metacognitive in their thinking. The findings consisted of candid testimonies by students. For purposes here, excerpts of student reflections are given which are exemplary of many of the entries submitted. The students gave permission to the professors to include their reflections.

Knowledge of Self. Two examples of this knowledge expressed by students in Reading I and Reading II respectively are:

> Before taking this course, I never really thought about myself as a reader/ learner, how to approach literacy tasks, or how to monitor and adjust my reading to achieve greater understanding and enjoyment. I now understand how the metacognition process works and why I do the

things I do when I read. When I pick up a book for pleasure or for school, I never thought about why some things I had read I understood automatically while others I stumbled over. It was not until this course pointed out why we do the things we do to achieve a better understanding of what we are reading that I realized what I was doing. I believe I have become a better reader.

and

During these courses, I thought I would learn techniques and tactics to educate children and get them interested in reading. To my surprise, that is not all I learned. I learned more about myself as a reader than I ever have before. I learned techniques to help me read that no teacher ever tried to teach me in the past. To be very honest, I never heard of metacognition before. I have always had a hard time reading expository texts. They never seemed to hold my attention and I always asked myself the question of "why do I have to read this when I am getting nothing out of it?" I would read and reread. I tried everything or so I thought. It was not until I learned about SQ3R that I actually started learning something from the expository texts I read. I was given the knowledge that I had to ask myself questions and start to find a purpose for reading the material. It has changed the way I look at many things. When I first started using this technique, I would write down the questions; but, now it seems as though it is automatic that I look for a question before I read something so I have a purpose.

Knowledge of Task. Two examples of this knowledge expressed by students in Reading I and Reading II respectively are:

I use the KWLSH Chart when reading about new ideas or even old ones. I do not make up a chart on paper, but I do it in my head. It helps me activate my schema and gives me a purpose for reading the material. I then can figure out what I do not know and find out where to find it. This strategy has been very useful to me. I also use more than one way to figure out unknown words rather than just trying to sound them out.

and

Before I began these classes, I would read a selection by just diving right into the print. I would never have gone through any of the pre- and post-reading strategies that are now helping me get more understanding from textbooks. I now look at headings, for important words, and constantly check for my understanding and predict what will happen next or what I will learn next from the selection. I use many ways now to attack words I don't know. After reading, I often question myself about the selection to be sure that what I have read makes sense to me. The KWLSH Strategy allows me to see what I know about a particular subject, ask myself what I want to know, see what I have learned after reading, think about what else I would like to know about the subject, and consider how I can gather additional information.

Knowledge of Ways to Self-Monitor. Two examples of this knowledge expressed by students in Reading I and Reading II respectively are:

I have learned a lot about my own literacy. I now know how to approach a book when I do not understand it. When I read, I use the SQ3R Strategy that I learned. I also predict in my head what will happen in a story. When I am writing papers, I try to make sure it makes sense and sounds right.

and

These courses have been valuable to me in seeing there is more to reading that just looking at words and sounding them out. I realized that my own difficulty with reading can be reduced. I did not know there were strategies that could help me with comprehension. My reading comprehension is low, and it is the major reason I did not attend law school because I know that, in law school, most of the work is reading comprehension. I have seen that my own distractions have been a major problem. I must force myself to be "present" when I read and not let other things distract me. I feel I now know ways to help myself and am more confident. . . . It is difficult to leave my old habits. I do know that going through chapters and reading summaries first helps me to know what I will be reading and to focus more fully.

Perceptions about whether a teacher needs to be metacognitive to encourage students to be metacognitive. Two examples of this knowledge expressed by students in Reading I and Reading II respectively are:

I think it is very important for teachers to have self-knowledge in the three areas of metacognitive knowledge. When teachers are aware of their own reading skills, they are better suited to help students become aware of their reading abilities. Teachers need to know the strategies for being better readers; and, I believe this course has taught me some great ones!

and

I believe teachers should recognize their own self-knowledge. If a teacher knows how s/he learns and solves reading problems, it will help her/him to realize students also learn in different ways. A teacher that knows how to approach literacy tasks will give that information to students.

Discussion

As we analyzed the findings, we were impressed with the growth students expressed and the differences between Reading I and Reading II students. A semester of emphasis on metacognition made awareness of one's literacy more apparent. It seemed that the essential difference was to continue overt metacognitive development into a second or even more sequential course if such might be offered. The differences of metacognitive awareness between the first and second reading courses was profound in terms of maturity and the ability to express what was now known about one's own literacy abilities and processes. The students they taught appeared to be much more aware of the three metacognitive areas than previous elementary students and to be able to verbalize effectively as we witnessed our own preservice students do.

During the literature search, Stewart and Tei (1983), Costa (1991), and Brown (1985) noted that age and reading experiences related to the degree of awareness. It was seen that regulation was not constant and that the post self-analysis by preservice students indicated change in the degree of their own self-regulation and their attitude of self-regulation was important for them to do when they read. They found if they scaffolded students gradually, the expectations of reading independence could increase which aligned with the findings of Babbs and Moe (1983).

Reflecting upon their literacy behaviors increased preservice students' awareness and the degree of verbalization about that awareness which reinforced the findings that Commander and Smith (1996) had when they required that university students keep logs to reflect upon and evaluated their learning and thinking growth. Concept mapping did extend schema and connect concepts learned which reflected the findings of Francisco, Nicoll, & Trautmann (1998), and Gravett and Swart (1998). This linkage seemed particularly useful to our preservice students as many will work in the school systems with second language learners who often have fragmented and partially developed concepts for which they see little or no relationship. By having our preservice students see how concept mapping and other taught strategies helped them link their understanding of the relationship of various concepts, they seemed to use some type of clustering or mapping when they planned for and worked with given elementary students and, especially, second language learners.

Although we did not use the checklists that Mack and Tama (1997) had their preservice teachers use in case studies, our preservice students did resemble this study's findings by increasing their own metacognitive awareness which, in turn, affected their sensitivity in activating a like awareness in their elementary students. Their own reading confidence and the implementation of appropriate strategies also increased which paralleled Risko's (1995) findings.

At the beginning of the semester, Reading I and Reading II students expressed some differences but these became more apparent as the Reading II students experienced the second reading course. The differences were most evident in what the students indicated should be experienced by elementary students during and after reading. The Reading II students were much more cognizant as to what should be done after reading such as retelling the selection in one's own words.. The Reading I students rarely moved beyond the question asking-answering stage. The Reading II students expressed more depth in their responses and required their students to participate more frequently in metacognitive oriented experiences. During reading, metacognitive strategies needed to be more substantively and strategically developed in both the Reading I and Reading II classes. There, however, was a predominant pattern of greater conceptual and maturational differences in the responses and actions of the Reading II students as compared to the Reading I students. Students in both classes used ideas other students shared during their cooperative group opportunities. The primary message to these professors was there needed to be a definite "continuity bridge" built between the two courses to provide both a developmental evenness and opportunities for one to grow metacognitively. The students, overwhelmingly, stated that it was their duty as well as their professional knowledge obligation to encourage the elementary students with whom they would have contact to become metacognitively aware. The universal lament shared by the majority of students reinforced the findings of Hollingworth (1998) when they queried why they did not get the same teaching in their elementary school training that they were gaining now in their university reading methods courses. They unanimously felt they were deprived because metacognitive instruction was not a focus during their earlier literacy training and development.

Summary

In the beginning of the semester, the degree of metacognition expressed between the Reading I students and the Reading II students was considerable. By the end of the semester, this span had greatly narrowed. The students were practicing metacognitive strategies such as rereading and predicting but they did not seem to be aware that these had anything to do with the term, metacognition. On the individual pre-assessment, both groups of students were strongest in what they knew to do and did before and after reading. The during reading segment was overlooked by the majority of both Reading I and Reading II students which may indicate that more instructional attention should be given on how to assist students during the reading process.

The group pre-assessment did provide a social context and sharing that

continued and strengthened in substance over the semester. The collaborative experiences encouraged students to share strategies that worked for them.
Some of those strategies were adopted by other students.

After approximately half a semester's instruction with a heavy emphasis
on metacognitive knowledge and strategies, the students worked during
regularly course scheduled sessions with elementary students at a public
school under the observations of their professors who kept anecdotal records.
The majority of the students in both Reading I and Reading II employed more
metacognitive strategies than had been observed previously. Think alouds,
graphic organizers, predicting and verifying predictions, modeling, fix-its,
reciprocal questioning, retelling, and group reflecting were among the most
frequent strategies used. Many of these strategies were not in their original
lesson plans. It was apparent that, as the semester progressed, the preservice
students were teaching elementary students and not inflexible lesson plans!

The Post Course Reflections were Detailed and Introspective

They revealed an increased sense of confidence about their own reading and thinking than was expressed by either group at the onset. Both the
Reading I and the Reading II students were unanimous in their beliefs that
the more metacognitive a teacher, the more effective she or he should be in
helping students become metacognitive thinkers and readers.

As we professors considered our data, we realized there was an un-
planned bonus in our findings. Just as Weir (1998) shared how her own
metacognition was jump started, so was ours. We became meta-aware of
our own metacognition! We found ourselves constantly reflecting and revising how we approached and instructed students. In order to do the modeling in the depth we did, we had to analyze and express publicly our own
knowledge and beliefs about literacy. Not only did our preservice students
increase their metacognitive base, but, so did their professors!

The ultimate accomplishment of this study is stated well by a Reading I
student:

> Most important of all, I have learned to love to read again! My
> metacognitive knowledge has expanded and now I am not just read-
> ing because I have to, but because it is fun to read! I have started to
> read the newspaper daily. In addition to taking five methods' classes,
> I found time to read *The Celestine Vision* and *Flowers for Algernon* this
> semester!

References

Alexander, J. M. & Manion, V. (1997). The benefits of peer collaboration on strategy use, metacognitive causal attribution, and recall. *Journal of Experimental Child Psychology,* 67, 2, 268-289,

Atkinson, P., Delamont, S., & Hammersley, M. (1988). Qualitative research traditions: A British response to Jacob. *Review of Educational Research,* 58 (12), 231-250.

Babbs, P. J. & Moe, A. G. (1983). Metacognition: A key for independent learning from text. *The Reading Teacher,* 36, 422-426.

Baker, L. & Brown, A. L. (1984). Metacognitive skills and reading. In D. Pearson (Ed.) *Handbook of reading research.* New York: Longman.

Barton, M. L. (1997). Addressing the literacy crisis: Teaching reading in the content areas. *NASSP Bulletin,* 81, 587, 22-30.

Baumann, J. F., Jones, L. A., & Seifert-Kessell (1993). Using think-alouds to enhance children's comprehension monitoring abilities. *The Reading Teacher,* 47, 3, 184-193.

Bean, T. W., Singer, H., and Cowen, S. (1985). Acquisition of a topic schema in high school biology through an analogical study guide. In J. A. Niles and R. V. Lalik (Eds.), Issues in literacy: A research perspective, *Thirty-Fourth Yearbook of the National Reading Conference.* Rochester, NY: National Reading Conference.

Beeth, M. E. (1998). Facilitating conceptual change learning: The need for teachers to support metacognition. *Journal of Science Teacher Education,* 9, 1, 49-61.

Bourner, T. (1998). More knowledge, new knowledge: The impact on education and training. *Education + Training,* 40, 1, 11-14.

Brown, A. L. (1985). Metacognition: The development of selective attention strategies for learning from texts. In H. Singer & R. B. Ruddell (Eds.), *Theoretical models and processes of reading* (3rd ed.) (pp.501-5267). Newark, DE: International Reading Association.

Brown, A. L. & Smiley, S. (1977). Rating the importance of structural units of prose passages: A problem of metacognitive development. *Child Development,* 48, 1-8.

Butler, D. L. (1997, March). *The roles of goal setting and self- monitoring in students' self-regulated engagement in tasks.* Paper presented at the meeting of the American Educational Research Association, Chicago, IL.

Chiu, C. W. T. (1998, April) *Synthesizing metacognitive interventions: What training characteristics can improve reading performance?* Paper presented at the meeting of the American Educational Research Association, San Diego, CA.

Commander, N. E. & Smith, B. D. (1996). Learning logs: A tool for cognitive monitoring. *Journal of Adolescent & Adult Literacy,* 39, 6, 446-453.

Costa, A. L. (1991). Mediating the metacognitive. In A. L. Costa (Ed.), *The school as a home for the mind.* Palatine, IL: Skylight.

Cunningham, A. E. (1990). Explicit versus implicit instruction in phonemic awareness. *Journal of Experimental Child Psychology,* 50, 429-444.

Flavell, J. H. (1978). Metacognitive development. In J. M. Scandura & C. J. Brainerd (Eds.) *Structural process theories of complex human behavior.* Alphen a. d. Rijn, The Netherlands: Sijthoff & Noordhoff.

Flood, J. (Ed.). (1984). *Understanding reading comprehension.* Newark, DE: International Reading Association.

Forget, M. A. & Morgan, R. F. (1997). A brain-compatible learning environment for improving student metacognition. *Reading Improvement,* 34, 4, 161-175.

Francisco, J. S., Nicoll, G., Trautmann, M. (1998). Integrating multiple teaching methods into a general chemistry classroom. *Journal of Chemical Education,* 75, 2, 210- 213.

Freeman, C. C. & Smith, D. L. (1997, March). *Active and engaged? Lessons from an interdisciplinary and collaborative college mathematics and science course for preservice teachers.* Paper presented at the meeting of the American Educational Research Association, Chicago, IL.

Garner, R. (1987). *Metacognition and Reading Comprehension.* Norwood, NJ: Ablex.

Geimer, T., Krzystofczyk, S., Luczak, C., and Talach, S. (1988). *Peer Assistance in Reading Strategies.* M.A. Action Research Project, Saint Xavier University and IRI/Skylight/Dissertation/thesis. Cincinnati, OH..

Gijselaers, W. H. (1996). Connecting problem-based practices with educational theory. *New Directions for Teaching and Learning, 68,* 13-21.

Graves, M. F., Penn, M. C. & Cooke, C. L. (1985). The coming attraction: Previewing short stories. *Journal of Reading, 28,* 594-598.

Gravett, S. J. & Swart, E. (1997). Concept mapping: A tool for promoting and assessing conceptual change. *South African Journal of Higher Education, 11, 2,* 122-126.

Hansen J. & Hubbard, R. (1984). Poor readers can draw inferences. *The Reading Teacher, 27,* 586-589.

Hansen, J. & Pearson, P. D. (1983). An instructional study: Improving the inferential comprehension of good and poor fourth grade readers. *Journal of Educational Psychology, 75,* 821-829.

Heller, M. F. (1986). How do you know what you know? Metacognitive modeling in the content areas. Journal of Reading, 29, 415-422.

Herber, H. (1978). *Teaching reading in the content areas* (2nd ed.). Englewood Cliffs, NJ: Prentice-Hall.

Hollingworth, R. W. (1998, July). *Chemistry problem solving and real world knowledge.* Paper presented at the meeting of the RACI Chemical Education Division National Conference, Rockhampton, Queensland, Australia.

Johnson, D., & Pearson, P. D. (1978). *Teaching Reading Vocabulary.* New York: Holt, Rinehart, and Winston.

Kintsch, W., & Van Dijk, T. A. (1978). Toward a model of text comprehension and production. *Psychological Review, 85,* 363-394.

Kirby, J. R., & Pedwell, D. (1991). Students' approaches to summarization. *Educational Psychology, 11,* 297- 307.

Langer, J. A., (1984). Examining background knowledge and text comprehension. *Reading Research Quarterly, 19,* 468- 481.

Lapp, D., & Flood, J. (1986). *Teaching students to read.* New York: Macmillan.

Lobel, A. (1971). *Frog and toad are friends.* New York: HarperCollins.

Mack, C. & Tama, M. C. (1997, December). Case studies as a means of exploring preservice teachers' use of content area literacy strategies in their subject area fieldwork. Paper presented at the meeting of the National Reading Conference, Scottsdale, AZ.

Masataka, K. (1997). Research on the complementarity of intuition and logical thinking in the process of understanding mathematics: An examination of the two-axes process model by analyzing an elementary school mathematics class. *Hiroshima Journal of Mathematics Education, 5,* 21-33.

Matanzo, J. B. (1997, November). *Literature, literature everywhere: The immersion of preservice teachers in a reading methodology course.* Paper presented at the meeting of the College Reading Association, Boston, MA.

McNeil, J. D. (1984). *Reading comprehension: New directions for classroom practice.* Scott, Foresman, & Co.

Murphy, P. (1997). Constructivism and primary science. *Primary Science Review,* 49, 3, 27-29.

Nagy, W. E. (1988). *Vocabulary instruction and reading comprehension.* (Tech. Rep. No. 431). Champaign, IL: University of Illinois, Center for the Study of Reading.

Ogle, D. (1986). K-W-L: A teaching model that develops active reading of expository text. *The Reading Teacher,* 39, 564-570.

Palincsar, A. M. & Brown, A. L. (1984) Reciprocal teaching of comprehension-monitoring activities. *Cognition and Instruction,* 1, 117-175.

Palincsar, A. S., & Brown, A. L. (1986). Interactive teaching to promote independent learning from text. *The Reading Teacher.* 39 (8), 771-777.

Paris, S. G., Lipson, M. Y. & Wixson, K. K. (1983). *Becoming a strategic reader, Contemporary Educational Psychology,* 8, pp. 293-316.

Pearson, P. D. & Gallagher, M. C. (1983). The instruction of reading comprehension. *Contemporary Educational Psychology,* 8, 317-344.

Pressley, M., El-Dinary, P., Brown, R., Schuder, T., Bergman, J., York, M., Gaskins, I., & Faculties and Administration of Benchmark School and the Montgomery County, MD, SAIL/SIA Programs. (1995). A transactional strategies instruction Christmas Carol. In A. McKeough, J. Lupart, & A. Marini (Eds.), *Teaching for transfer* (pp. 177 213). Mahwah, NJ: Erlbaum.

Raphael, T. (1986). Question-answering strategies for children. *The Reading Teacher,* 39, 186-190.

Ratekin, N., Simpson, M., Alvermann, D. E., & Dishner, E. K. (1985). Why content teachers resist reading instruction. *Journal of Reading,* 28, 432-437.

Risko, V. (1985). Using videodisc-based cases to promote preservice teacher's problem solving and mental model building. In W. M. Linek & E. G. Sturtevant (Eds.), Generations of Literacy, *The Seventeenth Yearbook of the College Reading Association* (pp. 173-187). Harrisonburg, VA: College Reading Association.

Sanacore, J. (1984). Metacognition and the improvement of reading: Some important links. *Journal of Reading,* 27, 706-712.

Schallert, D. L., & Kleiman, G. K. (1979). *Some reasons why teachers are easier to understand than textbooks* (Reading Education Report #9). Cambridge, MA: Bolt, Beranek, & Newman and Urbana, IL: Center for the Study of Reading.

Seng, SeokHoon (1997, April). *Using mediated learning experiences to enhance children's thinking.* Paper presented at the meeting of the International Study Conference of the Association for Childhood Education International, Portland, OR.

Shore, B. M., & Dover, A. C. (1987). Metacognition, intelligence and giftedness. *Gifted Child Quarterly,* 31, 37-39.

Stewart, O., & Tei, E. (1983). Some implications of metacognition for reading. *Journal of Reading.* 27, 36-43.

Stow, W. (1997). Concept mapping: A tool for self-assessment? *Primary Science Review,* 49, 12-15.

Tunmer, W. E., Herriman, M. L., & Nesdale, A. R. (1988). Metalinguistic abilities and beginning reading. *Reading Research Quarterly,* 23, 134- 158.

Underwood, T. (1997). On knowing what you know: Metacognition and the act of reading. *Clearing House,* 71, 77- 80.

Vacca J. A., Vacca, R. T. & Gove, M. K. (1991). *Reading and learning to read* (2nd ed.) (pp. 9-13). New York: HarperCollins Publishers Inc.

Weir, C. (1998). Using embedded questions to jump-start metacognition in middle school remedial readers. *Journal of Adolescent & Adult Literacy,* 41, 6, 458-467.

White, B. Y. & Frederiksen, J. R. (1998). Inquiry, modeling, and metacognition: Making science accessible to all students. *Cognition and Instruction,* 16, (1), 3-118.

White, E. B. (1953). Charlotte's Web. NY: HarperCollins.

Wixson, K. K. & Peters, C. W. (1987). Comprehension assessment: Implementing an interactive view of reading. *Educational Psychologist,* 22, 333-356.

Wong, J. A., & Au, K. H. (1984). The concept-text application approach. Helping elementary students comprehend expository text. *The Reading Teacher,* 38, 612-618.

Appendix A. The Individual Metacognitive Pre-Assessment

Twelve open ended items that relate to metacognition are listed below. Consider a response for each item. Briefly write your reflection. If more space is needed, attach additional pages.*

1. Metacognition is

2. Ways I would help a student be more metacognitive would be

3. When teaching students, before reading I would

4. When teaching students, during reading I would

5. When students encounter a problem during reading, I would teach them to

6. When teaching students, after reading I would

7. Things I do before I read are

8. Things I do during reading are

9. Have you ever read something that seemed unclear to you?
    Yes   No   Partially   If yes or partially, what did you do about it?

10. Things I do after reading are

11. Describe yourself as a reader:

12. You are asked to teach second graders to read and enjoy Frog and Toad are Friends (Lobel, 1971). Describe briefly what you would do in your lesson.

*Note: More response space was allowed on the original form.

Appendix B. The Group Metacognitive Pre-Assessment

Group # _____   Members: _____

Be candid in your responses. Do not say something just because you think you should. Be honest and express what you exactly do or know at this time. If more than one person has a similar response, put "tick" marks next to the given idea. Select a facilitator (time/task) and one or more recorders.*

1. You are assigned a chapter by a professor.
   A. First, you
   B. Next, you
   C. If you have trouble reading, concentrating, and/or understanding the text, you
   D. Next, you
   E. Finally, you

2. It is a rainy Sunday afternoon. Everyone else in your family has plans so you are not responsible for them, work, or anything else for about six hours. You have a fictional novel you've been wanting to read so you decide this is the time!
   A. First, you
   B. Next, you
   C. If something doesn't make sense to you, you
   D. Next, you
   E. Finally, you

3. Think about things you may think, do, or feel which are both similar and different when you read fiction and non-fiction materials.

Fiction:	Similarities	Non-Fiction:
Different things we think, do, feel		*Different things we think, do, feel*

4. What makes you like what you read?

5. What makes you dislike what you read?

6. You are asked to teach third graders to read and enjoy Chapter 1 of Charlotte's Web (White, 1953). Briefly outline the components of your lesson and include how you might make accommodations for the range of readers and understandings in your classroom.

7. You are asked to teach a chapter in a science text about rocks and minerals to fifth graders. During your lesson, you notice that a number of students are struggling to understand the text. You will

8. Things you feel you need to know most about in order to teach students to be literate are:

*Note: More response space was allotted on the original form.

Preservice Teachers Constructing Personal Understandings About Culture

Janelle B. Mathis

University of North Texas

Abstract

Advocating for learners includes empowering them to uncover insights into their own learning and the effects of personal culture and experiences on their learning. As preservice teachers in a reading/language arts block explore culture through children's literature, they are encouraged to grapple with understandings of their own perceptions of culture and multicultural education. Data sources analyzed were student responses in journal entries, taped and transcribed small group discussions, reflections on a multicultural unit, and mid-term and final reflections on personal learning within the course. The findings represent issues with which preservice teachers struggle as they respond to experiences with children's literature and class discussions around issues of diversity.

Introduction

As we prepare teachers to assume the responsibilities of increasingly diverse classrooms, we are consistently made aware of the need for these individuals to contemplate issues of culture and literacy. The demographics point to the fact that despite the continuous increase in children of diverse language and cultural backgrounds, the number of teachers from ethnic minority backgrounds has decreased (Delpit, 1995; King, 1993). While this concern calls for action in recruiting more minority teachers, it also begs for greater commitment to preparing teachers who more effectively can meet the needs of children whose linguistic and cultural backgrounds differ from their own. Banks (1992, p. 53) helps us to understand this need by stating:

Each of us becomes culturally encapsulated during our socialization in childhood. We accept the assumptions of our own community culture, internalize its values, views of the universe, misconceptions, and stereotypes. Students who are born and socialized within the mainstream culture of a society rarely have an opportunity to identify, question, and challenge their cultural assumptions, beliefs, values, and perspective because the school culture usually reinforces those that they learn at home and in their communities. Consequently, mainstream Americans have few opportunities to become free of cultural assumptions and perspectives that are monocultural . . .

Thus, considering the complexity of culture is not an easy task, although educators in all contexts are confronted with the need to be aware of the significant role that one's culture plays in literacy learning. To understand the role of culture in literacy learning students must first be given the opportunity to grapple with the significance of their own culture.

Context and Design

The present inquiry is part of a larger study which explored students' personal reflections and responses to experiences in an undergraduate reading/language arts block course. The participants of this particular semester were 22 students at a university in the southwest. Among these students were one male and 21 females. Ethnically, there was one Hispanic student and two African-American students with the remainder being European-American. Most students reside in homogeneous Caucasian suburban neighborhoods.

The methodology employed consisted of qualitative techniques set within the theoretical frame of teacher research (Cochran-Smith & Lytle, 1990). As a teacher researcher, I sought to critically examine the philosophical framework upon which the course is designed which includes:

1. Learning is an active, personal process;
2. Learning is a social process of collaborating with others (Vygotsky, 1978);
3. Choice allows learners to connect to their own experiences and feel ownership of the learning process;
4. Learning occurs when we make connections to our personal experiences;
5. Exploration of literature should take place through personal responses rather than through specific literary interpretation (Rosenblatt, 1983;1978);
6. Reflection is a vital part of the learning process;
7. Understandings and appreciation of diversity enhance learning;
8. Learning occurs through multiple ways of knowing.

The courses emphasize the collaborative nature of learning; educators share their responses and understandings with one another and serve as a support system for each other during both small and large group discussions. Throughout the course, participants explore the philosophical and theoretical underpinnings of reading and language arts instruction continuously supported by children's and young adolescent literature.

Questions guiding the larger study were:

1. Do student responses to their experiences within these courses reflect the beliefs about teaching and learning upon which the course is designed? What strategies empower them to both explore their own literacy and experience new ideas?
2. What new insights into culture and diversity do students construct? What role does literature play in these new insights?

The focus of the inquiry presented here is that of the second question.

Addressing Diversity Within the Course

Opportunities to contemplate diversity within public school classrooms were woven throughout the course. In addition to multicultural books having a predominant role in each class meeting, topics such as classroom contexts for ESL learners, home-school connections, and learner-centered instruction offered many opportunities to emphasize notions of diversity and how to address these differences within instructional planning. A focus on oral language/story-telling and writer's workshop invited class members to draw upon their own cultural experiences as they shared stories and responded to reading through art, music, and writing.

One focus within the semester was that of a multiethnic literature unit during which students were given the opportunity to explore numerous selected books representing various ethnicities within our society. While multicultural literature was continuously a part of other aspects of reading and literacy strategies, this particular focus identified literature that represented various genre and perspectives on ethnicity within children's books. At the same time, ideas of scholars were examined through articles and students were encouraged to contemplate what is meant by multicultural education, multicultural/multiethnic literature and the implications of this notion for classroom teachers. While exploring children's literature, students talked about evaluation of books, how to determine the best resources to use, and what experiences and literacy strategies are most significant in creating contexts for diverse learners. They were given an opportunity to share in reflective writing about their new knowledge and also to present their insights in a non-written presentation in the form of drama, art, music, technology, or any means they chose to express their learning.

Data Collection

Throughout the semester data was collected in the forms of an early literacy memory, journal responses, researcher field notes, audio-taped and transcribed discussions, reflection and response to the multiethnic literature unit and other course aspects, and a final self-evaluation. Data analysis took place on an informal level to inform teaching in order to make theory-based instructional choices. A more formal analysis took place at the end of the semester at which time the creation of categories was the key to analyzing the multiple data sources. This search for categories is described by Goetz and Lecompte (1984) as systematic, informed by the study's purpose, the researcher's orientation and knowledge, and the constructs generated by those within the study. Categories span each of the data sources and analysis was based on the constant comparative method (Glaser & Strauss, 1967). In keeping with the belief that teacher-research is "systematic and intentional inquiry" (Cochran Smith & Lytle, 1990, p. 3) numerous data sources collected consistently, reflection and review of findings by students and other teachers, triangulation of findings, and use of readings from theoretical frameworks promote validity (Mohr & MacLean, 1987).

Findings

Categories Regarding Culture

As data was analyzed four general categories emerged that indicated students' broadened notions of their own cultures and new insights into the meaning of cultural diversity. These were:

1. Perceptions of what "culture" is;
2. New understanding of the variety of cultural aspects that comprise their own lives;
3. New insights as to cultural pluralism in the classroom and in society;
4. Understandings as to the role of children's literature in creating learning environments.

In order to focus on the preconceptions and new insights that support these categories, five case studies are shared here. These student voices (pseudonyms are used) are taken from journal responses, responses to literature, self-evaluations, and class discussions.

Celia, Discovering Her Culture and Voices of Others Through Literature

As a child, Celia never saw herself reflected in the literature she read. Her excitement in class made her even more open to discovering other cultures as she realized that literature could authentically portray one's life style.

Not only did *Family Pictures* (Mora, 1990) mirror her childhood experiences, but *Too Many Tamales* (Soto, 1993) also invited her to reflect with humor on a family tradition. She wrote in her journal, "Wow, I saw all the books you brought dealing with the Hispanic culture. I love them!! My group read *Family Pictures* and it brought back memories of when I was small. I lived by the border, too, and many of the things shown in the book were seen at my home." Celia's exploration of the Asian culture created keen interest in the *pa'ndau*. *The Whispering Cloth* (Shea, 1995) helped her realize that other cultural groups were also struggling for voice and empowerment and that they, too, could be discovered in children's literature. She shared, "Being Hispanic, I always thought that there was nothing out there, such as children's books that reflected our culture. I was amazed to see all the ones that do exist. As a learner, I discovered many valuable things during this unit. First, there are more minorities other than Hispanics. I was always into my culture, only in class I discovered others as well. What was really unbelievable was that I could get so much information by reading a children's picture book. I didn't know that even as an adult I could get so much out of a picture book." While she was discovering various cultures reflected in children's literature she also was refining her definition of culture. Early in the semester, in a written response concerning the meaning of culture, Celia wrote, "I think culture means different races that shared or experienced the same thing throughout the education years." However in her self-evaluation a more finely tuned response was, "Culture is one's way of life. It involves a belief system, way of dress, religion, and tradition. Culture is about different economic systems, social skills and languages."

Flo, Realizing a Need for Culturally Relevant Resources

Flo represents those who are inundated with multicultural arguments and methods and who fail to see the practicality of it all within the classroom. Her own story reflects some of the reasoning behind her initial perceptions. "I was adopted and have never met my real parents. My adoptive parents were white middle class citizens of European descent. I have no idea what my specific heritage is. Does this mean I have no culture? Why is it so important to emphasize culture?" This portion of a journal entry continued. "I guess my question is why are we making multiculturalism this huge problem when we have other major problems with our education? I feel like we keep creating problems for ourselves without fixing our previous problems. We have students who are reaching college with a third grade reading level. Why is multiculturalism so important if the child can't read?" Flo's comments are a reminder that "When apparent similarities exist within school settings and home communities, there is often little perceived need to examine the cultural foundations of our own and others' literacy or the ways that literate practices differ among members of a diverse society" (Florio-Ruane, Raphael, Glazier, McVee, & Wallace, 1997, p. 452). Her connections to children's literature about others opened her thinking to the reality of those with diverse languages and literacy experiences. As a result she began to explore books that would help ESL students make connections between their home culture and that of the school. She realized that culturally relevant literature was significant in encouraging a child to make connections and comprehend while reading. Aliki's *Marianthe's Story* (1998) became significant to Flo's professional development as it tells of a child who immigrates to America and must learn English in school. Her response to our focus on multicultural literature was, "To be honest, I was very reluctant about starting up this whole multicultural thing in class. I'm just sort of burnt out on this topic because in every class I've been in we have had to do some type of multicultural unit . . . I've realized that by doing the multicultural ideas through literature, it's more enjoyable than other approaches." In addition to the learning experienced about literature, Flo's final self-evaluation stated, "Culture means differences between myself and another whether it is age, gender, race, religion, customs, beliefs and even my personality—my outlook. It all comes down to the development and nurturing of a spirit of justice that allows others their rights." She later continued, "I now see a difference in culture and ethnicity. We are all part of the American culture, but our ethnicity is where the African, Hispanic, Asian, and Native American comes in. Children now get a chance to learn about their ethnic background, except those like me, in my opinion. I don't know about my ethnic background that much. Where does that come in?" Although still seeking answers, Flo's understandings have evolved through reading and responding to both professional and children's literature.

Ted, Critically Contemplating Issues

Ted is aware that this "multicultural" notion is politically questionable in some circles. Literature both helped him define culture and realize its importance for the classroom. In the beginning he wrote, "I guess I get tired of people always talking about individual cultures. Why can't we all just be Americans?" Ted reconsiders his response during the semester while considering scholarly perspectives supporting the concept that culture (including race, gender, age and class) affects the reader's interpretation of story. *Grandfather's Journey* (Say, 1993) put readers such as Ted in touch with the feelings that an immigrant torn between countries might feel—feelings shared by many when life experiences are enmeshed between two or more places. After reading many books dealing with various Asian perspectives, Ted said, "Reading multicultural literature has made me aware of the other cultures. I can't believe how much I have learned about the Asian culture just by reading picture books. The only thing I was familiar with was Chinese food. Now I don't feel so ignorant. I don't know it all but I know something." Although enthusiastic about his discovery of the significance of children's literature, Ted is wise in drawing attention to the "labeling" of certain literature—an excellent point for discussion among peers. "This (children's literature) is a very interesting but sad part of the class, because I did not realize the lack of good materials out there. However, I am confused about it though. We tell our students not to discriminate and label yet we label this as *multicultural*. Is that because they don't think of it this way or this is the only way to approach it in our classroom?" As Ted's thinking becomes more focused during the course, he concludes with a final thought, "Children should be taught not to be biased to one way of learning or thinking, but to keep in mind many different ideas. A child or person can keep their opinion, but stay open-minded. Children's literature is a resource for this affective approach to teaching."

Dina, Supporting Her Beliefs About Culture With Children's Literature

Dina, an African-American middle-aged woman, has filtered all aspects of her culture through her ethnicity. She comes to class with strong feelings of the role of culture and the need for acknowledgment and appreciation of diverse literacy experiences. She wrote early in the course, "Multicultural education is education that meets the needs and goals of the diverse classroom today. It includes anti-bias materials, acknowledging different beliefs and celebrating the differences while realizing we are all similar." Dina had a strong sense of the significance of diversity from the beginning of class. The rich literature depicting her culture, however, was a valuable learning experience. Her discovery of the wealth of literature that did depict her culture encouraged her to seek other books representing other cultures as well as to critically evaluate her choices for the classroom. She was enthralled with the way various African American artists were able to put into pictures sections of Dr. Martin Luther King's speech *I Have a Dream* (1997). Likewise, during the course, Dina found *The Borning Room* (Fleischman, 1996) representative of her life experiences. Of concern to Dina was the response of other class members' conceptions of culture. "I was concerned in hearing some of the students refer to whole cultures as participating in traditions that are really a part of subcultures within the broader range. It also seemed that some older, out-dated traditions were described as occurring generally everywhere today." She expressed appreciation that we had open discussions during which such notions could be addressed. In her closing response concerning culture and ethnicity, Dina stated, "I came into class with a fairly solid knowledge base regarding culture and its implications for teaching yet I had a very limited (almost non-existent) knowledge of multicultural literature. I knew the recommended guidelines for evaluating literature but I was not familiar with the range of literature available. The time reading this semester has increased my awareness of what multicultural literature is and how it impacts children."

Katie, Experiencing Other Cultures Through Literature

Katie has lived all of her life in a homogeneous community of suburban America. "Culture, isn't that something in a foreign country?" was asked in earnestness in an early response to the meaning of culture. Through literature and discussion, Katie was invited to extend her sensitivity toward people to include those who are struggling for recognition and democracy in education. Tom Feelings in *The Middle Passage* (1995) portrays the struggle of Africans coming to America on slave ships. Katie followed this struggle through history as she discovered other literature with that theme and tried to understand the historical significance of the struggles in the lives of ethnic minority groups within our society. She shared in one discussion with peers, "The whole idea of multicultural literature is very new to me. It really is something that I never thought about." At the end of the semester she wrote, "The many books I read were very touching and informative, and I do hope they would be to my students. I learned from literature that our culture is more than just where your ancestors came from. It is a total picture of who you are and what you have become from all of your experiences. I learned a lot about how others see their own culture through multicultural books." Gordon Pradl (1996) emphasizes the significance of such reading when he says, "The democratic process of reading literature exists to widen the circle of readers of all ages. It accepts their experience, whatever it's been, and links it into new combinations of significance" (p. 143).

Discussion

The responses and insights of these five students are not unique. Teacher educators experience similar situations with their students as well as personally contemplate multicultural concepts in various contexts. The students described here have come closer to understanding culture by reading children's literature, discussing with others their concerns and insights, and reflecting on their own culture. As each student approached reading, reflecting, and discussions with varying prior experiences in considering culture, their new insights differed in the personal meaning for them as teachers. For Celia, realizing her own experiences reflected in children's literature was empowering. Exploration of other cultures created an awareness of other groups who, likewise, were struggling to gain a voice in society. She also realized that the meaning of culture includes but extends beyond race. Likewise, Flo gained initial perceptions as to what culture is and the importance of it in planning instruction. Ted's initial good intentions of considering everyone "American" reflected his lack of understanding about the experiences of various groups who have been under- and misrepresented. As he became aware of this, he critically contemplated the label multicultural and the need for anti-bias experiences. Dina had a very strong sense of her race and the struggles of African-American people. Her discovery of resources in literature have further empowered her to create the curriculum she desires. Katie was not aware that the culture she knew and found predominant in the schools she attended did not necessarily reflect or meet the needs of diverse learners. Powerful literature began to reveal to her the significance of experiences of different groups of people in considering their culture. Thus, the unsettling power of rich, authentic stories invited further contemplation and the construction of new insights.

Within each case study are major critical issues waiting for elaboration, discussion, and implementation. The general issues emerging from this data are ones that are highly discussed, debated, and used to ground pedagogy. These initial comments and early insights are only a beginning framework for students within a class whose focus is not solely multicultural education, but learning to create contexts for literacy learning. While cultural understandings are necessary in creating student centered learning environments and such reflection as described here creates a basis for grounding instruction, many other aspects of literacy must also be taught. The limitations of this study are centered around a lack of time to pursue in greater depth the issues that emerge and to look longitudinally at further growth and application of these gained perceptions. Because of the multiethnic literature emphasis during part of the semester, discussions of culture focused mainly on ethnicity. While other cultural aspects were part of discussions, the experiences with these books provided powerful ethnic considerations. Other issues, such as language, gender, and socio-economic aspects, were embedded about issues of race. Literacy strategies that invite more focused consideration and discussion of other cultural aspects are needed in future studies.

The experiences within this class are for some only the beginning of grappling with this notion of culture. For others, the significance of literature in creating learning communities that acknowledge the life experiences of its members are the major insights. Their voices speak to their new understandings and questions as well as to the value of personal inquiries into culture through literature. James Banks (1997) addresses the need for ". . . teachers to identify, examine, and reflect upon their attitudes toward different ethnic, racial, gender, and social-class groups" (p. 85). He calls attention to the fact that many educators are not aware of the extent their attitudes and behaviors are influenced by institutionalized conceptions of race, class, and gender. In support of the implementation of equity pedagogy—

teaching strategies that facilitate the learning process "to generate knowledge, construct interpretations, and create new understandings" (p. 80)—Banks emphasizes that good intentions are not enough and that "multicultural awareness can result only from in-depth work on the self" (p. 85). This can begin with preservice teachers identifying their initial perceptions and the influences on them. Such insights are critical for both future teachers and for the instructors who plan experiences that call for reflection, response, and revisiting literature with a more critical eye.

Another significance of this reflection on culture lies within the concept that literacy is a social construction. In preparing learning environments that are culturally responsive, interactive, and bridge home, community and school contexts, understandings about culture (beginning with one's own) include literacy acquisition. The work of Shirley Brice Heath (1983) and Victoria Purcell-Gates (1996) brings to attention the issue of functions of language and how culture often determines the ways in which print is used and the perceptions of different groups as to the uses of language. Our diverse classrooms need empowered teachers who realize the socio-cultural foundations of literacy and can sensitively and discerningly create curriculum accordingly. However, as the fabric of our society changes, this need also exists in homogeneous communities where students rarely have an opportunity to consider their biases and realize the pluralism of the greater society of which they are a part. The potential of children's literature as a vehicle to inform and nurture understandings of diversity depends on the experiences that young readers in schools have with this literature. The potential of preservice teachers to create these experiences in their future classrooms begins with the search for personal meaning as well as opportunities to construct knowledge supported by rich resources such as multicultural/multiethnic children's literature.

References

Aliki (1998). *Marianthe's story: Painted words, spoken memories.* New York: Greenwillow.

Banks, J. A. (1992). Multicultural education: For freedom's sake. *Educational Leadership, (4)*, 32-35.

Banks, J. A. (1997). *Educating citizens in a multicultural society.* New York: Teachers College Press.

Cochran-Smith & Lytle, S. L. (1990). Research on teaching and teacher research: The issues that divide. *Educational Researcher, 19*(2), 2-11.

Delpit, L. (1995). *Other people's children: Cultural conflict in the classroom.* New York: The New Press.

Feelings, T. (1995). *The middle passage.* New York: Dial.

Fleischman, P. (1991). *The borning room.* New York: HarperCollins.

Florio-Ruane, S., Raphael, T. E. Glazier, J., McVee, M. & Wallace, S. (1997). Discovering culture in discussion of autobiographical literature: Transforming the education of literacy teachers. In C. Kinzer, K. A. Hinchman, & D. J. Leu (Eds.), *Inquiries in literacy theory and practice, Forty-sixth yearbook of the national reading conference* (pp. 452-464). Chicago: National Reading Conference.

Glaser, B. & Strauss, A. (1967). *The discovery of grounded theory.* New York: Aldine.

Goetz, J. P. & LeCompte, M. D. (1984). *Ethnography and qualitative design in educational research.* Orlando: Academic Press.

Heath, S. B. (1983). *Way with words.* Cambridge: Cambridge University Press.

King, M. L. (1997). *I have a dream.* New York: Scholastic.

King, S. H. (1993). The limited presence of African-American teachers. *Review of Educational Research, 63*(2), 115-149.

Mohr & MacLean, M. (1987). *Working together: A guide for teacher researchers.* Urbana: National Council of Teachers of English.

Mora, P. (1990). *Family pictures.* San Francisco: Children's Book Press.

Pradl, G. M. (1996). *Literature for democracy.* Portsmouth: Heinemann.

Purcell-Gates, V. (1996). Stories, coupons, and the *TV Guide*: Relationships between home and literacy experiences and emergent literacy knowledge. *Reading Research Quarterly, 31*(4), 406-428.

Rosenblatt, L. (1983). *Literature as exploration.* 4th ed. New York: Modern Language Association.

Rosenblatt, L. (1978). *The reader, the text, the poem: The transactional theory of the literary work.* Carbondale, IL: Southern Illinois Press.

Say, A. (1993). *Grandfather's journey.* Boston: Houghton Mifflin.

Shea, P. D., Riggio, A., & Yang, Y. (1995). *The whispering cloth.* Honesdale, PN: Boyds Mills Press.

Soto, G. (1993). *Too many tamales.* New York: G. P. Putnam.

Vygotsky, L. (1978). *Mind in society: The development of higher psychological processes.* Cambridge, MA: MIT Press.

WRITING AND LITERACY
LEARNING CONNECTIONS

Traditional and Response-Based Writing Tasks in the Literature Classroom: A Comparison of Meaning-Making

Evangeline Newton

The University of Akron

Abstract

Traditional literature assignments focus on the text as an objective document for analysis. Reader response assignments invite students to investigate their own meaning-making processes through metacognitive exercises. Currently, many teachers assign both traditional and response-based writing tasks to their students. Using high school and college freshman essays written from both paradigms, this article explores epistemological differences that have significant learning implications for the student of literature. Ultimately, these differences raise complex questions about the nature of knowledge and the role of readers in a literate society.

In recent years, many of us have used reader response heuristics to expand the scope of writing assignments in our English classes (Applebee, 1992; Langer, 1994; Newton, 1991). We encourage students to investigate their own meaning-making processes through expressive journals and other metacognitive activities. Unlike traditional writing assignments which focus on the text as an "objective" document for analysis, response-based approaches shift pedagogical focus from text to reader (Cooper, 1985). Consequently, they call into question standard assumptions and practices which have buttressed the teaching of literature for most of this century.

Tompkins (1980) argues that a response-based approach mandates a new view of texts and readers, one that alters distinctions between them. This alteration forces literature teachers to "redefine the aims and methods of literary study" (p. x). But despite the growing popularity of response-based approaches, redefinition efforts are still in their infancy. Langer (1994) observes that as teachers explore the use of various response-centered approaches, they are "uncertain about the place of instruction in these paradigms" and about the role that they, as teachers, should play (p. 203).

In fact, extensive research indicates that teachers use response-based techniques most often in the early stages of textual interaction to "foster student involvement," but ultimately focus on more traditional interpretive approaches (Applebee, 1992; Langer, 1994, Zancanella, 1988). This suggests that while teachers encourage students to write personal responses to literature in a journal or informal discourse, at some point they feel compelled to intercept personal meaning-making with objective or "correct" interpretations.

So while theorists have indicated that response mandates new purposes for teaching literature, in practice many of us are using written response only to supplement traditional approaches to literary analysis (Applebee, 1992; Langer, 1994; Zancanella, 1988). Since the writing tasks we assign influence how students approach texts and "ultimately what they will take from those texts" close examination of those tasks seems an important step in evaluating the appropriateness of current practice (Newell, Suszynski & Weingart, 1989, p. 50).

The purpose of this article, then, is to compare the epistemological underpinnings of traditional and response-based approaches to writing assignments using passages from high school and college freshman essays about literature. The student work was collected during field observation in classrooms taught from either a traditional or response-based perspective. The following questions were used to guide this comparison: How do response-based writing tasks differ in purpose from traditional literary criticism? What are some implications of each approach for teaching and learning? Ultimately, are these paradigms truly compatible in the English classroom?

Traditional Writing Tasks

In 1938, Rosenblatt argued in *Literature as Exploration* that all literary interpretation depended essentially on the unique personality of the person who was reading the text. Yet Rosenblatt's (1938) innovative theory of the relationship between reader and text was eclipsed for years by the text-centered fervor of New Criticism. Based on T.S. Eliot's declaration in 1919 that the poem (i.e., the literary text) was really an "objective correlative" of the poet's experience, the New Critics warned against corrupting literary interpretation through a subjective analysis (Harrison, 1959, p. 846). Their curricular agenda included the study of genre and literary technique so readers could interpret text "correctly." Consequently, most literary instruction in American classrooms has promoted student mastery of a "special vocabulary" and correct "methods of explication" (Tompkins, 1980, p. 223).

Note the following passage from a conventional writing assignment on the "use of language" in Frost's "Out, Out-" (Taylor & Hall, 1970). The writer, Janet, is a high school senior:

> Frost also uses personification to give the reader a sense of meaningless urgency. Frost uses personification in describing the saw, and the subsequent accident: "the saw . . . leaped out at the boy's hand, or seemed to leap— . . . However it was, neither refused the meeting." By personifying the accident in this way Frost gives the reader the idea that the accident was inevitable, just as death is inevitable. The reader is left with the feeling that nothing could be done to help the boy. Consequently, the boy's pleas to his sister are rendered completely futile, which adds to the normality of the boy and to the reader's sympathy for him. Through this use of language Frost creates a tone of urgency, yet the reader is able to understand that it is useless urgency, and that nothing can be done to stop the approaching death.

In this passage, Janet shows an awareness of standard methods of explication: good literature must have a main point or truth about the human condition ("death is inevitable"). In fact, she invokes Frost's name four times, noting that he "uses," "gives" or "creates" his images for specific purposes. Moreover, Janet understands that her interpretive task is to discover those purposes. Her discussion of personification enlists the special vocabulary of poetry to enhance that interpretive process.

But perhaps most intriguing are Janet's frequent references to "the reader," an amorphous presence who is "left with the feeling" and "able to understand" the poem because of Frost's linguistic expertise. Curiously, there is nothing to suggest that these emotions and insights are bound in any way to the specific reader who wrote this essay. In fact, Janet has volunteered no personal opinions; her own voice and disposition are not integral to the process of literary analysis or to her purposes for writing. Meaning is objective and outside the self.

The following example from Amy, a college freshman, also demonstrates conventional purposes for writing. Amy was asked to analyze the theme in Hemingway's "A Clean, Well-Lighted Place" (Kennedy, 1991):

> Hemingway in this particular short story is neither complex nor overexaggerated. He told a simple story of growing old and how we are born being afraid of the dark, yet we go back to being afraid after we have finished living out our bright and glorious dreams. Hemingway did not want to confuse his readers or dissuade them from the main point. Society is terrified of aging and more importantly afraid of dying . . . a point so realistic and effective as this it carries more meaning than other writer's trivial tales of their own pains. Hemingway identifies with the human population as a whole . . ."

From her first sentence, Amy's pursuit of theme demonstrates a mastery of New Critical values. She draws on story grammar to reveal the text's main point about society and "the human population as a whole": it fears "aging" and "dying." And like Janet, her high school senior counterpart, Amy believes that Hemingway, the text's progenitor, is the authority; Amy's purpose as student-reader is to discover his intent. In fact, she offers here a series of rhetorical generalizations through which Amy hopes to identify the critical theme Hemingway intended—or at least her instructor is seeking. Again conspicuously absent from the process of literary analysis is Amy's own voice, beliefs or disposition.

Writing assignments such as these suggest that the purpose for writing about a literary work is to discover its indigenous truth, often interpreted by students as determining what the author intended. But ownership of that process is impossible for a student who has not already mastered the specialized vocabulary and New Critical interpretive methodology that has dominated the teaching of literature in this century (Tompkins, 1980). Moreover, according to this approach, any intrusion of a writer's own life experience or view of the world—his or her "voice"—tacitly pollutes the discovery process.

"Response-Based" Writing Tasks

During the sixties, Cooper (1985) writes, "new developments in psycholinguistics and cognitive psychology . . . made possible a new view of reading," one in which a reader's literary and life schemata fuse with the "constraints in connected discourse" (p, xii). Because of these "new developments," reading research began to observe learners' cognitive processes. As new perspectives were extended to literary study, Rosenblatt's (1938) seminal work was revived and elaborated upon by others. Eventually the term "reader response" became shorthand for ways of defining the reader-text relationship which highlighted the role of readers in the meaning making process.

While response-based reading theorists sometimes disagree over the sources of individual reaction to literary text, they all recognize that the reader-text relationship is complex and idiosyncratic (Beach, 1993; Mailloux, 1990; Rosenblatt, 1978). Moreover, they also recognize readers as primary agents in construction of textual meaning, so the "comprehension of text . . . is more an act of composition" (Petrosky, 1982, p. 19). The construction of each composition, therefore, must vary according to readers' life and literary schema. It must also vary according to the context and purpose of each reading event (Mailloux, 1990). In the following passage from a response-based assignment Tom examines his personal impressions of Hayden's "Those Winter Sundays" (Kennedy, 1991). A college freshman, Tom was asked to describe any personal feelings or associations he had while reading the poem:

This is talking about my Dad. The man who always takes care of things. It's hard to explain but it is Dad in this poem. My Dad and I don't talk much and I must hug and/or kiss him first. But I know he loves me. . . . The part about the cracked hands reminds me of a story my Dad told me. It was about his grandfather and how in the winter his hands would get such deep cracks that his grandmother would have to sew the cracks up. (His grandfather was a farmer naturally.)

By establishing a direct link between his own life and the text, Tom has used experience to enrich his understanding of the poem. His interpretation is neither objective nor dependent on the poet or teacher for validation. "Self-knowledge" and "understanding others" are unmistakably his purposes for writing.

Note the following passage from a response-based essay by Sarah, a high school senior. When asked to describe her initial reaction to Jackson's short story "The Lottery" (Kennedy, 1991) Sarah writes:

I did not like "The Lottery" because the story seemed senseless. The people seemed senseless. I do not understand why a town would annually kill a citizen just for the hell of it. I don't see how this can be compared to anything in real life. Even the Holocaust isn't the same. They weren't killing their own family by luck of the draw...Growing up in a rural town myself, I see all the things at home in this story. This is probably another reason why I disliked it so much. It shows how narrow-minded people in the country can be. If something is a tradition, no matter how stupid or dangerous it may be, it will remain a tradition. God forbid if anyone should try to change anything in these small towns. It scares me to think that if one of these "traditions" was to stone someone in the community every year, they would still do it. These attitudes are what made me want to leave so desperately and never go back, but even so, I still have ties to my home (Vacca & Newton, 1995, pg. 289-90).

Sarah begins by dismissing the "Lottery" as "senseless," perhaps in an effort to resolve the dissonance its premise had created for her. Most striking in this passage is the reluctant interpretation which evolves. As she draws on her own knowledge, feelings and experience of small town life, Sarah admits to seeing "all the things at home in this story." Writing from that perspective, she constructs an understanding of the story and recognizes its insights into small town life. Sarah has indeed created a unique text; in the process, perhaps, she has also gained some understanding of herself and of the human condition.

Petrosky (1982) notes that the response-based perception of meaning construction is "quite a radical change" from an understanding of reading as the "straightforward retrieval of information" (p. 23). Although the purpose of traditional writing assignments is usually to "show you got the point," such a purpose is inviable when interpretive focus is on the reader and not the text, because "the point" is a unique construction for each individual reader. In order to accommodate this new perception of the reader-text relationship, then, Petrosky (1982) has endorsed a "schema-theoretic" approach to composition where readers "put together their comprehension from not just the text, but from the interactions of their personal knowledge, feelings, and experiences with the text under the constraints of the context for reading" (p. 23).

Writing Tasks at Cross-Purposes?

Given the antithetical nature of the response-based and New Critical approaches, then, any "redefinition" of aims and methods must also wrestle with the apparent incongruity of mixing these paradigms in our classroom assignments. Response-based writing tasks encourage students to establish direct links between themselves and a text; traditional writing tasks discourage those links. When we invite students initially to connect their experiences with text but ultimately value New Critical approaches, do we send them confusing messages about whose "meaning" really counts? Furthermore, since making meaning from printed symbol is the fundamental disciplinary activity of literary study, this issue of whose meaning "counts" has great significance for how students will understand what it means to read literature.

Certainly response-based approaches are more compatible with current views of reading as a sociopsycholinguistic process of meaning-making. But there is also a well-established tradition favoring text-based or New Critical interpretive strategies. Ridings (1995) found, for example, that secondary level preservice teachers are primarily taught to view literature as "artifact" in their English courses. They are asked to analyze canonized texts from a critical and objective perspective. In their methods courses, however, these same students are increasingly urged to view literature as "expression." They are asked to generate personal connections, drawing heavily on their own experiences.

When preservice teachers receive such polar messages about where meaning resides they run the risk of becoming atheoretical practitioners. Since the university faculty who prepare future teachers hold such divergent beliefs about how literary meaning is made (Ridings, 1995), perhaps we should begin to reconsider the goals of literary study in ways which will accommodate and augment both these positions.

Redefining Pedagogical Objectives

Newell, Suszynski, and Weingart (1989) believe that writing about literature "can be either an endpoint that tests for a specific form of response or a point of departure for exploring and elaborating on students' responses to literature" (p. 38). While this statement accurately represents most writing assignments in school today, perhaps we have limited ourselves—and our students—with too few methods of writing about literature.

Noting the decline in the popularity of literary study, Emig (1990) wonders if it is not in part due to the preoccupation of university English instructors with critical theories of textual interpretation. She has urged them to study learning theory, believing that insights into the developmental nature of learning might offer a "redefinition of theory that organically brings our students into the dialogue" (Emig, 1990, p. 89).

Emig (1990) further recommends that instructors initially help students uncover their own constructs and use those as the framework for understanding. After "conscious theorizing" about their own learning, students will understand the "principles they follow" and are likely "to transfer what they learn" to other paradigms (Emig, 1990, p. 93). Once they have examined their own theories of reading, for example, students can turn to the "established theories of noted literary critics more openly and comprehendingly" (p. 93).

In a similar vein, Bleich (1985) advocates a new learning paradigm in the literature classroom, one which sees "developing knowledge" as a purpose for writing. A paradigm of developing knowledge demonstrates "that learning about language and literature is a process of self-regulation" (Bleich, 1985, p. 270).

The following excerpts from essays about Thurber's "The Catbird Seat" demonstrate the concept of "developing knowledge" by applying personal constructs to conventional literary devices. The assignment asked students to generate their own criteria for excellence in a short story. Note the three unconventional criteria identified by Angela in the following passage:

> First, a short story should capture my attention. Second it should keep my interest. Third, the characters should develop with the story. . . . As I began reading "The Catbird Seat," Mr. Martin's thought: "If any of the staff at F & S had seen him buy cigarettes, they would have been astonished, for it was generally known that Mr. Martin did no smoke . . ." aroused my curiosity. My first thought was: Why was he buying cigarettes when he did not smoke? I had to read on to find out the answer . . .

Another student, Nick, chose "diction"—a conventional literary device—as an important criterion, but note his unorthodox motivation:

> The reason diction is so critical to me is because it will make the difference in reading through a short story and enjoying it or having to stop every few lines to look up a word for its meaning. Also good diction will make a description vivid and clear and impress upon you the feelings the characters

have towards each other . . . Thurber does this with two small and brief passages early in the story . . .

The difference in voice and perspective between these passages and those of Janet who wrote on Frost's use of language or Amy who wrote on Hemingway's use of theme is striking. While both assignments tackle literary analysis through textual criticism, the assignments suggest different purposes for writing. In the first examples, Janet and Amy were asked to examine the text. In the second set of examples, Tom and Sarah were asked to examine their response to the text. In these, however, Angela and Nick were asked to examine their *relationship* to text. For students of literature, this is a critical revision of interpretive stance. Moreover, it incorporates features of both interpretive modes.

Conclusion

Finally, then, are writing assignments based on these dissimilar paradigms compatible in a contemporary American literature classroom? As we currently use them, probably not. Response-based assignments privilege the reader; traditional assignments privilege the text. Regardless of our predilection, sociopsycholinguistic and response theory have provided new understandings of the meaning-making process that validate Tompkins' (1980) call for a "redefinition of aims and methods" of literary study (p.x). Sociopsycholinguistic insights include a belief that readers initiate and control the reading event by applying both linguistic and life experience to the process of reading (Goodman, 1976, 1987). As Smith (1988) explains, "reading "is less a matter of extracting sound from print than of bringing meaning to print" (p. 2).

Bleich's (1985) paradigm of developing knowledge and Emig's (1990) suggestion that we use learning theory as both a personal and interpretive construct are a starting point for serious consideration of alternative ways of approaching literary interpretation. But the task of exploring new ways of meaning-making is enormous and complex. Further complicating the reader-text debate, for example, is the relatively unexplored role of context in the interpretive process. The reader-text relationship does not occur in a vacuum. It is sensitive to both tacit and explicit features of the learning community. Readers are influenced by teacher and peer values as well as their larger socioethnic culture. Even texts are constructed within a historical and literary context. Exploration of the role of context may also yield interpretive options that move beyond the reader-text debate.

Whatever the outcome, efforts to redefine the "aims and methods" of literary analysis will not be easy. As we dialogue with one another, we will raise tough questions about the nature of knowledge and the role of readers in a literate society: For what purpose should we ask students to write about the literature they read? To school them in the "poetic medium"? To help them discover knowledge or truth of the human condition artfully tucked into canonized text? To promote their own "self knowledge" and their "understanding others"? Perhaps to demonstrate cultural literacy, as it is articulated in our school district's curriculum guide? And ultimately, our answers may require some pedagogical consensus from us about where ownership of the interpretive process truly lies.

Beach and Hynds (1991) believe that our fundamental instructional challenge lies in "recognizing and preserving the integrity of each student's response within a highly technological and bureaucratic culture that demands standardization and accountability" (p. 480). In fact, perhaps all American educators have a paradoxical mission: to nurture and develop the potential of each individual while also dispensing information and inculcating values regarded as essential for life in our society. Viewed from this perspective, the tension between response-based and traditional writing tasks may be a powerful metaphor for a greater incongruity.

References

Applebee, A. (1992). "The background for reform." In J. A. Langer (Ed.), *Literature instruction: A focus on student response* (pp. 1-18). Urbana, IL: National Council of Teachers of English.

Beach, R., & Hynds, S. (1991). Research on response to literature." In R. Barr, M. L. Kamil, P. Mosenthal, & D. Pearson (Eds.), *Handbook of reading research II* (pp. 453-489). New York: Longman Publishing Group.

Beach, R. (1993). *A teacher's introduction to reader-response theory.* Urbana, IL: National Council of Teachers of English.

Bleich, D. (1985). The identity of pedagogy and research in the study of response to literature. In C. Cooper (Ed.), *Researching response to literature and the teaching of literature: Points of departure* (pp. 253-272). Norwood, NJ: Ablex Publishing Corporation.

Cooper, C. (1985). *Researching response to literature and the teaching of literature: Points of departure.* Norwood, NJ: Ablex Publishing Corporation.

Eliot, T. S. (1959). The problem of Hamlet. In G. B. Harrison (Ed.), *Major British writers II* (pp. 845-847). New York: Harcourt, Brace.

Emig, J. (1990). Our missing theory. In C. Moran & E. Penfield (Eds.), *Conversations: Contemporary critical theory and the teaching of literature* (pp. 87-96). Urbana, IL: National Council of Teachers of English.

Goodman, K. S. (1976). Behind the eye: What happens in reading. In H. Singer & R. B. Ruddell (Eds.), *Theoretical models and processes of reading* (2nd ed.) (pp. 470-496). Newark, DE: International Reading Association.

Goodman, K. S. (1987). Transactional psycholinguistic model. In H. Singer and R. B. Ruddell (Eds.), *Theoretical Models and Process of Reading* (3rd ed.) (pp. 813-839). Newark, DE: International Reading Association.

Harrison, G. B. (1959). *Major British writers II.* New York: Harcourt, Brace.

Kennedy, X. J. (Ed.) (1991). *Literature: An introduction to fiction, poetry, and drama* (5th ed.). New York: Harper Collins.

Langer, J. (1990). Understanding literature. *Language Arts, 67,* 812-816.

Langer, J. (1994). A response-based approach to reading literature. *Language Arts, 71,* 203-211.

Mailloux, S. 1990. The turns of reader-response criticism. In C. Moran & E. Penfield (Eds.), *Conversations: Contemporary critical theory and the teaching of literature* (pp. 38-54). Urbana, IL: National Council of Teachers of English.

Newell, G., Suszynski, K., & Weingart, R. (1989). The effects of writing in a reader-based and text-based mode on students' understanding of two short stories. *Journal of Reading Behavior, 21*(1), 37-57.

Newton, E. V. (1991). Developing metacognitive awareness: The response journal in college composition. *Journal of Reading, (34)*6, 476-478.

Petrosky, A. (1982). From story to essay: Reading and writing. *College Composition and Communication, 33*(1), 19-36.

Ridings, R. (1993). Literature as expression—literature as artifact: Which pedagogy did our English teachers choose? (ERIC Document Reproduction Service No. ED 287 172).

Rosenblatt, L. (1938). *Literature as exploration* (lst ed). New York: D. Appleton-Century, Co., Inc.

Rosenblatt, L. (1978). *The reader, the text, the poem: The transactional theory of the literary work.* Carbondale: Southern Illinois University Press.

Smith, F. (1988). *Understanding reading: A psycholinguistic analysis of reading and learning to read* (4th ed.). Hillsdale, NJ: Lawrence Erlbaum Associates.

Taylor, W., & Hall, D. (Eds.) (1970). *Poetry in English* (2nd ed.) New York: The Macmillan Company.

Thurber, J. (1987). The catbird seat. In X. J. Kennedy (Ed.), *Literature: An introduction to fiction, poetry, and drama* (4th ed) (pp. 48-54). Boston, MA: Little, Brown.

Tompkins, J. (1980). *Reader-response criticism: From formalism to post-structuralism.* Baltimore, MD: Johns Hopkins University Press.

Vacca, R. T., & Newton, E. (1995). Responding to literary text. In C.N. Hedley, P. Antonacci, & M. Rabinowitz (Eds.), *Thinking and literacy: The mind at work* (pp. 283-302). Hillsdale, NJ: Erlbaum.

Zancanella, D. A. (1988). Relationships between five teachers' personal approaches to literature and their teaching of literature. *Dissertation Abstracts International, 49,* 3293-A.

Movement and Motif Writing: Relationships to Language Development

Heidi Allen   **Timothy G. Morrison**
Patrick Debenham   **Pamela S. Musil**

Brigham Young University

Margery Baudin

Alpine School District

Abstract

Schools have traditionally emphasized oral and written language as the primary vehicle for instruction. Recognizing that there are multiple ways of knowing and communicating, teachers should provide various options for their students to communicate in their classrooms. Motif writing is a notation system used to record movement in much the same way written language is used to record speech. This article describes how motif writing was introduced to third grade students through creative dance classes. Results of how they learned to record and read movement are presented, with particular attention paid to individual students' acquisition of motif writing ability. Discussion centers around symbol systems and thinking, development of motif writing ability, and values of learning motif writing. Possible applications of motif writing in elementary classroom content areas are presented as well.

A merican classrooms have traditionally required children to use their linguistic expertise, perhaps to the detriment of other forms of expression. Linguistic intelligence has been required almost exclusively, resulting in what some have termed a "verbocentric" bias in school (Dyson, 1986; Fueyo, 1992; Gallas, 1994; Hubbard, 1989; Leland & Harste, 1994; Moffett, 1992; Siegel, 1995; Smagorinsky, 1995). Language is regarded as the sole or at best the primary means through which learning occurs in schools.

Despite the emphasis on language in schools, other systems of communication should not be ignored as means by which children can come to understand and express themselves. "Music can express feelings we cannot put into words; language is a better medium for humor than math; yet math can represent concepts that are not easily represented in art, and so on" (Berghoff, 1993, p. 218). Each communication form has potential to express meaning and each should be attended to in school. Since individuals possess varying degrees of ability and interest in various intelligences, access and validity for each should be offered in school. Harste, Short, and Burke (1988) caution that "if we encourage only those [communication systems] that highlight language, many types of meaning will necessarily be neglected because they simply are not amenable to linguistic expression" (p. 339). Perhaps teachers should identify children's strengths and abilities and focus on them for instruction. The result could be academic achievement, as well as increased interest and motivation for learning (Gardner, 1983).

Despite the rational argument for use of alternate communication systems in the schools, the use of the written word remains paramount. Perhaps other systems of written language related to various forms of expression would be beneficial for children. Notation systems have been developed in several fields to represent meaning in permanent form. As a musical score represents various aspects of music, so movement symbols represent a variety of body actions. Much of what is expressed through movement is momentary, fleeting, and easily forgotten, or at best it may be preserved through memory or videotape recording. Just as writing preserves oral language, movement symbols can capture body movement. If written symbols are important for expression of oral language, then they may also be important to expression of movement. Perhaps use of written symbols to represent movement can serve the same purposes as other forms of writing: to preserve, to communicate, and to clarify.

Motif Writing

One of the oldest forms of movement notation is Labanotation. Originally called Kinetography, Labanotation was developed by Rudolf von Laban in 1928 (Hutchinson, 1977). Out of this complex system stems what is known as motif writing, a simpler written code for dance and movement (Lohmiller, 1977). Figure 1 presents basic motif notation symbols.

Motif symbols serve as a new written sign system, encouraging children to learn and analyze movement in a new way. As children learn motif writing, movement is no longer merely something they do; movement becomes a series of specific actions that are combined to make a unique movement statement. By recording their movements, children become more aware of

Figure 1. Basic Motif Symbols Presented to the Students

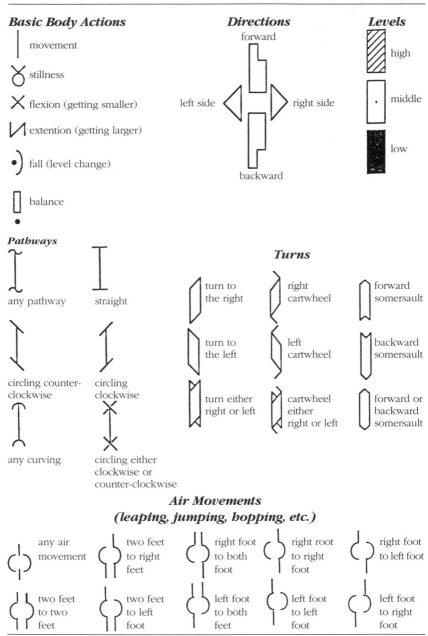

From *Your move: A new approach to the study of movement and dance* by A.H. Guest, 1983, New York: Gordon and Breach)

the processes they use to express themselves through movement. Writers of language complete a first draft of their writing so they can have a tangible record to which they can return for revision. In similar fashion, dancers can record on paper symbols to represent their movements. They can then return to the written record to continue creating and reworking movement phrases.

Children who are taught motif writing at a young age have a head start in movement communication. Dulieu (personal communication, March, 1996) found that with motif writing "the younger the student, the quicker they learn and the more they retain." By developing an additional way to understand and communicate, children will be better able to communicate with others. Children for whom spoken or written language is not an easy mode of communication may develop expertise in a new form of communication that could open up new understandings for them. In contrast, by combining physical expression with a symbolic written expression of the movement, students who struggle with bodily-kinesthetic intelligence are given a new opportunity to make meaning more concrete. They can understand their movement through writing, a more familiar form of communication for them. Through the act of recording movement, they come to understand and value movement as a means of expression.

Dance educators (Bashaw, 1995; Burke, 1993; *Dance Philosophy,* 1991; Groves, 1993; Guest, 1994; Morse, 1994; Pierce, 1995) have found that motif writing provides a logical way of learning and recording movement. Dulieu (personal communication, March, 1996) found that "the visual aid of symbols provided a handle for the children to understand the abstract to the concrete" and that "motif writing gives the non-dancer confidence to create" (personal communication). Motif writing provides children with a symbolic language that gives them "words" to articulate the actions of their bodies. "It is the first step toward dance literacy" (Groves, 1993, p. 9). Just as writing can clarify thinking (Vygotsky, 1978), motif writing can help clarify understanding of movement.

Motif Writing in a Third Grade Classroom

To discover ways children explore movement and use motif symbols as written expressions of movement, we decided to work with a class of third graders. Our interest in selecting these children was to describe in greater detail their successes and struggles as they learned to deal with a new form of written expression and to explore additional uses for motif writing in the elementary classroom. We understand that this study is descriptive in nature and that the results cannot be generalized to the entire population of third graders in the United States; indeed, results are specific to the students with whom we worked.

These third grade students were ideal for these purposes because they had already developed oral and written language ability. We anticipated that the students' ability to use written language to express ideas originating in oral language would help them understand how to use motif symbols to express ideas originating in movement. Third grade children were also well suited for this work because their levels of physical, mental, and social development could enhance their creative dance experiences.

> Nine to twelve year olds can control their moves with greater physical ability. With their heightened mental awareness, they can explore in depth all the elements of dance in all facets. They enjoy group work because of their social development and their space-time awareness, and they can readily experiment with relationships. (Joyce, 1994, p. 17)

Twenty creative dance lessons were taught by one of the authors over a fourteen-week period from November to February. The students in this school were from middle to upper-middle class families. All of the third grade students used English as their preferred language, and all were literate in English. These one hour lessons included creative movement, motif writing, and journal writing experiences. The lessons were arranged into four groups of five lessons each.

The first set of lessons helped students explore basic actions of the body, using authentic movement choices. During these lessons, children were asked to explore basic movement concepts, such as jumping, turning, stillness, and balance, based on their prior knowledge of movement.

The second set of lessons included oral and/or written observation and description of students' own and others' movements through shared writing and reading experiences. For example, the students worked with individual and group composition of small movement phrases. The students were given pictures of different animals and asked to create movement phrases that depicted the animals' qualities of movement. These phrases were then shown to the class as a whole. Class members described their observations of the movement phrase verbally and recorded their experience as best they could in their journals.

The third group of lessons introduced the children to basic motif writing structures, such as bottom-to-top orientation and timing. Figure 2 provides an example how a motif movement phrase begins, continues, and ends. Included in the example are symbols that show timing (short and long) and symbol layering (an action that moves in a straight, low pathway). Children were introduced to creating movement phrases through modeled writing and were then asked to approximate motif writing using invented spelling. The teacher modeled a movement phrase and the children tried to record the movement they observed using the newly introduced motif symbols. The teacher also modeled for the students how to write the movement phrase with motif symbols.

The last five lessons were designed to further develop children's motif

Figure 2. Motif Writing Structure.

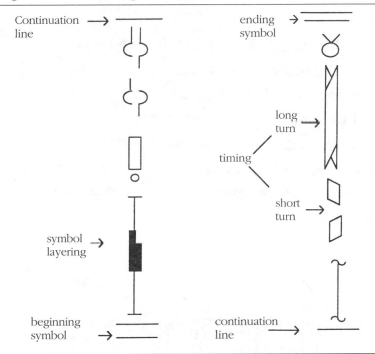

Represented in the illustration are basic elements of beginning and ending symbols, continuation lines, symbol layering, and timing.

writing skills through continued use of the symbols with teacher feedback. During these lessons, the children were asked to observe and record movements of others and to document their own movement phrases with motif writing. They demonstrated their ability to read and write using motif symbols. During one class experience, each child was given a story with movement words deleted. Students filled in the missing words in a story using motif symbols to indicate movement (see Figure 3). In small groups of four, students shared their stories. One child read another child's story with the inserted motif symbols, while that child performed the actions suggested by the motif symbols. The two remaining children recorded what was seen and heard. The stories were then examined to evaluate students' understanding of both motif writing and reading.

As a culminating event, the students held an informal performance-dem-

Figure 3. Small Group Motif Story Writing Activity

Keith and Billy's Motif Adventure

Keith and Billy ________ through the field that led to the forest. They ________ over a log and ________ under a hanging branch. They love to ________ in between the trees. Every time they heard a sound they would ________. They ________ when they came to a large river. After a long day of ________ and ________, they decided it was time to go home. On their way back home, they ________ and ________.

The End

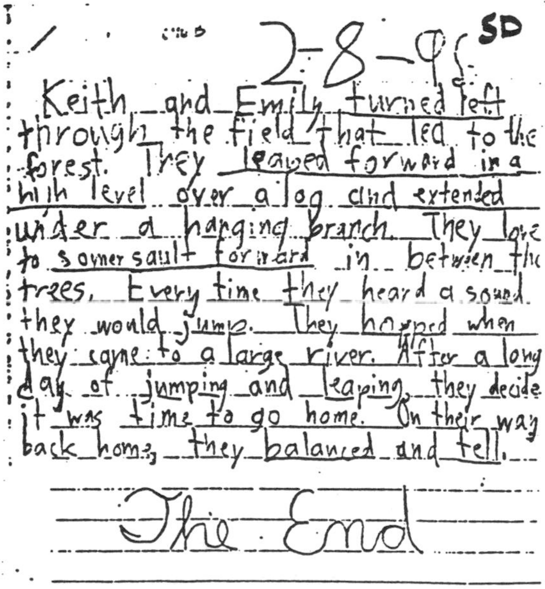

2-8-95 SD

Keith and Emily turned left through the field that led to the forest. They leaped forward in a hih level over a log and extended under a hanging branch. They love to somersault forward in between the trees. Every time they heard a sound they would jump. They hopped when they same to a large river. After a long day of jumping and leaping, they decide it was time to go home. On their way back homes, they balanced and fell.

The End

onstration for their parents and other invited guests. Through this activity the students shared their knowledge of motif writing by observing, recording, and performing basic motif movement phrases.

Results—Learning Motif Symbols
Writing Development—Whole Class

The students' motif writing development became apparent as the journal entries were examined and students were observed in the classroom. Over the 14-week period, students kept journals of their involvement with movement and motif writing. These journal entries were examined using coding procedures suggested by Strauss and Corbin (1990). As a result of this coding, five stages of motif writing development became apparent. Each of the five stages is described below and sample journal entries representing each of the five stages of motif writing development are included in Figures 4-a through 4-e.

Stage 1—Use of Pictures/Signs/Words In their first journal entries

Figure 4a. Stage 1—Use of Pictures/Signs/Words

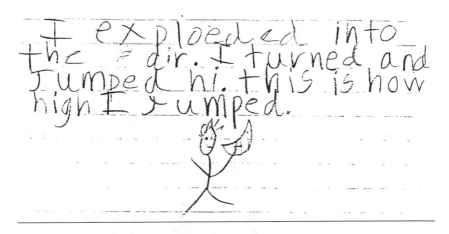

students depicted their movements by drawing pictures and/or writing words. In many cases students used a combination of words and pictures. Since they had not yet been introduced to motif symbols, they used the sign systems most familiar to them. Most students moved to the next stage at about the same time, but others continued writing at this stage for some time (See Figure 4-a).

Figure 4b. Stage 2—Movement Labels/Floor Patterns/Random Motif Symbols

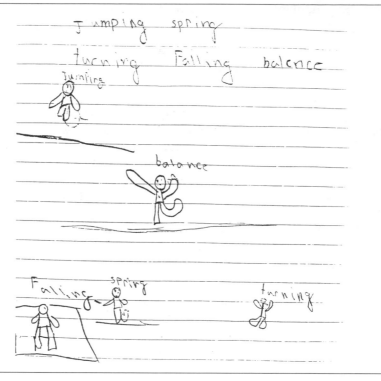

Stage 2—Movement Labels/Floor Patterns/Random Motif Symbols. In the second stage, students demonstrated awareness of what they had been taught by adding motif symbols and/or floor patterns to their repertoire. Pictures were still common in many journal entries, but students frequently added words to label the movements (See Figure 4-b).

Stage 3—Simple Motif Symbols with Words. By the time they reached the third stage, students had begun to follow the conventional bottom-to-top print orientation of motif writing, although their appropriate use of motif symbols was still less than fifty percent. Interspersed with these new innovations were vestiges of the pictures and labels from the previous stage (See Figure 4-c).

Stage 4—More Consistent and Correct Use of Motif Symbols. The fourth stage found the students able to more correctly form and use motif symbols (approximately 80% correct formation), use correct orientation symbols, and appropriately use motif symbols to represent movement sequences.

The students at this stage were becoming more conventional in their use of motif symbols (See Figure 4-d).

Stage 5—Use of Conventional Motif Symbols. The final stage of development was represented by near perfect formation and use of motif symbols (over 80% correct formation), consistent orientation of the symbols, and conventional symbol layering (i.e., combining two movements, such as turning and jumping). It appears that a process of acquisition took place for both receptive and productive use of motif symbols, as occurs with both oral and written language acquisition (See Figure 4-e).

Figure 4c. Stage 3—Simple Motif Symbols with Words

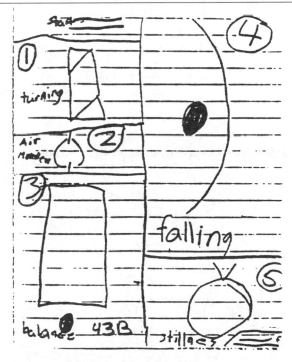

Figure 4d. Stage 4—More Consistent and Correct Use of Motif Symbols

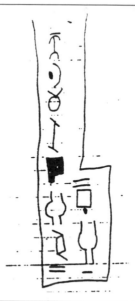

Figure 4e. Stage 5—Use of Conventional Motif Symbols

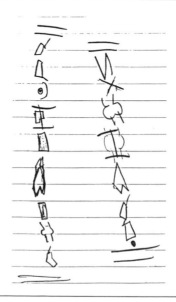

Writing Development—Individual

Although it became apparent that the third graders were able to acquire ability to read and write motif symbols, individual differences among the children provided greater insight into the process. For example, one of the students, Cathy, was described by her teacher as a low ability reader and writer who had been referred to the school resource teacher for assistance. Cathy was able to read some of the small function words (e.g., *and*, *the*, and *is*), but was unable to read enough content words with fluency to comprehend efficiently. She was a quiet, on-task student who rarely caused disruptions in class. Although she had a sense of her body and was coordinated in her movement, she lacked confidence to fully express herself in movement and did not want to be the center of attention. When she began to use motif symbols to express movement, Cathy used an arrow to show that her face was performing the action. Other students in the early stages of motif writing development used words or pictures to express similar ideas. Cathy, who felt less able to use words to express herself, used other symbols.

At the end of her exposure to motif writing, Cathy not only used the motif

Figure 5. A Movement Drawing by Cathy

She uses an arrow to show that her face is performing the action

symbols correctly, but was willing to demonstrate her skills by writing them in front of her classmates. She would never have volunteered to do this with reading or writing. Motif writing gave her a means by which she could relate her experiences in a written form. In fact, during one session where over 80% of the students chose to record their movement experiences with words and pictures, Cathy was one of the few who felt comfortable enough to use only motif symbols. Not only did motif writing give her a way to record her experiences, but she was also able to read other students' recorded movement phrases. During a final motif story experience, she struggled to pronounce and interpret each word written in English, but, when she came to a movement symbol, she immediately recognized it and was able to read it.

In general, the students were excited to learn new symbols and to explore new movement. One student, Greg, constantly thought of new ways to describe movement. One of his most clever invented spellings using motif symbols was his idea of how a cartwheel symbol could be created (see Figure 6). He described a cartwheel as an air moment that went from two feet, to two hands, and back to two feet. This student was able to combine his knowledge of motif symbols with his creativity. A number of students dem-

Figure 6. Greg Invents His Own Motif Symbol for Cartwheel

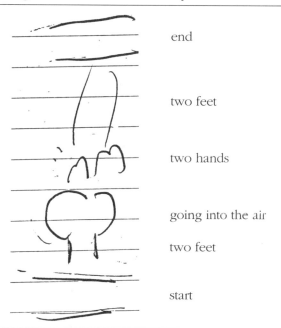

	end
	two feet
	two hands
	going into the air
	two feet
	start

The invented symbol depicts the child going from two feet, into the air, landing on two hands, and then back to two feet.

onstrated willingness and ability to invent their own symbols using a combination of motif symbols, or a combination of motif symbols and pictures,
words, and/or other symbols.

Frank was an active, impulsive student who struggled to stay on-task.
He was physically aggressive and very talkative in class. However, he enthusiastically participated in movement experiences. He became able to identify his exact movements during class activities. Usually he recorded his
movements by use of illustration. His movement journal was filled with
unrecognizable drawings, except for the one drawing of himself sliding along
the ground, reaching to get a ball. Both his writing and his drawings were
hard to decipher. But for some reason, Frank was able to develop some degree
of ability with motif writing. His only clear journal entries were those in which
he chose to use motif symbols to represent his movements.

Ashley was well above average in her language abilities. She was an
avid reader and was able to express herself well in writing. She did not re
quire extrinsic motivation to read. She was basically well-behaved in school
and tried hard to do her best. Although she demonstrated high ability with
oral and written language, her movements could best be described as "ordi-
nary" or even "awkward" at times. She was enthusiastic in her participation,
but her movements were not as fluid or controlled as those of many other
students. However, Ashley became more aware of movement as she broke

Figure 7. Ashley's Conventional Use of Motif Writing

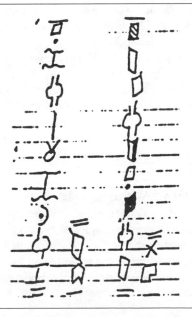

movement sequences into parts by using motif symbols. She also became very skilled in her use of motif symbols. Figure 7 shows Ashley's conventional use of motif symbols. Her symbols not only accurately record her movements, but they are also formed neatly and legibly.

Conclusions. As we completed our work with the third graders, we concluded that all the students were able to acquire some ability with motif symbols. As expected, students did not attain equal levels of competence, but showed individual differences in their acquisition. They appeared to follow certain stages of development in using motif symbols similar to oral and written language development.

We also found that many students used very creative ways to use their understanding of motif symbols, as evidenced by Greg's creation of a cartwheel symbol. Motif writing seemed to promote creative thinking among these children and gave them another tool to use in creative expression. In Frank's case, motif writing became a more effective form of written communication than conventional writing. He was able to form the motif symbols more legibly than the letters of the alphabet.

Some children have greater ability with movement than others. Some who were not as fluid and graceful in their movements, would analyze these movements through motif writing. Through careful observation, these children were able to become more aware of their movement. Ashley not only showed ability to use the motif symbols but also came to a greater understanding of movement.

The final outcome of our work with the third graders concerns those students who experience difficulty with conventional written language. Smagorinsky (1995) argues that individuals have many tools available to them to learn, although writing has achieved a preferred status among them. Since writing is the privileged sign system in schools, children must learn to write to be successful. Motif writing showed children who experienced difficulty with writing a new way to express themselves in written language. By examining writing from this new perspective of movement and motif writing, children for whom movement is a primary source of understanding may discover new insights about written language.

Applications of Motif Writing to the Content Areas

Although many teachers do not include movement instruction as part of their curriculum, creative movement exploration can be employed as a means of learning in any subject area from reading to math to science to art. The elements that comprise movement (space, time, and force) are universal. They can be manipulated and expressed through the body instrument to reinforce learning in almost any setting.

A teacher can demonstrate how to perform a movement, then show how to represent that movement in written form. For example, a teacher could model a movement phrase that includes a right turn, a leap, and stillness, and then represent the movement sequence using motif symbols. The teacher could describe the movements as he or she demonstrates them and also explain the symbols while writing them. These two steps of writing and moving can also be reversed, demonstrating the symbols first, then performing the movement. However, the movement and the written expression of the movement should occur together. When this is done, children may begin to make connections between the symbols and the movements they represent (Pierce, 1995).

For example, emerging readers and writers must come to some understanding of relationships between sounds and letters. Letter shape can be explored within a movement context, allowing children to internalize concepts such as the difference between lines that are straight and curved, as well as rounded and angular.

Basic math facts can be explored in the movement class by using variation of rhythm and timing. For example, the teacher could ask students to perform actions of equal timing in nine counts, or perform an action four times the duration of another. The movement may assist some children in feeling the division of the sequence into equal parts. Additionally, by using motif symbols, others who are more visual may also *see* the division of the parts in a new way.

Movement exploration which involves increasing and decreasing amounts of energy output can assist the child in conceptualizing an abstract math idea by giving it concrete meaning. Even difficult concepts, such as fractions, can be more easily understood when explored using the element of time and the sub-elements of rhythm, meter, and note-value. While these concepts are somewhat abstract and outside the conscious experience of most students, they can become more meaningful through movement exploration.

Science concepts, such as differences among solids, liquids, and gases, can be given more concrete meaning through movement explorations that relate to the molecular properties of each substance. For example, cell bonding could be easier to understand in terms of children connecting their movements together. A leap and a turn could be bonded together as a movement sequence. Layering motif symbols may enable some students to see how cells could come together to bond. Cell division could be demonstrated through movement by having students stretch or reach until they "split" apart and create two separate cells. This science concept could be clarified for some students by representing the ideas using motif symbols.

Other possible applications of movement and motif writing to the science classroom include representing changes in the weather. For example, a tornado could be demonstrated by turning and pathway movements. Evaporation could be shown by rising and extensional movements. Falling and trailing pathways could be used to represent rainfall.

Motif writing also has many possible applications to the language arts classroom. For example, our third graders were offered several enrichment activities after they had read a story. These activities included drama, art, and writing activities, as well as a motif writing activity. In the movement activity choice, students wrote a motif phrase that described the story or a part of the story. After the motif phrases had been written, students performed their movement sequences. Other students observed the movements and compared them with the motif symbols.

Students were also encouraged to write a poem that suggested movement (e.g., snowflakes falling to the ground, fish swimming in the ocean, etc.). They wrote the poem using any form they wished, but then symbolized the movements using motif writing. The students then performed the movements with other students observing, commenting, and recording the movements using motif symbols. The two motif symbol versions of the movements were compared to see if both used appropriate symbols.

Students also participated in a pre-writing activity which involved movement adventure. They imagined that they were being held captive in a castle and needed to create a way to escape. In finding a pathway out of the castle, the students shared their movements with others. Through this activity, students found that movement itself is a powerful learning tool. A motif writing activity naturally followed as well. Students recorded each others' movements using motif symbols. They also used motif symbols to represent their own movement phrases. Once again, the students had the opportunity to compare their own motif writing with other students' writing.

The addition of motif writing to the movement experience creates another dimension in the learning process. The student records experiences using motif symbols. The act of writing reinforces understanding of the original concept.

Discussion

The use of motif symbols to express movements has implications that reach several areas of literacy development. We will discuss three areas: use of sign systems to think, learn, and understand; development of children's ability to appropriately use motif writing; and the value of a notation system for movement.

Sign Systems and Thinking

Writing and thinking are closely related processes. Zinsser (1988) explains that "writing is thinking on paper" (p. 1). He goes on to assert that "writing enables us to find out what we know—and what we don't know—

about what we're trying to learn" (p. 16). The process of writing causes individuals to formulate thoughts and ideas in ways that are comprehensible to others. As they write, new doors can open, and writers may begin to see things in new, enlightening ways. Just as conventional writing serves to clarify thinking, motif writing may also help students develop thinking skills. When children have opportunities to develop their ideas and actions using motif symbols they learn about important aspects of their own thinking processes.

Motif writing, when combined with creative movement exploration, can also provide significant opportunities for children to learn how to communicate more effectively. Although communication is a major focus of writing, perhaps even more fundamental is that writing can "provide the basis of a developing system of personal thought" (Langer, 1986, p. 2).When cognitive understanding of movement accompanies the psychomotor and affective learning processes that are more often associated with movement, learning is more complete.

For some of our third graders motif writing offered new, exciting ways to see things. For example, many became better observers through this experience. They saw more clearly and distinctly the component parts to movement phrases. Previously, they had considered a movement as a whole, but through work with motif writing, they were able to identify, describe, and record the parts that made up the whole movement. After going through this process, the whole movement sequence became much more meaningful to them. Their understanding had been enlightened.

It also may be true that learning to communicate in one writing system can facilitate development in another. Cathy, the student who had experienced feelings of frustration and failure with written language, felt great success with motif writing. She began to see how written symbols and movement actions are related to each other. Because of this insight, she may also learn to see relationships between spoken and written language in new ways that will enhance her language development.

Development of Motif Writing Ability

Development of any cognitive ability occurs gradually over a long period. When infants are born they know no language; but after a few short years virtually all have mastered their first language. In doing so, children proceed through several predictable stages of oral language development (Glazer, 1989). Although the process seems the same for all children and developmental stages are anticipated, each child develops language in his or her own way.

Several stage models of reading acquisition have also developed to explain the gradual development of reading ability observed in young children(Chall, 1983; Ehri & Wilce, 1985); Gough & Hillinger, 1980; Mason,

1984). In general, these models describe three phases of beginning reading development: first, a selective-cue stage, followed by a spelling-sound stage, and finally an automatic stage. Similarly, writing develops in consistent ways over time. Spelling develops in predictable ways (Sulzby & Teale, 1985), as well as children's tendencies to become less self-oriented in their writing over time (Moffett, 1968).

Just as oral language proficiency and ability to read and write develop over time, so too does children's ability to use motif symbols to express movement. As we found in this study, children appear to develop motif writing ability by progressing gradually and individually through several stages. As with other cognitive processes, motif writing ability is idiosyncratic and follows stages of development in general ways.

Value of Motif Writing

As students explore their own movement and create movement individually or with others, they can use motif symbols to record and preserve their movements. Writers can come back to earlier drafts to revise, add, and delete from their writing; individuals working with movement can do this as well. Motif symbols provide a way for students to use "place holders" as they compose movement phrases. Movement, like language, does not need to be momentary; both can be recorded and held for future use. In our work with third graders, we found that in many activities students were able to revisit their movement work using motif writing. They did not feel that their movements were lost. Rather, they seemed to feel liberated in that they knew they could return to any motif phrase they had written and create meaning from it.

Motif symbols not only provide a logical system to represent movement, but they can also facilitate movement. Children can examine all that is included in a movement sequence by associating motif symbols with each part of the sequence. They can also observe and rehearse so that all the parts of the movement sequence are noted and practiced. Although some students were not as able to perform movements as others, as the third graders practiced movement by identifying all the parts that comprised a movement sequence, they became more fluid and graceful in their movements.

Many posible forms of communication exist for individuals to understand and express meaning. Although traditional language arts in all forms—listening, speaking, reading, and writing—are very common in the classroom and constitute the bulk of instructional time, alternative forms of communication also appear to serve students well. Motif writing may provide a vehicle for students to combine movement and writing as forms of expression, allowing children to obtain deeper understandings and experience subtle nuances of communication.

References

Bashaw, B. (1995). Summer motif magic in Ohio. *Program in Dance and Dance Education Newsletter*, 4-5.

Berghoff, B. (1993). Moving toward aesthetic literacy in the first grade. In D. J. Leu & C. K. Kinzer (Eds.), *Examining central issues in literacy research, theory, and practice* (pp. 217-233). Chicago: National Reading Conference.

Burke, M. (1993). Your move in Christchurch, New Zealand. *LODA-NEWS, 2,* 3-4.

Chall, J. S. (1983). *Stages of reading development.* New York: McGraw-Hill.

Dance philosophy. (1991, August). Columbus, OH: Columbus Public Schools.

Dyson, A. H. (1986). Transition and tensions: Interrelationships between the drawing, talking, and dictating of young children. *Research in the Teaching of English, 20,* 379-409.

Ehri, L. C., & Wilce, L. S. (1985). Movement into reading: Is the first stage of printed word learning visual or phonetic? *Reading Research Quarterly, 20,* 163-179.

Fueyo, J. (1992). Reading "literate sensibilities": Resisting a verbocentric classroom. *Language Arts, 68,* 641-648.

Gallas, K. (1994). *The language of learning.* New York: Teachers College Press.

Gardner, H. (1983). *Frames of mind: The theory of multiple intelligences.* New York: Basic Books.

Glazer, S. M. (1989). Oral language and literacy development. In D. S. Strickland & L. M. Morrow (eds.), *Emerging literacy: Young children learn to read and write* (pp. 16-26). Newark, DE: International Reading Association.

Gough, P. B., & Hillinger, M. L. (1980). Learning to read: An unnatural act. *Bulletin of the Orton Society, 30,* 179-196.

Groves, M. (1993). A new approach to creative dance. *LODA-NEWS, 1,* 7-9.

Guest, A. H. (1994). Language of dance at Nutmeg Ballet School. *LODA-NEWS, 3,* 11.

Harste, J., Short, K., with Burke, C. (1988). *Creating classrooms for authors.* Portsmouth, NH: Heinemann.

Hubbard, R. (1989). *Authors of pictures, draughtsmen of words.* Portsmouth, NH: Heinemann.

Hutchinson, A. (1977). *Labanotation or kinetography Laban: The system of analyzing and recording movement* (3rd ed.). New York: Routledge/Theatre Arts Books.

Joyce, M. (1994). *First steps in teaching creative dance to children* (3rd ed.). Palo Alto, CA: Mayfield.

Langer, J. (1986). *Children reading and writing: Structures and strategies.* Norwood, NJ: Ablex.

LeLand, C. H., & Harste, J. C. (1994). Multiple ways of knowing: Curriculum in a new key. *Language Arts, 71,* 337-345.

Lohmiller, M. (1977). Motif writing: A creative tool. *Journal of Physical Education and Recreation, 48,* 60, 62.

Mason, J. M. (1984). Early reading from a developmental perspective. In P. D. Pearson, R. Barr, M. L. Kamil, & P. Mosenthal (eds.), *Handbook of reading research,* (vol. 1) (pp. 505-543). White Plains, NY: Longman.

Morse, I. (1994). Language of dance foundation course. *LODA-NEWS, 4,* 3-4.

Moffett, J. (1968). *Teaching the universe of discourse.* Boston: Houghton Mifflin.

Moffett, J. (1992). *Harmonic learning: Keynoting school reform.* Portsmouth, NH: Boynton/Cook Heinemann.

Pierce, A. (1995). Language of dance at Mulberry School. *LODA-NEWS, 5,* 3-5.

Siegel, M. (1995). More than words: The generative power of transmediation for learning. *Canadian Journal of Education, 20,* 455-475.

Smagorinsky, P. (1995). Constructing meaning in the disciplines: Reconceptualizing writing across the curriculum as composing across the curriculum. *American Journal of Education, 103,* 160-184.

Strauss, A. L., & Corbin, J. (1990). *Basics of qualitative research: Grounded theory procedures and techniques.* Newbury Park, CA: Sage Publications.

Sulzby, E. , & Teale, W. H. (1985). Writing development in early childhood. *Educational Horizons, 64,* 8-12.

Vygotsky, L. S. (1978). *Mind in society: The development of higher psychological processes.* M. Cole, V. Joh-Steiner, S. Scribner, & E. Souberman (Eds.). Cambridge, MA: Harvard University Press.

Zinsser, W. (1988). *Writing to learn.* New York: Harper Row.

Improving Preservice Teachers' Attitudes Toward Writing

Susan Davis Lenski

Illinois State University

Sherrie Pardieck

Bradley University

Abstract

This study reports the effects of incorporating writing workshop activities in a language arts methods classes. Forty-two elementary education students in a large midwestern university attended one of two classes. The students were given a Writing Apprehension Survey at the beginning and at the end of the semester. During the course, students participated in writing workshops and were encouraged to develop their individual writing identities. Data from the pretest and posttest surveys were analyzed. The group as a whole significantly improved its attitudes toward writing (t = 5.96, p < .05). Additionally, students who had strongly held beliefs about themselves as writers, either positive (t = 2.26, p < .05) or negative (t = 4.03, p < .05), significantly improved their writing attitudes.

As teachers enter the new millennium, the ability to teach writing will become even more important than it has been in the final decades of the twentieth century. With the advent of new technologies, writing is becoming the preferred method of communicating, replacing telephone calls and face-to-face conversations. New teachers entering the teaching profession, therefore, must have a positive feeling about writing and a strong identity as a writer. The purpose of this article is to suggest that teacher education courses should implement writing workshops to improve the attitudes preservice teachers hold about writing.

Theoretical Framework

Attitudes About Writing

The attitudes teachers hold about writing are important. Teachers are expected to model joyfully literate behavior in their classrooms and are expected to exemplify "more learned others" who enjoy writing, are able to write well, and have the knowledge to assist students who are novice writers. But, do teachers have positive attitudes about themselves as writers? Research indicates that many preservice and practicing teachers perceive themselves as poor writers and are not sure how to teach and develop writing skills (Bowie, 1996, Brinkley, 1993).

Writing Apprehension

Many teachers who have a negative feeling about writing actually exhibit dispositional writing apprehension. Writing apprehension is a construct that refers to whether a person will undertake or avoid writing tasks (Daly, Vangelisti, & Witte, 1988). The degree of writing apprehension a person experiences can range from complete absence of any apprehension to debilitation. Some people have no fear of writing; in fact, they welcome opportunities to write. Others find writing to be mildly enjoyable; some are ambivalent; others try to avoid writing but are not really apprehensive; and still others panic when they are asked to write. Apprehension toward writing tends to remain fairly stable over time and task (Daly, 1985), which indicates that those who have writing apprehension do not lose their fear of writing when they receive a teaching degree or a classroom of students to teach.

The degree of writing apprehension writers feel is formed, in part, by their background experiences with writing. The writing environment that students experience is one of the determinants of their feelings about writing (Smith, 1982). Students who have had their writing attempts criticized often feel defensive about their writing. This defensive attitude sets off a causal chain that may lead to a dread of writing activities (Daly, 1985).

Traditionally, teachers have evaluated student writing by pointing out writing errors, often with a red pen, which leads to "bloody papers." Although process writing advocates have discouraged this practice for years (Graves, 1994), many practicing teachers, some of whom use components of writing workshops, feel obligated to mark all errors. Several studies have shed light on reasons why this type of evaluative practice may lead to writing apprehension. Writing fear is generated when the possibility of evaluation arises. Bishop (1989) suggests that students may become highly apprehensive about writing evaluation and, in turn, may write shorter texts. Students may feel that writing is hard work and discouraging. Students facing criticism of their writing become apprehensive, and, consequently, avoid writing tasks

(Brinkley, 1993). Furthermore, one of the primary factors contributing to writing apprehension is negative self-talk (Madigan, Linton, & Johnson, 1996). Teacher criticism of writing can lead students who experience primarily negative input, to increase their negative self-talk about writing.

Instructional Effectiveness

A teacher's attitude toward writing can influence his or her effectiveness as a writing teacher (Daly, 1985). Research in writing apprehension indicates that a positive correlation exists between high writing apprehension and a teacher's perception about the relevance of writing, the teacher's instructional methods, the teacher's emphasis on classroom writing, and the teacher's own writing behavior (Faigley, Daly, & Witte, 1981). Highly anxious teachers also tend to be more traditional writing teachers. They tend to emphasize rigid grammar rules at the expense of teaching the writing process (Gere, Schuessler, & Abbott, 1984). Highly apprehensive teachers may avoid any physical contact with students during writing time (Bizzaro & Toler, 1986). Furthermore, teachers who do not like to write tend to assign fewer writing tasks than do teachers with a positive attitude toward writing (Claypool, 1980). In turn, the concepts students develop about writing are influenced by the teacher's view of writing (Wing, 1989).

Preservice Teachers' Attitudes Toward Writing

Research has demonstrated that writing apprehension can limit the writing skills of teachers and their instructional practices. Many of the preservice teachers that we have in classes today have experienced writing instruction that leads to negative beliefs about themselves as writers. Even though the process writing movement is in its third decade, writing workshops have not made their way into all classrooms from which our students have graduated. However, writing workshops that are incorporated in preservice education classes seem to be successful in changing the writing attitudes of preservice teachers (Fox, 1980, Lenski, 1994).

Purpose and Pilot Study

The purpose of this study was to determine whether the attitudes preservice teachers have about writing would change after they experienced a language arts class that included a writing workshop. A secondary purpose was to determine whether the attitudes of students who held strong writing identities change more or less than that of students who had less clear writing identities. The present study is the second in a series that investigates the writing apprehension of preservice teachers. In the first study (Lenski, 1994), the Daly-Miller Writing Apprehension Survey (Daly, & Miller, 1975) was administered as a pretest and posttest to two classes of undergraduate students in a large mid-western university. One class experienced writing workshops and a comparison group read about writing workshops. A comparison of the pretest and posttest scores indicated increased mean scores in both groups at a level that was near significance. However, the participants in the study found that the instrument was not entirely applicable to their situation. The first study, therefore, was considered a pilot study for the present study.

Design of the Study
Participants
The participants in this study were elementary education majors attending a large midwestern university and taking a required course in language arts teaching methods. The participants were in two different classes taught by the same instructor, one of the investigators. Of the 42 students completing the study, 40 were female and two were male. All of the students were between the ages of 21 and 26, and all of the students were Caucasian.

Procedures
To determine whether preservice teachers improved their attitudes toward writing, an adapted Daly-Miller Writing Apprehension Survey was administered to two classes of students taking an undergraduate language arts class (see Appendix). The Daly-Miller Writing Apprehension Survey is a list of 26 items that query the participants' attitudes about writing on a five point Likert scale from "strongly disagree" to "strongly agree." The survey has robust internal and external validity and reliability (Daly, & Miller, 1975) and was considered an appropriate measure for this study.

The Daly-Miller Writing Apprehension Survey adapted for the present study incorporated students' suggestions from the pilot study. The substance of the survey was not changed in significant ways. Most of the changes dealt with wording that made the items more relevant for teacher education students. The wording of nine of the survey items was changed. For example, "I expect to do poorly in composition classes even before I enter them" was changed to " I expect to do poorly on writing assignments." A second example, "I have a terrible time organizing my ideas in a composition course," was changed to "I have a terrible time organizing my ideas for a piece of writing."

A second change in the survey that was used in the present context was in the numbering scale. The numbering scale on the Daly-Miller Writing Apprehension Survey ranged from 1 (strongly agree) to 5 (strongly disagree). The students at this university were used to taking surveys that used 5 (strongly agree) and 1 (strongly disagree). The survey was changed to make its use more compatible with students' expectations of surveys. This change, however, makes it difficult to compare the mean scores of the students in this study with the scores from previous studies using the original scale.

The survey was given both at the beginning and at the end of the language arts course. Both groups experienced writing workshops within the class. Because of the students' positive reactions to experiencing writing workshops in the pilot study, the investigators decided not to use one class as a comparison group. Certainly, a single group pretest/posttest design is not a strong research design. But, it can be argued that to deprive one class of an educational experience that could make them better teachers is not a good instructional decision. Therefore, the investigators opted for a weaker research design and a stronger language arts class.

In addition to administering a writing apprehension survey, students were asked to respond to questions about their writing identity. The questions that the students were asked follow.

1. What is a good writer?
2. What is the easiest part of writing for you? What do you do well?
3. What is the hardest part of writing for you? What do you need to work on?

Students then participated in a four-week writing workshop. The class met three times a week for an hour at each class meeting. During the classes, the instructor spent 5 to 10 minutes describing a stage in the writing process. After the instruction, the instructor gave students time to work on a self-selected piece of writing. Students met in writing groups for approximately 40 minutes. At the conclusion of the class, the instructor asked the students to react to their experiences and to apply their experiences to teaching. Each student completed at least one piece of writing. At the end of the four-week period, the students were asked to write a response to the following question: "Do you consider yourself a writer?"

Results
Writing Identities

The results of the answers to questions about writing identities were read by one of the investigators and a research assistant and separated into three categories: strongly held positive writing identity, strongly held negative writing identity, and weak writing identity. The decisions about category placement were primarily determined by the answer to the question "Do you consider yourself a writer?" and supplemented with information from the preliminary questions about writing. Discussions about students' responses were held until the investigator and research assistant agreed on the category placement. Of the 42 responses from students, only two engendered much discussion.

Nineteen of the 42 students evidenced strongly held positive writing identities. When asked whether they considered themselves writers, they answered that they enjoyed writing, felt confident about writing, and looked forward to teaching writing. Two students' examples follow.

Student #1: Strongly held positive writing identity
I consider myself to be a highly effective writer. This consideration comes from others informing me that they enjoy my writing and can understand the meaning. I, however, feel that the most important factor of being an effective writer is that writing is something I truly enjoy.

Student #2: Strongly held positive writing identity
I love writing. I write letters, stories, poems, journals entries, and I love it. I feel that I am a writer simply because I find writing be a great experience. For me, writing is like a vacation. I write to relax, think, and escape.

Fourteen of the 42 students had strongly held negative writing identities. These students expressed a strong dislike of writing and had little confidence in their ability to write as exemplified by these two students' examples.

Student #3: Strongly held negative writing identity
No, I do not see myself as a writer. I never enjoyed writing in school because I didn't (and don't) have the imagination for it. I also think that because from Jr. High on, if we had six errors or more, we got an automatic *F*. I was very discouraged. No matter how hard I worked or how good my paper was, I could never be perfect and get an *A*.

Student #4: Strongly held negative writing identity
I don't view myself as a writer, because I don't enjoy writing. In grade school, my writing was always evaluated, judged and given a grade. I still have that idea of writing, and, therefore, get no enjoyment out of it.

Nine of the students had ambivalent feelings toward writing. When they were asked whether they considered themselves to be writers, they answered that they were not sure or that they didn't know. These students did not identify with the students who had positive writing identities, nor did they identify with students who had negative writing identities. Examples of two students' answers follow.

Student #5: Weak writing identity
I feel that I am capable of writing, yet I have little confidence. I am always afraid to share the things which I write. I feel that if I had more confidence in my writing, then I would improve as a writer. I don't know if that makes me a writer or not.

Student #6: Weak writing identity
I consider myself to be a very average writer, and I'm not sure if I consider myself a writer or not. I have always had great thoughts and ideas in my head, but trying to write them down on paper seems to be quite a task.

Writing Apprehension Survey

The Writing Apprehension Survey scores of the pretest and posttest were calculated. The mean score of the entire group at the beginning of the study was 92.88. This mean score indicates a relatively low degree of writing apprehension. Consistent with Daly and Shamo (1978), people with debilitating writing apprehension typically select occupations that do not require much writing. Since elementary education majors know they will be required to teach writing, people with higher degrees of writing apprehension may not select a career as an elementary teacher. The mean score of the total group, however, was encouraging. The preservice teachers in this group have a more positive attitude toward writing than did the students in the pilot study (Lenski, 1994).

The mean scores were then analyzed by writing identity. That calculation revealed predictable mean scores. Students with strongly held positive writing identities had a beginning mean score of 97.57, students with strongly held negative writing identities had a beginning mean score of 75.57, and students with a weak writing identity had a mean score of 89.12 as reported in Table 1.

Table 1. Writing Apprehension Survey Scores

Writing Identity	Number of Students	Pretest Mean	Pretest SD	Posttest Mean	Posttest SD	t
Strongly held positive identity	19	97.57	23.47	109.68	8.62	2.26*
Strongly held negative identity	14	75.57	25.16	83.85	7.39	4.03*
Weak identity	9	89.12	5.54	89.25	6.75	.09
Total	42	92.88	13.92	98.95	14.17	5.96*

*p<.05

The scores of the pretest and posttest Writing Apprehension Surveys were analyzed using a paired t-test to determine whether a significant change in writing apprehension occurred after experiencing a language arts course that included a writing workshop. Forty-two pairs of scores were recorded and analyzed. The results indicated significant gains for the group as a whole (t=5.96). For students with strongly held positive writing identities (t=2.26) and for students with strongly-held negative writing identities (t=4.03), the results were also significant. For students who had weak writing identities (t=.09), the results were not significant.

Discussion

The present study was based on the assumption that improving writing attitudes, whether for students who already have positive writing identities or for students with negative writing identities, is an important aspect of teacher education. If one of the components of effective writing instruction is predicated on the writing attitude of the teacher, addressing writing attitudes in preservice education courses is imperative. Previous studies have indicated that preservice teachers' attitudes toward writing are amenable to change (Bowie, 1996). Therefore, it behooves teacher educators to identify the instructional interventions that will best lead to improving writing attitudes of preservice teachers.

Engaging preservice teachers in writing activities such as writing workshops has been one of the innovations that has been effective in improving preservice teachers' attitudes toward writing (Bass & Chambless, 1994, Chambless & Bass, 1995). This study adds to that body of research that advances the idea of incorporating writing activities in preservice education courses. In this study, students experiencing writing workshops improved their writing attitude scores by an average of 6.07 points. Although the changes in scores do not provide educators with the reasons why the scores changed, an hypothesis based on current studies on writing apprehension can be made.

Writing apprehension seems to be more of a function of a writer's self-talk than it is of the writing task or the writer's ability to write well (Madigan, Linton, & Johnson, 1996). Therefore, writing apprehension is a cognitive disposition. Writers who are self-critical and experience self-deprecating thoughts raise their apprehension about writing tasks, whether or not they are actually poor writers. This negative self-talk may be a function of an attributional style that attributes success or failure to luck. Writers with high apprehension often explain their anxiety by luck rather than by effort (Daly, 1985). When writers attribute feelings to luck, they prevent themselves from developing their writing abilities. As a result, they are unable to develop either their confidence or their writing skills.

Assuming, therefore, that an important factor in a writers' attitude is self-talk during writing activities, it follows that a positive writing workshop experience could influence a writer's self-talk in a positive direction. Rather than thinking about how difficult writing can be, writers in a writing workshop can share their feelings about writing and can gain the support of other writers. A study of the ways preservice teachers attribute success or failure as they experience a writing workshop, therefore, could be a fruitful area of future study.

This study also indicates that preservice teachers should examine their own writing identities. The preservice teachers in this study who held strong notions about themselves as writers showed greater improvements as a group than did the students who did not have firm beliefs about their writing identities. The students who held positive writing identities improved their writing apprehension mean scores an average of 12.10 points. Students who held negative writing identities improved their mean scores an average of 8.28 points. The students who did not have strong writing identities, positive or negative, scored virtually the same on the pretest and posttest measures.

While we cannot be certain why students holding stronger writing identities made more gains than students who were unsure of themselves, a hypothesis can be suggested. Students who were unsure about themselves as writers may have attributed success or failure to the task at hand rather than to a belief about their writing abilities. Although the sample in this study of unsure writers was small, there is some evidence that the students who did not have strong feelings about writing used the task as a measure of their confidence. For example, one student wrote: "Sometimes I consider myself a writer. If I'm writing about something I know or truly care about, my writing will reflect this. However if I have to write about something I'm not interested in or I believe is boring, my paper will show this." It is possible that students who rely on the task for their writing identities are not as amenable to improving their writing attitudes as students who attribute their writing success or failure to themselves.

Implications

This study underscores the need to incorporate writing activities such as writing workshops in preservice education courses. In discussions about using writing workshops to improve preservice attitudes toward writing, however, many teacher educators express the concern that they do not have enough time to participate in such a time-consuming activity. Certainly time in teacher education courses is limited. However, the benefits of implementing activities that improve students' attitudes toward writing more than justify the time they take.

Teachers of preservice education courses should also take time to help preservice teachers develop positive writing identities. The preservice teachers in this study who held positive writing identities continued to improve their attitudes toward writing as they experienced the language arts course.

These beginning teachers will be armed with positive beliefs about themselves as writers and will be more able to become positive role models for their students. Teacher educators should also emphasize to students that everyone can become a writer, including all of the preservice teachers. Furthermore, teacher educators should help students learn how to develop positive self-talk as they face writing assignments.

Conclusions

Encouraging new teachers to embrace a positive attitude toward writing is a crucial step in breaking the cycle of negative feelings toward writing. When new teachers feel confident about themselves as writers, they will provide better writing instruction and better role models for the next generation of students. To help preservice teachers develop more positive attitudes toward writing, teacher education courses should include at least one course that has writing workshop activities. Along with having preservice teachers experience writing workshops, teacher educators should make a conscious effort to help preservice teachers develop positive writing identities. Helping preservice teachers learn to love to write should be an important goal of teacher education programs.

References

Bass, J. A., & Chambless, M. S. (1994). Modeling in teacher education: The effects on writing attitude. *Action in Teacher Education, 16,* 37-44.

Bishop, W. 1989). We're all basic writers: Tutors talking about writing apprehension. *The Writing Center Journal, 9,* 31-42.

Bizzaro, P., & Toler, H. (1986). The effects of writing apprehension on the teaching behaviors of writing center tutors. *The Writing Center Journal, 7,* 37-43.

Bowie, R. L. (1996). *Future teachers' perception of themselves as writers and teachers of writing: Implications for teacher education programs.* Paper presented at the Annual Meeting of the College Reading Association, Charleston, SC.

Brinkley, E. H. (1993). Passing on the joy of literacy: Students become writing teachers. In L. Patterson, C. M. Santa, K. G. Short, & K. Smith (Eds.), *Teachers as researchers: Reflection and action* (pp. 210-219). Newark, DE: International Reading Association.

Chambless, M. S., & Bass, J. A. (1995). Effecting changes in student teachers' attitudes toward writing. *Reading Research and Instruction, 35,* 153-160.

Claypool, S. H. (1980). *Teacher writing apprehension: Does it affect writing assignments across the curriculum?* Washington, DC: Educational Research Information Center. (ERIC Document Reproduction Service No. ED 216 387)

Daly, J. A. (1985). Writing apprehension. In M. Rose (Ed.), *When a writer can't write* (pp. 43-82). NY: Guilford.

Daly, J. A., & Miller, M. D. (1975). The empirical development of an instrument to measure writing apprehension. *Research in the Teaching of English, 9,* 242-249.

Daly, J. A., & Shamo, W. (1978). Academic decisions as a function of writing apprehension. *Research in the Teaching of English, 12,* 119-126.

Daly, J. A., Vangelisti, A., & Witte, S. P. (1988). Writing apprehension in the classroom context. In B. Rafoth & D. L. Rubin (Eds.), *The social construction of written communication* (pp. 1-36). Norwood, NJ: Ablex.

Faigley, L., Daly, J. A., & Witte, S. P. (1981). The role of writing apprehension in writing performance and competence. *Journal of Educational Research, 75,* 16-21.

Fox, R. F. (1980). Treatment of writing apprehension and its effects on composition. *Research in the Teaching of English, 14,* 39-49.

Gere, A. R., Schuesslet, B. R., & Abbott, R. D. (1984). Measuring teachers' attitudes toward writing instruction. In R. Beach & L. Bridwell (Eds.), *New directions in composition research* (pp. 348-361). NY: Guilford.

Graves, D. H. (1994). *A fresh look at writing.* Portsmouth, NH: Heinemann.

Lenski, S. D. (1994). *Effect of participation in writing workshops on the dispositional writing apprehension preservice teachers.* Paper presented at the College Reading Association National Conference, New Orleans, LA.

Madigan, R., Linton, P., & Johnson, S. (1996). The paradox of writing apprehension. In C. M. Levy & S. Ransdell (Eds.), *The science of writing* (pp. 295-308). Mahwah, NJ: Erlbaum.

Smith, F. (1982). *Writing and the writer.* NY: Holt, Rinehart, & Winston.

Wing, L. A. (1989). The influence of preschool teachers' beliefs on young children's conceptions of reading and writing. *Early Childhood Research Quarterly, 4,* 61-74.

Appendix. Writing Apprehension Scale*

Name _____ Date _____

	Strongly Agree	Agree	Undecided	Disagree	Strongly Disagree
1. I avoid writing.	5	4	3	2	1
2. I have no fear of my writing being evaluated.	5	4	3	2	1
3. I look forward to writing down my ideas.	5	4	3	2	1
4. I am afraid of writing when I know it will be evaluated.	5	4	3	2	1
5. Writing is an intimidating experience for me.	5	4	3	2	1
6. Finishing a piece of writing makes me feel good.	5	4	3	2	1
7. My mind seems to go blank when I start to work on a piece of writing.	5	4	3	2	1
8. Expressing ideas through writing seems to be a waste of time.	5	4	3	2	1
9. I would enjoy submitting my writing for publication.	5	4	3	2	1
10. I like to write my ideas down.	5	4	3	2	1
11. I feel confident in my ability to clearly express my ideas in writing.	5	4	3	2	1
12. I like to have my friends read what I have written.	5	4	3	2	1

13. I'm nervous about writing.   5   4   3   2   1

14. People seem to enjoy what I write. 5   4   3   2   1

15. I enjoy writing.   5   4   3   2   1

16. I never seem to be able to clearly
    write down my ideas.   5   4   3   2   1

17. Writing is fun for me.   5   4   3   2   1

18. I expect to do poorly
    on writing assignments.   5   4   3   2   1

19. I like seeing my thoughts
    on paper.   5   4   3   2   1

20. Discussing my writing with
    others is an enjoyable experience. 5   4   3   2   1

21. I have a terrible time organizing
    my ideas for a piece of writing.   5   4   3   2   1

22. When I finish a piece of writing,
    I know it's not good.   5   4   3   2   1

23. It's easy for me to write well.   5   4   3   2   1

24. I don't think I write as well as
    most of my friends.   5   4   3   2   1

25. I don't like my writing
    to be evaluated.   5   4   3   2   1

26. I'm not good at writing.   5   4   3   2   1

* Adapted from Daly, J. A., & Miller, M. D. (1975). The empirical development of an instrument to measure writing apprehension. *Research in the
Teaching of English, 9,* 242-249.